# The
## **Lovers**

## Also by Amitava Kumar

# The
# Lovers

*A Novel*

AMITAVA KUMAR

ALEPH

**ALEPH**

ALEPH BOOK COMPANY
An independent publishing firm
promoted by *Rupa Publications India*

First published in India in 2017
by Aleph Book Company
7/16 Ansari Road, Daryaganj
New Delhi 110 002

ISBN: 978-93-86021-00-7

1 3 5 7 9 10 8 6 4 2

For sale in the Indian subcontinent only.

Printed and bound in India Replika Press Pvt. Ltd

For Teju

'The Revolution smells of sexual organs.'
—Boris Pilnyak, 'Ivan and Maria'


'Oh, he *loves* her: just as the English loved India and Africa and Ireland;
it is the love that is the problem, people treat their lovers badly.'
—Zadie Smith, *White Teeth*

*Part I*
_____

# Jennifer

*Researchers found that people are attracted to people who are attracted to them. This from a clipping pasted in a notebook kept while writing this book.*

I was a new immigrant, eager to shine, and, if self-abuse were to be omitted from the reckoning, pure of body and heart. The letters I sent my parents in India were full of enthusiasm for the marvels of my new life. To those who welcomed me to Reagan's America, I wanted to say, without even being asked, that *E.T.* ought to have won the Oscar over *Gandhi*. I had found the latter insufficiently authentic but more crucially I felt insufficiently authentic myself. Not so much fake as insubstantial. I understood that I needed a suitable narrative to present to the people I was meeting. There was only contempt in my heart for my fellow Indian students who repeated stories about telling off ignorant Americans in barbershops who had asked how come they spoke such good English or if they belonged to tribes or grew up among tigers. The nostalgia I had come to treasure was a hypertrophied sense of the past as a place, a place with street signs and a figure atop a staircase that I recognized. This desire had nothing to do with the kinds of claims to civilizational superiority that make men demolish places of worship or want to bomb cities into oblivion. I knew this and yet I was uncertain about my story. I lacked calm self-knowledge. If a woman spoke to me, particularly if she was attractive, I grew excited and talked too much.

I'm talking of what happened more than two decades ago; this is the story of my first years here and my first loves. But the reality of my becoming who I am now, this *evolution*, as it were, goes back in time to the monkeys that surrounded me as an infant. This is my own, personal *Origin of Species*. In such a forensic way did I begin this investigation into my past before recent events cast a shadow over my work—but more of that later.

I first told a woman seated next to me on a Greyhound bus the story about the red-bottomed monkeys of my childhood. The monkeys would leave the branches of the big tamarind tree and peel the oranges left unattended on the balcony of Lotan Mamaji's house. This was in Ara in the late sixties. A war with

Pakistan was over and another loomed in the distance. Nehru had been dead only a few years. In the language of the history books, *the nation was in turmoil.*

Lotan Mamaji was my mother's younger brother. A giant of a man, immense and bearded, paan tucked under one dark cheek like a secret he didn't want to share. One winter morning, while everyone on the balcony sat listening to the radio, following the cricket commentary from Eden Gardens, Bedi in a pink patka about to claim his seventh Australian wicket in a match that India would go on to lose heavily, a monkey stole into Mamaji's room. He climbed on the huge white bed and finding Mamaji's pistol, brandished it, they say, at my cousin, born two months after me and still in her crib. No one moved. Then, turning the pistol around, the primate brain prompting the opposable thumb to grasp the trigger, the monkey blew his brains out. He was a medium-sized young male. Bits of flesh, bone, and hair had to be cleaned from the pictures of long-dead family patriarchs hanging on the wall.

There were so many lies repeated in the family, so many half-secrets, I don't know why I never asked anyone if the monkey story was true. For a long time, it had been lodged in my mind as a baptismal tale that taught me the nature of fear, or maybe provided a lesson about fate. But then the past lost its authority and the meaning of the story changed. I had by then come out of my teen years. The main questions now were about the fiction of the past, the idea I had of myself as a person, and what it meant for me to become a writer.

For so many years, the idea of writing has meant for me recognizing and even addressing a division in my life: the gap between India, the land of my birth, and the US, where I came as a young adult. If and when I imagine an audience for my writing, it is also a divided one. But the two places are connected in reality, not only by those histories that cultural organizations celebrate through endlessly dull annual gatherings but by millions of individual yearnings, all those stories of consummated or thwarted desire. There are many of my populous tribe who have examined the wonder and the mystery of this condition.*

Consider the monkeys in Ara—*rhesus macaques*. They were not just visitors to my maternal uncle's home. They have a place in my imagination because they, too, were unheralded immigrants in America. A few years ago, I read in a newspaper report that the problem Delhi residents were having with monkeys went back to the early years of Indian independence when thousands from that region started being sent to America to be used for science. As many as twenty thousand to fifty thousand monkeys were exported each year. A newly independent India was in need of foreign exchange. The Americans needed middle-aged male monkeys for their experiments. The result of the selective trapping, according to a primatologist interviewed for the report, was the disruption of the ecological balance. The disruption took place because the family unit was broken and the monkey groups entered a process of division that the primatologist termed 'chaotic fission'.

But let's take a step back from the political and enter the riskier domain of the personal. I want to focus on why monkeys came to mind when I started work on this book. I claim kinship with the monkeys of my childhood because of what I read in a magazine in 2010: *Rhesus macaques, who normally are not self-*

---

*In literature, diverse testaments to distant love. 'In 1964, the year Nehru died, the year V. S. Naipaul's *An Area of Darkness* was published, I was sitting in darkness's heart, in a bungalow in Allahabad, in a railway waiting room in Bilaspur, and as scores of Indian poets—from Henry Derozio to Srinivas Rayaprol—had done before me, I was taking my bearings from distant stars. The two I took mine from were e.e. cummings and Kahlil Gibran.' Poet Arvind Krishna Mehrotra quoted in A. Kumar, ed., *Away: The Indian Writer As Expatriate* (New York: Routledge, 2004. The writers in the above volume go beyond literary influences to record links that are also historical, cultural, economic. And personal. On the one hand, in a poem by A. K. Ramanujan, Indian Fulbright scholars in Egypt coming across millennia-old mummies swathed in muslin from Calicut. And, on the other, a young Sarojini Naidu, homesick and feverish with love in Cambridge, writing letter after letter to a doctor in the Nizam's army who would later become her husband.

*aware, will, following brain surgery, examine their genitals in a mirror. Similar evidence of self-awareness was previously limited to higher primates, dolphins, magpies, and an elephant named Happy.* ('Findings', *Harper's* magazine, December 2010, p. 84.)

✓

In America, the land of the free and home of the brave, it was possible, figuratively speaking, to examine genitalia in public.\* I discovered this when I turned on the radio one day and heard a woman's voice. A foreign accent, except the surprise was that she was talking about sex. She sounded like Henry Kissinger. Her name was Dr Ruth. Unlike Kissinger, she wanted us to make love, not war.

In India, the only public mentions of sex were the advertisements painted on the walls that ran beside the railway tracks. I read the ads when I travelled from Patna to Delhi for college, and was filled with anxiety about what awaited me when, at last, I would experience sex. On the brick walls near the tracks, large white letters in Hindi urging you to call a phone number if you suffered from premature ejaculation or erectile dysfunction or nightly emissions. A nation of silent sufferers! Men with worried brows holding their heads in their offices during the day, and, back at home, lying miserably awake beside quiet and disappointed wives in the dark.

But not in America where Dr Ruth was talking to you cheerfully on the air. I had no accurate idea of what *epiglottis* and *guttural* really meant, but those words vibrated in my mind when

---

\*Bill Clinton on President Obama's re-election: 'He's luckier than a dog with two dicks.'

Of course, Bill Clinton deserves a footnote in any book on love. My writing notebook also has this quote in it: 'I—but you know, love can mean different things, too, Mr. Bittman. I have—there are a lot of women with whom I have never had any inappropriate conduct, who were friends of mine, who will say from time to time, "I love you". And I know that they don't mean anything wrong by that.'—Bill Clinton, Testimony Before Grand Jury.

I listened to Dr Ruth. Her voice on the small, black radio-cum-cassette-player in the privacy of my room offering advice to the males among her audience. Even if they themselves had already climaxed, they could help their female partners achieve orgasm.

—You can just pleasure her.

I hadn't heard that word used as a verb before. I also spoke in an accented English; I wondered if Dr Ruth's usage was correct.

—And for women out there, a man wants an orgasm. Big deal! Give him an orgasm, it takes two minutes!

*Such relief.* For more than one reason.

There were details about her that I discovered later. Dr Ruth grew up in an orphanage. Her parents perished at Auschwitz. She was very short but had fought in a war. She was once a guerrilla in the Haganah and now, in this country, she was famous for talking about masturbation and penises and vaginas on the radio. An extraordinary and busy life. She was on her third marriage.

You will understand when I say that listening to Dr Ruth that night in my room on Morningside Drive I was back in Delhi where it was morning and we were enjoying three days of spring. The year I left, 1990. My friends were in my room in the college dorm. The daughter of the warden walked past the window on her way to work, her hair still hanging damp on her yellow dupatta. She was a post-doc in history and would become a lecturer soon. And then we were running to the end of the corridor to watch the warden's daughter open the little wooden gate on her way to the bus stop. Her prepossessing calm, her very indifference to the existence of gawking others, was an incitement to collective lust. She was soon gone and, still excited but also somewhat let down, the group returned to my small room with its dirty, whitewashed walls.

—There is nothing purer than the love for your landlord's daughter, said Bheem.

—No, said Santosh, after an appropriate pause. If you are looking for innocence, the purest gangajal, you have to be in love with your teacher's wife.

As if to sort out the matter, we looked at Noni, a Sikh from

Patiala. He was the only one amongst us who wasn't a virgin.

Noni took off his turban and his long hair fell over his shoulders.

—You bastards should stop pretending. The only true love, true first love, is the love for your maidservant.

This was duly appreciated. But Noni was not done yet.

—She has to be older than you, though not by too much, and while it's not necessary for you to have fucked her, it is important that she take your hand in hers and put it on her breast.

There was the usual silence that greets the utterance of grand truth. Three bodies were sprawled next to each other on the bed, their heads pillowed against the wall behind them. Aureoles of dark, oily smudges indicated where other heads had pressed against that wall. Then, someone started laughing.

—You are a bunch of pussies, Noni said, to dismiss the laughing. When you went back home during the winter, did any one of you get laid?

He smiled and announced his own success with another question.

—Has anyone slept with a friend's mother?

—I have, Bheem said. He had light-coloured eyes. He was smiling a soft, secret smile.

—Whose mother, Noni asked.

—Yours.

Noni was my Dr Ruth before Dr Ruth. My naiveté was the price of admission I paid for his tutorials. Noni had discovered that the medical definition of a kiss was 'the anatomical juxtaposition of two orbicularis oris muscles in a state of contraction'. This made the unfamiliar even more unfamiliar. He told me that the word 'fuck' was an acronym derived from 'for unlawful carnal knowledge'; this terminology was itself a rewriting, Noni said, of the medieval rule to which 'fuck' owed its origins, 'fornication under consent of the King.' Noni was completely wrong; at that time, however, I marvelled at his knowledge of sex.

Until I met Noni in Delhi, my familiarity with sex was limited to what I had learned from the censored movies screened on

Saturdays in Patna. I'd be sitting with others in the dark, the air warm, the smell of sweat around me, and somewhere a cigarette being smoked. There were probably two hundred others in the theatre, almost all men and most of them older than me. In the local paper the theatre advertised itself as 'air-cooled' but what you breathed was the effluvia of restless groins shifting in fixed seats that had coir-stuffing poking out of torn rexine covers. It was no doubt cooler in the apartment in Prague where the on-screen action was taking place. A middle-aged man had unclasped the hook of the bra that an impossibly young woman was wearing. She turned to face him, her breasts milk-white, with pale pink drowsy nipples. There was a cut and a jump in the film there. The duo was now in an open car on an empty road, driving under leafy trees, in bright sunlight.

But a child had started crying in the audience near me.

—*Scene dikha, baccha ro raha hai*, a man shouted from a further seat, wanting us to return to the bedroom. 'Show a breast. Because if you don't [offer the nipple], the baby will cry.' The rough remark, bewildering at that time, soon lost its confusing aspect: glinting like mica in a piece of granite, it sat for a while in the nostalgic narrative about my late teenage years.

Ten years later, for the benefit of a later generation, a sex advice column in *Mumbai Mirror* had become popular in India. I made this discovery when my laundry came back to my hotel room wrapped in newspaper.

*Q. My girlfriend kissed the tip of my penis and the next day she suffered a stomach-ache. Could she be pregnant? Should she take some pills?*

A. She must have had dinner afterwards and that probably led to the stomach-ache. Oral sex does not cause pregnancy and she need not take any pills.

*Q. I am a 25-year-old man. Please tell me if regular masturbation can increase the size of one's butt.*

A. Just as your nose, fingers and tongue will not increase in size, neither will the butt.

*Q. When it comes to sex, my partner allows me to use only a finger for just a few seconds. Please tell me why. Also, when I hold my bowels for too long, my testicles swell and hurt. What could be the reason for this?*

The good doctor, the Sexpert, had once again exercised a grim matter-of-factness, the humour in his eyes hidden under the thick glasses he wore in the grainy photograph.

A. She is probably scared by your intentions—pregnancy or an infection. Why not ask her? And, do you mean 'balls'? 'Bowels' refers to the intestines. Why would you want to hold them? Please explain.

The *New York Times* carried a story on the Sexpert. His name is Dr Mahinder Watsa and he recently turned ninety-three. His editor says the doctor has received more than 40,000 letters seeking advice. He has tried to promote sex education but many of his own colleagues say it is pornography. Dr Watsa was the first to use words like penis and vagina in the newspapers. A reader filed an obscenity suit against the doctor, charging that the editors fabricated letters to increase readership. In response, the editor delivered a sack of unopened letters at the judge's table. 'He read them over the lunch hour and dismissed the case.'

The Sexpert column can now be read on the Internet. There was nothing like this when I was growing up in India. If, at the time, I could have written one, which letter would have been mine? The range of problems people present to the doctor is stunning but yes, this one:

*Q. In the last semester, I failed one subject. My parents got worried and took me to an astrologer. He asked me to remove my pants. He said the ejaculate after masturbation is equal to 100 ml of blood, hence my weakness. I am regretting showing him my penis. Please help.*

A. The astrologer is a hoax and completely ignorant of sexual matters. Masturbation is completely normal. Visit your college counsellor instead to discuss your not doing well in one subject.

⌣

After arriving in New York, I would have a constant conversation in my head with a judge who was asking me questions. The judge was white; we were in a court for those accused of false pretenses and indecent acts. Standing quietly in a dock, I rehearsed lines. *Sisters and Brothers of America*, Swami Vivekananda had said, in Chicago in 1893, at the Parliament of the World's Religions, *I thank you in the name of the mother of religions, and I thank you in the name of millions and millions of Hindu people of all classes and sects.* Unlike Vivekananda, I addressed the judge from a less exalted place but I wasn't lacking for conviction. *I am telling you all this in Immigration Court, Your Honour, because I want to assert that I knew about sex, or at least discoursed about sex, prior to my arrival on these shores. I have chosen to speak in personal terms, the most intimate terms, Your Honour, because it seems to me that it is this crucial part of humanity that is denied to the immigrant. You look at a dark immigrant in that long line at JFK, the new clothes crumpled from a long flight, a ripe smell accompanying him, his eyes haunted, and you wonder whether he can speak English. It is far from your thoughts and your assumptions to ask whether he has ever spoken soft phrases filled with yearning or what hot, dirty words he utters in his wife's ear as she laughs and embraces him in bed. You look at him and think that he wants your job and not that he just wants to get laid. I offer you the truth without shame and thank you, Your Honour, in the name of the dark hordes that have nothing to declare but their desire.*

ſ

Despite such declarations, I remained as celibate as Swami Vivekananda. But I was picking up a friendship with a woman named Jennifer.

   While waiting for classes to begin, I got a job at the university bookstore. My fellowship payment wasn't going to start till a month and a half later. I liked working among books. Jennifer had been employed there for years and was now in charge of the humanities section. She was tall and thin and she tied her long brown hair at the back in a ponytail. I guessed she was about ten years older than me but I could be wrong. I never asked her because I had been told it would be impolite. I learned that Jennifer had suffered a nervous breakdown on the night before her master's exam and quit grad school. I was told this by our Zambian co-worker, who had also dropped out. His name was Godfrey, and everyone just called him God. He had worked in the bookstore beside Jennifer for years, and they both knew all the professors, some of whom had been their teachers long ago.

—It was very tragic, very tragic, God said about Jennifer, the vivid whites of his eyes expanding with a fine appreciation of horror.

He said Jennifer's boyfriend used to bartend at a place downtown. He was killed in a motorcycle accident on FDR Drive late one night. She was riding pillion and her lover died in her arms.

This bit about her tragic past gave Jennifer's life depth. But I was more immediately drawn to her clear skin and wondered what she smelled like. Jennifer dressed simply and while standing across from her on the packing floor I was conscious of the slope of her breasts under her pale cotton shirts. When I was alone, I imagined the white of her thighs inside her blue jeans. I had never seen a woman's naked thighs before. Everyone at the bookstore liked Jennifer because she was smart and had read more widely than any of us. She was also kind to me. When I complained to her once that I didn't want to go to the International Students' social, she took me instead to a screening of Michael Moore's documentary *Roger & Me*.

Moore wanted the chief of General Motors, Roger Smith, to come back to his Michigan hometown and meet the people who were losing their jobs. The film confirmed what I was already discovering about America. Poverty or homelessness wasn't something I needed to associate only with India. *Roger & Me* explained the reality I had seen outside the university gates. Only a hundred yards from the Cathedral of St. John the Divine where people with cameras stood in line to gain entry, I saw an old white woman walking along slowly with shit running down her swollen legs. A middle-aged woman passed me with her little girl. As she came close to the old woman, the mother covered her daughter's eyes.

The film rescued me from my passivity. It made me think about the outside world but I was thinking also of Jennifer. I would have liked to kiss her as she lay naked in my arms; I also wanted her to see me as a man with a camera. Michael Moore was honest and funny even while he seemed to embody a shambling slovenliness. I aspired to be a witty raconteur, open about wanting to seduce Jennifer with sparkling essays about ordinary people dropped in the maw of late capitalism. And that wasn't probably how Jennifer saw me. Near the checkout counter at the bookstore, there was a postcard stand and one day she picked up a card and called out to me.

—Is this you? She looked amused. She said, I recognized the hair.

I looked at the card. There was a sketch of a man sitting at a table, holding a mug, his eyes downcast. He had black curly hair. Below the sketch was a short story:

> The waitress came over and
> took his order for iced tea. She did so
> without flirting at all, something that
> disappointed and depressed him.
> —R. Kevin Maler, *Counterfeit*

The story made me laugh and, though I was happy that I was the cause of Jennifer's amusement, I knew that she was being critical. Her remark made me feel shallow. I decided I would spend more time with her. And even after classes had started, and I no longer worked at the bookstore, I stopped by each Tuesday and Thursday to eat lunch with Jennifer.

—Kailash, have you ever gone apple picking?

When Jennifer put this question to me I explained that apples in India grew in the mountains, in Kashmir, or in hill stations like Shimla. I had never been north of Delhi.

—I am from the burning plains, I said to her melodramatically, and she smiled at me then, kindly, but with enough restraint to stop me from going further.

Jennifer was one of the few people who called me by my full

name. In one of my classes, a fellow graduate student had given me a nickname. Although names were shortened in America, this wasn't true in my case. My German friend Peter had begun calling me Kalashnikov instead of Kailash. It was a mouthful, but he got enough laughs each time and so he never gave up on the joke. Then, someone shortened Kalashnikov to AK-47. On occasion, people called me AK or, sometimes, just 47.

On a Saturday morning, Jennifer rang the downstairs bell and called my name on the intercom. This was another thing about her; she never took her own name, even on the phone. This was a lesson to me in intimacy. You gave someone you loved a new name, or you uttered their name as if it were your own.

We left in her beaten-up blue Volvo, driving an hour or more north of the city. I had no idea that apples grow on short trees so close to the ground or that there are so many different varieties. We picked our apples and then bought cider doughnuts. I returned that evening with two paper sacks filled with fruit. When I bit into one and the sweet juice filled my mouth I immediately sat down to write a letter to my parents in Patna. I told them that my room smelled fresh and sweet. At least for the moment, I forgot my anxiety about money, forgot too the necessary practice of converting dollars into rupees, or apples into the dwindling balance in the account book—will I again be nine or ninety dollars short at the end of the month? While I was writing the letter, my worries receded. Even my loneliness acquired a pleasant hue, the way objects appear to glow in the light of the setting sun. Earlier that day, I wrote, I had walked between the long rows of trees and I had plucked apples with my own hands. I talked about autumn and the way in which the leaves changed colour in this country. I did not say anything about Jennifer.

⁓

'Hello, USA, 212-866-5826?' That is how the telephone operator from India began. Yes, I shouted, yes. It appeared that the ocean that lay between us was roaring in my ear. I switched to Hindi but the operator kept speaking English and next confirmed my name. Then, my father hurriedly greeted me, and asked me how I was, before giving the phone to my mother. These calls were expensive, I knew. When my parents requested the call, they would have paid for the first four minutes at the post office. After those minutes were up, the operator would break in to ask if we wanted to continue talking. This was now the second phone conversation with my parents. The first conversation had been about my having reached New York City.

—Why have you not written? No word for so many days.

—I have, I said to my mother. I did, just last night.

—Is it very cold there?

—No, no. I went to an apple orchard yesterday.

—We took a rickshaw and came here to call you because I woke up from a dream...

She wouldn't tell me what she had seen in her dream, and so I told her that the only reason I hadn't written was because of my classes. I had been busy. I knew the cost of the call was prohibitive but felt secretly happy when my mother said, 'Extension, please.'

They were going to visit my grandmother in the village for Diwali.

—Send her a postcard too, my mother said. You don't need to write anything much. Just write, *Mataji, I am well.* Just four words and she will be happy.

My grandmother couldn't read or write. She would have asked someone in the village, perhaps a kid walking back from school, to read my letter aloud to her. Or my cousins Deepak and Suneeta, if they weren't stealing anything at that time from her garden or her granary. About once a month, I sent my grandmother a postcard. I would sit down to write and then imagine a school-going child reading out my words. To bring to the young student a sense of wonder I would add a line or two about life in America:

*When it is midnight in India, it is the middle of the day here. Even the people who collect garbage have their own truck.*

*You cannot travel in a train without a ticket.*

*To go from one part of the city to another, I use the train that runs underground.*

*When I cook, the supply of gas is just like water. It is delivered through a pipe connected to my stove. No standing in long lines here for gas cylinders.*

⌁

Jennifer and I took the subway down to Lincoln Center. It was an early Saturday afternoon. The plan was that we would walk across Central Park and emerge on the other side near Hunter College. We were going to Asia Society to see an exhibition of photographs by Raghu Rai. As we were coming out of the subway station at Lincoln Center, Jennifer caught sight of a sign that said: 'Gandhi was a great and charitable man.' Beneath, in smaller type, were the words: 'However, he could have used some work on his triceps.' The sign was an advertisement for a gym. If you joined early, the sign said, you could save 150 dollars.

I said to Jennifer that the Mahatma would have found the price of the package a bit steep. But he would have liked the thriftiness of the early-membership plan. Gandhi came from a family of traders. He was inclined toward austerity but he was also a man of the world. Jennifer asked if I was offended by the ad, but I wasn't.

In India, Gandhi had been a face smiling from the walls of the decrepit offices in the small towns of Bihar. This use of his image for a New York City gym returned me to a different use of Gandhi, one that took the Mahatma out of the museum. This use wasn't unknown in India, it was just ignored by official pieties. This was the irreverent Gandhi of the Indian marketplace. Long live Gandhi Safety-Match. Long live Bapu Mark Jute Bag. Long live Mahatma Brand Mustard Oil.

A poster with the arrow pointing down to the exhibition space had a quote from Raghu Rai: 'A photograph has picked up a fact of life, and that fact will live forever.' The exhibition, made up exclusively of black and white images, was in a long room in the basement of the building. Upon entering, our eyes fell on the photographs on the facing wall. These were pictures from the Union Carbide disaster in Bhopal from six years ago. On the walls on the side were images that Rai had made in Delhi and Bombay. We went up to the Bhopal pictures first. There were three of them. One was the iconic image of an unknown child being buried, its eyes wide open, the small body nearly covered by ash and rubble. A hand near the child's forehead gave to the picture a touch of tenderness, a human presence among the stones. There was a second picture of a child's corpse. Here one could tell the gender of the child. And there was confirmation because the small girl had a piece of paper pasted on her forehead. Her name, Leela, was written in Hindi, and also her father's name, Dayaram. A white piece of cotton covered her body but she too lay on a bed of dark stones that could be coal. I hadn't seen the third picture before. It showed a man on a deserted road carrying a bundle on his shoulder. Behind the man was the equally deserted Union Carbide factory. Jennifer took my hand in hers when I went closer to the picture to read the caption. Then I saw what she had already seen. What I had at first thought was a quilt or a heavy blanket was the man's dead wife. The gas had killed her the night before. I now saw the pair of stiff, naked feet protruding from under the paisley pattern of the sari.

The pictures from Delhi were on a wall on the right. In the centre was a photograph of Indira Gandhi sitting in her office with her back to the camera. She was the prime minister at that time. Around her were about twenty men in white dhoti-kurtas, Nehru caps on their head, all of them caught in poses of genuine servility. A startling photo. Another of a young swimmer, outlined against the sky, about to leap into the pond inside a sixteenth-century monument. In the background, in the far distance, the modern monuments, the tall skyscrapers of Connaught Place. My favorite image was one that Rai had shot from a rooftop in Old Delhi. The dome of Jama Masjid, its minarets, and the tops of other buildings formed the far horizon; dusk was creeping in, evident from the lights that had come on, and, occupying the foreground but still far away, so that one didn't seem to disturb the privacy of the act, was a woman in an illuminated room. It appeared that the call for the evening namaz had just come from the mosque. The tile-work and the trellis formed a delicate pattern around her, while the woman herself, or what we saw of her, was bathed in white light. She had her head covered, her hands open in front of her in prayer.

Jennifer and I walked over to the Bombay pictures. These were new to me, a different order of urbanity. Two men reading newspapers, islands of stillness, while around them were the moving, blurry bodies of commuters at the Churchgate railway station. Women arguing at a fish market; a socialite sitting in her living room in front of a giant, expensive oil painting; men in crisp white holding dark briefcases near the Jehangir Art Gallery; dabbawallahs; workers building a skyscraper in Colaba. In this air-conditioned space in New York, you didn't feel the heat in which the photos had been clicked; perhaps because Rai had made expert use of the flash, the pictures were so evenly lit, you seemed to have stepped into a land without shadows. Jennifer wasn't saying anything but, as I've said, she had taken my hand in hers. I liked this. We stood in front of an image of thin-limbed boys playing a game of marbles in a backstreet. All around them were crumbling walls, tin roofs, and dirt, but Rai had caught the fluid movement of the boys and their extended limbs.

When I was in school in Patna, I wanted to be an artist because the placid expanse of the River Ganga close to my home, and sometimes a solitary boat with a dirty sail or a red pennant, looked beautiful and somehow easy to draw. It wasn't easy, of course. But even my failures perhaps were teaching me how to see the world around me. I could be sitting in a crowded bus bringing me back from school and a voice running in my head would name the objects I saw being sold on the street, their colours, the look in the eyes of the sellers.

Jennifer and I were standing in front of a Raghu Rai photo that showed about a dozen buffaloes feeding in a khatal (in Bihar and Bengal, khatal or khataal is the word for a cow pen) in Bombay. Hanging above the dark beasts that were linked together by chains, and suspended from the roof of the shack, were cots on which men sat or slept. Around them, from hooks and nails, dangled buckets for milk and also items of clothing. Small, cramped lives, but I was familiar from my childhood with what was shown here. I knew the smell of that khatal, the stink of animal waste and the hum and buzz of flies, and I knew I could speak the language used by those men sitting bare-chested near the buffaloes. I turned to Jennifer.

—If I ever write a book, I want this picture on the cover. It will be called *Migrants*.

—It is an amazing picture, she said. There's so much happening here.

Jennifer brought me sandwiches made of hummus and olives. I had never eaten this food before. We crossed the university quad and sat on the stone steps of the library. Just the previous week the weather had been chilly, and one night I had seen the glitter of raindrops on my window, but this day was unseasonably warm. Bright sunlight falling on the windows of the buildings and on the faces and limbs of students sprawled on the grass. The day felt a little like those days in India when the exams were over and you could sit out in the sun peeling an orange. Jennifer took off her blue sweater. She was wearing a t-shirt with thin black horizontal stripes. I studied the freckles on her pale arm and then I took off my jacket too.

—On this day, last year, Jennifer said, I returned from a three-week trip to Nicaragua.

—*Nicaragua?*

—I went there with my friend Lee. We stayed with campesinos and worked on a farm and then on a small dam near Managua.

This little detail produced a twinge of jealousy.

—Is Lee a man?

—Interesting question. Lee used to be a woman. Laura. She

went to school with me. Then, she decided she would prefer to be a man.

New food, new knowledge.

—Tell me something about your childhood, she said to me after a while.

I didn't have a story like the one about Lee. I found myself describing the red-bottomed monkeys outside Lotan Mamaji's home. I had told the story to a few others before, about the monkey finding my uncle's gun and pointing it at my cousin in her crib, and maybe the story had been told too often, because Jennifer wasn't as surprised as I had hoped she'd be.

—Kailash, what happened to your cousin, where is she now? That was all she wanted to know.

She wouldn't have thought of it as a very big deal, so I didn't tell Jennifer that I couldn't even make it to my cousin's wedding. But I had felt guilty about it for years. I couldn't tell her that in a photo I saw of the ceremony years later, the sign that the painter had put up outside, with a lotus flower and a colourful pot with a coconut in it, contained a spelling mistake: *Rajesh Wets Shalini*. So, instead, I told Jennifer about the summer afternoons when I was a kid and my cousin was a teenager and she would listen to sad Hindi songs on her radio: songs of unrequited love during those months when we waited for rain. The heat of the summer. In the blind alley below us, a cycle-rickshaw parked to the side, the sun's glare reflecting off the metal rims of its wheels. The rickshaw appeared defeated, skeletal, because it was now missing both a rider and a driver. With a gurgle, the water supply from the municipality would resume at three each afternoon. My cousin sighed when a favourite song of hers, from the film *Guide*, started playing on the radio. If we were lucky, there would be another sound—louder, more insistent, filled with greater yearning than any sound heard all afternoon—the call of the koel hiding in a mango tree. The heat left everyone lethargic, even stoic, but not this koel who was unafraid to make a spectacle of his suffering. No, not just spectacle, he was making a song. Such unabashed glory, such art. Years later, in college in Delhi, I wrote a short poem about the koel and mailed it in a yellow envelope to Khushwant Singh. I was surprised that the old writer sent back a letter, praising the poem's simplicity and my art, encouragement enough for me to wax poetic when, sitting on the steps of the library, Jennifer asked me what I missed most about India. That afternoon, I was only imitating the koel.

The next day, she put a simple white card in my mailbox at the bookstore. It had a haiku by the poet Basho.

*Even when I am in Kyoto*
*When I hear the call of the cuckoo*
*I miss Kyoto*

To show my gratitude for her gift of lunch and the card, I gave Jennifer a packet of jasmine incense. It had sat unopened in the suitcase that I had brought with me from India. She put the roll up to her nose and thanked me sweetly, and then said that one day she'd have me come over to her apartment for dinner. That remark made me think that Jennifer liked me, although she never said anything to me about the matter.

The semester's work took up my time. Once or twice, we went to campus events together. A Diwali festival organized by the South Asian students, chaat and spicy chana masala from a Bangladeshi restaurant close by, each plate costing three dollars. Pepsi and Sprite in small plastic cups for a quarter. The organizers asked everyone attending to pick rose petals from a plate and throw them at the plastic idols of Ram and Sita while they screamed 'Happy Diwali!' One of the women, an undergrad wearing a salwar-kameez from Jackson Heights, went around putting red tikas on our foreheads. When I thanked her, she laughed nervously and said loudly that when we went back to our apartments the other students would say that we had ketchup on our foreheads.

I talked to a couple of the Indian girls there, and I caught them looking at Jennifer while they spoke to me. During that first semester, there was at least one girl in my class that I liked. Well, there were several that I liked, but there was one in particular. I hadn't spoken to her much. Her name was Nina. I would have found the prospect of talking to Nina daunting, but Jennifer was easier to be with. She had gone down in life when she dropped out of school. It made her approachable. Or maybe it was because she was older and lived frugally. Is that what I thought at that time? More than once, off-handedly, Jennifer had indicated that she found me good company, and I felt pleased, as if she had recognized a hidden part of me.

One evening, we went to listen to Edward Said playing Bach piano concertos in the chapel. Jennifer had taken classes with the famous professor. I spotted two of my own professors there, including Ehsaan Ali, who had come with his wife who was white. Western music was new to me but I saw that Jennifer was moved by it. I was in classes where Said's writings were discussed and in the weeks to come I would come to speak of my own identity in ways that were influenced by him, but on that night, the night of his performance, Jennifer introduced me to what she had borrowed from Said to understand music.

This was during dinner at my apartment after the concert. We were eating the mattar-paneer and biryani I had prepared for her, and she was speaking about music in an even, clear way, telling me about polyphony and counterpoint. This kind of talk made her at once more interesting and mysterious to me. If this were a movie, I imagine it would be a montage of scenes, like this one, that introduced me to America—a discussion about Bach, the first taste of Mexican food, the first rock concert, lectures by the teachers I came to admire. And the footage of the first snowfall. The blue of the cold afternoon and, as if someone had cut the sound from the universe, snow drifting down in the stillness. When it stopped snowing, we went sledding down a hill in a park on the other side of Morningside Drive. This was new to me, but even as I was riding down the slope on a sled I asked myself if what I had with Jennifer was love. Every week, I spent time with my other friends, those who I used to see in my classes. I didn't discuss Jennifer with them. In the beginning at least, I wouldn't have known what to say.

The one activity that was perhaps the most stable part of my identity that first semester was the seminar I was taking with Ehsaan Ali. His class on 'Colonial Encounters' was held on Friday afternoons. The seminar participants were required to get his special permission to join. I had heard that he brought two bottles of red wine each week to his classes and you sat around discussing the day's readings while sipping wine from small plastic cups. When the semester began, I went to Ehsaan's office in Philosophy Hall to get his signature. Third floor, after the set of dual radiators, next to the notice board covered with announcements. The door was open and I saw that he was on the phone. With his right hand, he pointed to a chair. The tenor of the exchange suggested that he was being interviewed. Then it became clear that the interview was about the Iraqi invasion of Kuwait.

—Well, our president has said that a line has been drawn in the sand. He claims that he has no dispute with the Iraqi people. His war is going to be against Saddam. Do you believe the ordinary Iraqi, suffering in her home or in a hospital, is going to think our president is being honest? No, let me explain…

While he was speaking on the phone, he was looking directly at me, and I found myself nodding my head. The window was open behind him and on the wall to his right was a framed poster of *The Battle of Algiers*. I had watched the film, when I was in my teens, in Pragati Maidan in Delhi. The poster's background showed grainy black-and-white warren-like homes in the qasba, and leaning into the frame from the sides were the Algerian Ali La Pointe on the left, and, on the right, the French military colonel Mathieu.

The film's director Gillo Pontecorvo had sought out Ehsaan when making the film. Pontecorvo had arrived in Algeria with his screenplay, but accidentally left it on the top of a car. Parts of the screenplay soon appeared in a right-wing paper. So Pontecorvo had recast the story, basing it on interviews with revolutionaries: 'a fiction written under the dictatorship of facts'. Ehsaan was in Algeria then and became one of his advisers. Except that the student who told me all this, a thin, saturnine man from Gujarat, was not a credible source. He would even have put Ehsaan in the film as the main actor, a man from a scrappy background emerging, not without charisma but mainly because of the pressure of history, into the forefront of a glorious struggle. Truth be told, I wasn't too far from holding the same view myself.

Ehsaan was a man born in a village not too far from mine. He migrated to Pakistan during the bloody Partition, and later came to America on a scholarship. Awarded a doctorate at Princeton, he toured the globe and made friends with Third World leaders, especially in Africa. He had been tried in court for having conspired in a plot to kidnap Kissinger! How could I not look up to him? He was our hero—and thus, all heroic. He had crossed boundaries. He was a man who was without a nation, and a friend to the oppressed peoples of the world.* A few years later, when Ehsaan died, after a battle with cancer, Kofi Annan would pay tribute at his funeral. But all this was still in the future. Even the immediate deaths in Iraq were far away. Two days after the ceasefire went into effect, planes from the USS *Ranger* bombed and strafed thousands of Iraqi fighters fleeing in their vehicles. That road came to be called the Highway of Death. How did the men die? I would know the answer when a photograph was published many months later, showing

---

*I wanted to title this book *The Man Without A Nation*. I even applied for a grant but got rejected: that made me regard the title with suspicion. But the title was inappropriate for a novel. It seemed more suited to a non-fiction study about a kind of discrepant cosmopolitanism that develops as an antidote to sectarian conflicts and murderous nationalism. For a brief while I thought the book would be called *The History of Pleasure*. I had picked up the phrase in a Philip Roth novel where the narrator had this to say about himself: 'But I was a fearless sort of boy back in my early twenties. More daring than most, especially for the woebegone era in the history of pleasure. I actually did what the jerk-off artists dreamed about. Back when I started out on my own in the world, I was, if I may say so, something of a sexual prodigy.' *Sexual prodigy? Your Honour, a hunger artist, more likely.* The proposed title overwhelmed me with its ironies and so it, too, was abandoned.

an Iraqi soldier burned alive while reaching out of his truck. But on the day that I met Ehsaan for the first time, this massacre had not yet taken place. The Iraqi soldier was still sitting on a chair outside the barracks listening to music or to the excited report of horses galloping around the old racetrack in Baghdad.

—You can do the math, yes? Clearly, some kids can die to make us feel safer. And the tragedy is doubled because we are not going to be safe... Listen, I have a student waiting to see me. I have to go. But if you have any questions about what I have said, call me back. I'll be here till four.

Without saying anything, Ehsaan reached out and took the yellow form that I was holding in my hand. He quickly signed it and then leaned back in his chair.

—Where were you born?

—India.

—That is obvious. Where in India? My guess is Uttar Pradesh.

—Next door, sir, in Bihar.

—A fellow Bihari. I was born near Bodh Gaya.

He was grinning when he said this. I smiled too but I didn't want to tell Ehsaan that I already knew a lot about him. There was a reason for my silence. I had read in an interview that as a boy Ehsaan had witnessed his father's murder. This was a few years before Ehsaan left for Pakistan, travelling alone in a column of refugees. He was only five and lying in bed next to his father when his father's cousin and his sons came in with knives. Ehsaan's father knew they were going to kill him, but he covered the child's body with his own. I didn't want to acknowledge my awareness of the sadness in Ehsaan's past. I didn't know then, or knew but hadn't acknowledged it, that as the weeks turned into months, and then into years, the details of Ehsaan's life would become a part of my life and the life of a woman I loved.

⁓

One night Jennifer called me to ask if I'd go ice skating. She said that we could rent skates at the rink. Back in Patna, I had learned to use roller skates on the smooth, straight road, lined with gulmohar trees, that led to Governor House. Ice skating required a different kind of movement and control. I held Jennifer's hand and skated around, following her instruction that we sketch the figure eight on ice. Jennifer was wearing a woollen hat, and so was I. We wore scarves. The hands that we extended towards each other were gloved. Jennifer was offering me a lesson because she wanted me to try to skate on my own. Just then a tight group of men wearing fluorescent suits winged by like a flock of geese. I gave chase, hamming it up, and inevitably, stumbled and fell. I was laughing, and Jennifer was too, and when I was back on my feet with her help, I kissed her, first on the cheek and then, my gloved right hand cupping the back of her head, on her lips. It seemed the most natural act in the world, and yet it filled me with intolerable excitement. We skated for a while longer on the hard ice and, as we went in widening circles under the night sky surrounded by the lights of the city, I felt a euphoria that made me weightless and lifted me to the stars.

—Are you in a hurry to get home? We were in the subway when Jennifer asked this question.

—No, no, I have nothing to do. *The effort required, Your Honour, to not sound overexcited and instead only a bit bored.*

When I tasted the scotch in Jennifer's apartment, I imagined that her mouth, too, would soon offer the same taste to my tongue. Yet she didn't kiss me. Saturday Night Live was on, an actor imitating President Bush. I kept my eye on the television and then, weak from waiting for something to happen, I stretched out on the futon. Jennifer came closer to me and, leaning down, unbuckled my belt and smiled through sleepy eyes. Then she took me in her mouth. I hardly dared look down at her head, and even less at her open mouth and her tongue that she extended to lick me. I didn't dare to look, yes, but I did, amazed. Her eyes were closed. I stared at her lips and at my cock in her hand. Could she sense that I was looking? I jerked my eyes away, noticing on the side table a new book by Geoffrey Wolff that I had seen at the bookstore, and the glass of scotch beside it, and further away, beside the door, the dark stain of melted snow where Jennifer had taken off her leather boots. For weeks I had asked myself if the two of us would have sex. It had often seemed possible, at least in my fantasies, and then not. But now it really had happened and I wanted to be able to tell someone and didn't know whom. That's what I thought when I looked down at Jennifer's head again, her hair golden and shiny except for four or five, I didn't count them, grey hairs, her body close to me but also distant in my mind, removed far enough to allow me to compose an excited report from the front. And then none of these thoughts mattered.

Before I left India for America, one of my friends made me promise that as soon as I had finally fucked someone, I would send a postcard saying 'I have eaten cherry.' I had mailed the postcard after only my second week in the country, as a joke, laughing to myself. Now, I wished I had waited.

Ↄ

Jennifer would shop at a co-op close to her house, buying half a dozen kinds of tea. Peppermint tea, green tea, and also black tea with chocolate or blood orange, the more austere sencha, the cloying and unpalatable cinnamon spice, and the smoky flavour of Lapsang Souchong that I came to prize. She would get me to try foods that she thought I would like. Pasta, baby corn with lemon juice and tarragon, roasted leg of lamb without the spices I was accustomed to, or shrimp sautéed lightly and served with chopped scallion. One afternoon, in the green plastic basket, she also added a strip of condoms. I recognized the brand; she kept a similar strip under a mattress. I had never made such a purchase. The woman at the counter didn't even look up when she rang up the condoms, a bar of Kiss My Face soap, a candle, celery sticks, a cucumber, a bottle of tomato sauce, and a packet of ravioli. In Jennifer's apartment, I learned to enjoy tea from China and South Africa and Malaysia; I liked sitting on her rocking chair which I would drag into a rectangle of sunlight; I spent afternoons reading books from her shelves, writers like Jean Genet and Angela Carter whom I hadn't encountered before.

She had a black cat and this was new too, stroking the cat as she lay on the wooden floor. I discovered that Jennifer had played the piano since she was a child, and gave lessons to little kids on the weekends. Young mothers, who appeared to be of Jennifer's age, brought their children to the apartment. When they saw me, they hesitated at the door, hands resting on their children.

The enquiring gazes of those white suburban women made me ask the question: were we now *an item?* This was a phrase that I had recently acquired; the words appeared strange to me. And also the sentiment. The truth was that even at the end of the summer, although I hadn't told anyone at the bookstore that we spent time with each other, people had noticed. Often, I would be asked where Jennifer was, or what time she was coming to work. Jennifer hadn't changed her behaviour with me—or she had changed it in ways that only I noticed. I was content with this; I didn't want anything more at that time. There was an imbalance in our histories. I felt she had lived a full life and I hadn't; I had only begun to experience life, which is to say, sexual life. If I were living in Patna, I'd have immediately thought of marriage, but not here. Here, I was finally leading a fuller existence. I understood that this newness couldn't be shared with those I had left behind. I couldn't imagine writing and telling my friends in Delhi, those who had sat laughing and hooting in the dorm only a few months ago, that I was sleeping with Jennifer. At least I couldn't tell them anything about her that wouldn't appear a betrayal. The reverse was also true. Was there any way of introducing my friends from Delhi into my conversations with Jennifer without turning them into sex-obsessed hooligans? Twenty-year-olds who looked at women and acted like the two adolescents I was to later encounter on American TV, Beavis and Butthead. It was easier to keep the worlds apart, even if it meant seeing myself as split or divided. Except that one day I looked in the mirror and felt the sudden clutch of vertigo. I saw a future in which Jennifer and I would be married, living in a small town, maybe in Ohio, where I'd find a job teaching at a college while trying to write during weekends.

During family holidays we would drive to her parents' home and each year someone would look at me and repeat the joke about Indians coming to Thanksgiving. We would return home the next day, the road winding endlessly into the future. Were there hills in Ohio? I felt I was rising and sinking with each passing breath. Then I realized that the mirror was moving. The wind made the sound a kite makes when struggling to get off the ground. When I looked outside through the grimy bathroom window I saw that the few leaves left on the branches of the trees outside were in danger of being swept away. I was safe in my apartment, and there was no immediate peril of any sort, but I was overcome by a feeling that took root then and has never left me, the feeling that in this place that was someone else's country, I did not have a place to stand.

# Part II
## Nina

Another clipping in the notebook for this novel. This one from a magazine essay by Abraham Verghese:

His voice took on a conspiratorial tone. 'I heard that one of our buggers, when he landed at Kennedy, he met a beautiful woman—a deadly blonde—and her brother outside baggage claim. She was very, very friendly. They offered him a lift in a white convertible. They took him to their apartment, and then you know what the brother did? Pulled a bloody gun out and said, "Screw my sister or I'll kill you." Can you imagine? What a country!'

(In the Verghese quote, I had identified with the fantasy but reading it now what catches my eye is the music of that insistent—because it springs from what is dubious—detail: very, very.)

Then there is this too. Another clipping pasted among the pages. The underside of the fantasy:

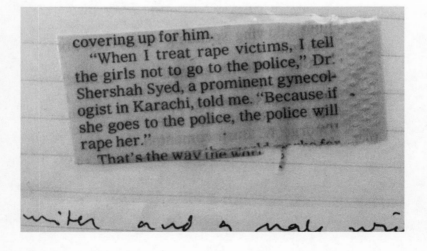

covering up for him.
"When I treat rape victims, I tell the girls not to go to the police," Dr. Shershah Syed, a prominent gynecologist in Karachi, told me. "Because if she goes to the police, the police will rape her."
That's the way the world

Two or even three times each week that semester, I would be at Jennifer's apartment. I preferred going to her place rather than having her come over to my cramped room. Her apartment was a two-room space, in the shape of an L, and it was located above a drugstore off 148th Street in Harlem.

On a Friday morning, while I was there, Jennifer went downstairs to the store to buy a pregnancy-test kit. She had called me late the previous evening and said she wanted me to be with her. I didn't ask any questions. I thought perhaps her father in Ohio, who had suffered a mild stroke the previous May, had taken a turn for the worse. But when we were getting ready for bed, she said, matter-of-factly, that her period was delayed. I felt ashamed. Here I was, standing close to her, thinking that we were soon going to fuck. And now this news. I didn't know what to say. Then I asked whether she had seen a doctor. She shook her head and turned off the light. In the dark, I tried to work out when she had become pregnant. There was a calendar with empty black and white squares on her kitchen wall that Jennifer would consult before deciding whether or not we ought to use a condom. What had gone wrong?

In the morning, I woke up first and began making coffee. Jennifer lay in bed longer than was usual, perhaps more than an hour. When she got up, she opened the front door and said she'd be back in a minute.

She appeared carrying a blue-and-white paper bag in her hand. Through the half-open bathroom door I caught sight of her sitting on the toilet bowl. After a few moments, she shut the door.

The bookstore provided its employees access to three gynaecologists and Jennifer chose one with a clinic on 78th Street. The name sounded Hispanic. The receptionist on the phone said that we could wait another week but Jennifer didn't want that. An appointment was made for Monday morning.

—Stay in the waiting room. I don't want you to come inside with me.

—Do they allow others to come in?

—I don't know. I haven't done this before.

I thought I should protest, just in case Jennifer was doing this to spare me. But spare me what exactly? I didn't know, but also felt that I couldn't ask. She was brittle, maybe she was angry and blamed me. I felt I ought to show that I was big enough to understand this.

A five-minute walk from the subway station and we were standing outside the clinic's beige-coloured walls. The first floor had three large rectangular windows with one-way mirrors. For a minute or two, Jennifer searched in her bag and then took a card out.

We passed through a metal detector and, once inside, we waited together in silence. After maybe twenty minutes, a nurse called out her name and held the door open for her. Jennifer didn't look at me as she left. I picked up a *National Geographic* from the stack of magazines. I was skimming through the pages, looking at pictures of crocodiles in Australia, when I suddenly saw Jennifer's Doc Martens Mary Janes next to me. She had come to tell me that I could go. There wouldn't be a procedure today, only a consultation and blood tests and an ultrasound. It was going to take hours.

Are you sure, etc.

We waited. Was it two weeks? I didn't keep a journal until another year had passed and I don't have any records with me now. Nevertheless, I remember that the next time we went to the clinic it was again a Friday. I left during Ehsaan's lecture on *Heart of Darkness* to meet Jennifer at the bookstore at two in the afternoon. This time she had brought her car. She broke the silence to say that her friend Jill, who worked at the campus ID card office, had said that she ought to have made the appointment for the morning. I didn't ask her why. We were late by about five minutes. A man had been standing outside, his head bowed, and it was only because Jennifer stepped away from him that I even looked at him a second time. The man was praying. Inside, the same guard we had seen the other day, a middle-aged, grey-uniformed black man, fat, with gold-rimmed glasses, checked a register in front of him and said that he didn't have Jennifer's name on it. He spoke in sonorous tones and acted officious, as if he were calling Congress to session.

—I've been talking to someone called Colleen, Jennifer said to the man.

He picked up the phone and dialed three digits.

—Yes, I have an individual named Jennifer here for a two-thirty, but I don't see her name on the list here… No, you see, I cannot properly do my work if you don't do yours…

He looked up.

—You go ahead, ma'am. You have to understand we keep this list here for your safety. It has to match what is inside. We have security—

But Jennifer wasn't going to wait for him to finish.

Once again, I stayed in the waiting area. Although I had expected to see other men there, the only others in the room were two heavy-set women, maybe in their forties, sitting together with their bags in their lap. One of them wore a bright red sweater and the other a dazzling white one. I was reading a book by Rachel Carson but now and then my eye wandered outside. The man who had been praying near the door hadn't moved at all. What would happen if he said anything to Jennifer? She was a quiet person but religion brought out her rage.

A young woman came in alone, wearing dark glasses, teetering on high heels, giving to the room a sudden, slightly illicit air. After a while, I stopped looking at her and went back to my reading. More than two hours passed. I began to worry why Jennifer wasn't coming out. The woman called Colleen had told Jennifer on the phone that the actual procedure wouldn't take long. They were going to run a couple of tests but that was 'merely procedural' and that part lasted only a few minutes. Colleen had said the whole affair would take an hour. Then, the door to the inside opened and a young woman and a man in a camouflage t-shirt came out. They headed for the two women seated together. The women got up and hugged the couple. It was unclear whether the woman had been operated upon, or whether she had only gone in for a consultation. I thought she looked fine. I began to pretend I was reading, aware that my stomach was churning. At least another hour passed. Then, the door opened again but it was only the nurse.

—I went back to my reading and the nurse came closer and said to me, Are you with Jennifer?

What had happened to her? Who was to be called in case of an emergency? People died during childbirth in India, I had heard this all the time when I was a boy. Just a few years ago, Smita Patil had died soon after giving birth. But this was only an abortion, what had gone wrong?

The nurse's tag said Paula. She was in her forties.

—Jennifer would like you to come inside.

A door opened into a narrow hallway and Paula allowed me to walk into the room alone. Jennifer was lying on a bed, a sheet covering her up to her waist. She had been crying, her eyes were red. An untouched cookie and a cup of water waited on the side table. When I asked if she was in a lot of pain, she shook her head and, as if she was cold, pulled the sheet up to her neck.

—I don't want the car to get towed. Can you put more quarters in the meter?

Why hadn't I thought of this myself?

—Yes, yes. Do you want anything else? Would you like me to get you some tea or juice? Why did it take so long?

Jennifer wasn't really saying anything and that is why my questions were so rushed and jumbled together. I went out in a hurry, not waiting at the door for the Middle Eastern woman who was coming into the clinic. She wore the hijab and holding the door for her was a thin man with a toddler in his arms. I shouted back an apology. There was a ticket under the wiper. Twenty-five dollars. I put it in my pocket, telling myself that I would pay it immediately but wouldn't tell Jennifer about it. And, with my hand still inside the pocket of my jacket, I thought I'd cook basmati rice and chicken in coriander for Jennifer. She liked that. And I'd make some dal. Keep some red wine handy, if she wanted it. I must bring her flowers. And wash her sheets if they were bloody. Would the sheets have blood on them? I didn't know the answer to the question but I was certainly going to be generous and attentive.

I didn't recognize at that moment what I already knew, that nothing I could do would ever be adequate. It seemed that Jennifer had made a discovery about me, a discovery that I wasn't privy to. It was as if a policeman had stopped by one evening when I wasn't there and asked a few disturbing questions about me. And at the end of the conversation, Jennifer had risen and gone to a drawer in my room and found the evidence. All that was required now was for an accusation to be aired in the open.

Early evening. I had placed a bouquet of fresh flowers near her bedroom window, white and red carnations, a couple of asters and yellow daisies, a stem of tiny white spray roses. Now I brought her dinner with a small glass of red wine on the tray. Jennifer sat up on the bed and looked at me.

—I appreciate what you're doing but really I'd just like to be alone. Will you please take that bottle of wine and leave?

—I'll go in a bit. Why don't you eat first? I want to make sure you eat something.

—No, I'm sorry... *Why am I even saying sorry?* I'd like to be alone. Go. Please go.

My first thought, Thank god, I'm wearing these sandals. I had brought them from India. They were inappropriate for the season. But they were proving useful now, I didn't at least have to upset her by taking time to put on my shoes.

Stepping out of her door, I wondered why she had insisted that I take the wine. Was it because I had bought a bottle that only cost seven bucks? But she drank cheap wine all the time. Then I realized that such questions were unimportant. I had failed. I knew I had failed in the way one knows one has failed in a dream: you might not know the cause, but the proof is available to you, the train is coming closer, you hear a clanging, there is only the feeling of vast regret that you have no legs and you can't possibly snatch away to safety the small bundle lying on the tracks.

A man was sitting at the bottom of the steps that led up to Jennifer's apartment. He didn't move when I came out. His right hand, with a large sore on one of the fingers, was on a shopping cart filled with black garbage bags spilling with rags. I pulled the door shut a bit too forcefully and stepped on to the street telling myself that I needed to eat some rice and chicken curry. The bottle of wine was in my hand. I would eat a bit and drink, and yet, as I said this to myself, I also experienced a clutching sadness.

The world had darkened. A giant hand had painted the world around me with a black, smudgy substance. Two blocks down, I saw that a basement door opened to a tiny Lebanese restaurant and when I was seated I asked for lentil soup and bread. The food and the wine disappeared in some empty place inside me. I called Jennifer's number the next day and for several days that followed but the phone just rang in her apartment. Once I called the bookstore, and God said Jennifer was sick, and that she wouldn't be back before Christmas. Did he know what was wrong with her? He had heard it was pneumonia. But that couldn't have been correct.

A week passed and I got a card from Jennifer. The first line said that she was sorry but she couldn't talk to me anymore. I didn't read any further than the next line that said *All possibilities are stillborn*. The language appeared heavy-handed to me, the too-deliberate, and somewhat inaccurate, metaphor dragging me into waters muddy with misery. I understood that Jennifer was upset and disappointed. I also knew that it wasn't anything I had said, but instead everything that I had left unsaid. She knew that I didn't love her in a deep or lasting way. I felt guilty at first but then another thought took its place. Over the coming weeks, I would start telling myself that it had been a good thing we had done by getting together. We had seized an opportunity for happiness. A part of me would always feel that I had been shallow and opportunistic. But we had also been happy. She had changed me, and I had changed her. This part of what had happened had been a gift.

I was not to see Jennifer till a year had passed and it was winter again. I was with Nina. We had gone in for a hurried lunch at Ollie's, the Chinese restaurant near the university gates. We had eaten spicy mock duck with steaming bowls of rice. When we stepped out in the cold, I put my arm around Nina. I was about to tell her that I wished I had drunk a Tsingtao. I stayed silent because I was looking at Jennifer. I knew the coat she was wearing and also the gloves. Our eyes met. She didn't acknowledge me but her upper lip curled up over her teeth in such distress that I was transported to the room in the clinic where I had seen her lying on the bed with the sheet drawn up to her neck. I looked away and walked briskly ahead of Nina, who, incidentally, never asked me anything about Jennifer and so we never discussed what had happened between us.

Coming down the steps outside his apartment building, Ehsaan fell down and twisted his ankle. Walking turned out to be difficult for him and our seminar temporarily shifted to his home. We still had the wine and the plastic cups. The subjects of discussion that day were issues of displacement and exile, focused on the writings of Edward Said ('Reflections on Exile'), Assia Djebar ('There is No Exile'), and Anton Shammas ('Amérka, Amérka'). One of the students in the seminar, Negin, who was Iranian and had grown up in Los Angeles, said she had really liked Djebar. There is no exile for women. When women lose their country and live somewhere else, the customs of the old country follow them there. They are never able to escape it. Negin's mother had said to Negin's elder sister, who was studying law, 'Don't be a whore.' The mother wanted a marriage in which the family would play a part. But the sister was fighting back. Like one of Djebar's characters, Negin's sister told her parents, 'I won't marry.'

Ehsaan was sitting in a chair with his hurt leg raised and resting on a stool. He tilted his head toward Negin as she told her story and then, when she stopped, he told us about his mother. When Ehsaan left his village Irki in 1947, to accompany refugees going across to Pakistan, his mother stayed back in India. Her exile was different from Djebar's. Ehsaan said his mother saw the people who were fighting for Pakistan as reactionary and insufficiently anticolonial. That was one side of the picture. On the other side, unlike Ehsaan's older brothers who had eager plans about what they wanted to do in the new country, their mother was faced with a simpler task. Ehsaan's sister Aba had fallen sick. She had typhoid.

—My mother decided to take care of my sister who would not have been able to make that arduous journey.

—When did you see them again? Negin asked.

—I didn't, not my sister at least. She died. This was about ten-eleven years later. I saw my mother then. She came to Pakistan for a while before returning again to the village in India. She had liked the life there. We brought her back when she fell ill. She died in Pakistan.

He became silent. I thought of my mother in Patna. She was waiting for me to come back after I had received my degree. Soon, she would be old too. And my grandmother in the village, whom I could see in my mind's eye placing two or three red hibiscus flowers on the shrine in her courtyard. The shrine was a dark stone, no bigger than a fist, on a brick and cement pedestal about four feet high that had projecting from it a tall bamboo with a red jhandi on the top. The brief morning prayer was my grandmother's first act of the day after her bath, her hair still wet, a fresh cotton sari wrapped around her. As it happened, I was never to see her again. On my second Diwali in America, I called my neighbours' phone in Patna so that I could speak to my parents. My sister came on the phone and said that our parents had gone to the village to take care of my grandmother who was very sick.

—She was asking about you—that's what Ma said.

—Why didn't you go?

—I just got back today. I have my exams in three days.

—Are you celebrating Diwali?

—No fireworks in the house this year.

My sister, older than me, was telling me that our grandmother had died. This clear thought came to me only after I had hung up the phone. My next thought was that my sister must have rushed home from our neighbours', crying. When I imagined this, my own tears came. Before I left India, my grandmother had joked that I would marry a white woman and become a sahib. I would never return home. But I'm going to bring my white bride to the village, I said to her. And she said, No, no, don't do that. She will ask you why your grandmother has got such a flat nose. It is flat like a bedbug's back.

A letter from my mother arrived two weeks later. It wasn't an aerogramme letter. Instead, it was an envelope with a photograph inside of my dead grandmother's face with a white garland around her head. My mother had written that I shouldn't feel bad, that my grandmother had passed away peacefully. I was asked to pray for her peace. Light an agarbatti and put it near the photograph. *Think good thoughts*, my mother wrote.

The discussion at Ehsaan's house that day began with Said's line that 'exile is strangely compelling to think about but terrible to experience'. Said was Ehsaan's friend; we all knew that both had worked together for the rights of dispossessed Palestinians. But the story that Ehsaan was telling us about his mother and his sister made me think of him as an exile too, suffering what Said had described as 'crippling sorrow of estrangement'. *Your Honour, I've been asked, when did it all start? When did I start becoming the person I am today? I don't know whether there is a simple answer to that question. But it was perhaps during that seminar session in Ehsaan's house that, under the influence of Said's words, I started to think of everything heroic or glorious in Ehsaan's life as nothing more than efforts meant to overcome that great sorrow.*

For this class, we had also read a recent magazine piece by Anton Shammas, a Palestinian writer who grew up in Israel. Ehsaan wanted us to tell him whether the idea of a 'portable homeland', the things that migrants carry with them, appealed to us. I spoke up. I said that I had found very moving the story that Shammas had told of a Palestinian man bringing to

San Francisco the small plants and seeds that were native to
the West Bank. And, hidden in his heavy black coat, the seven
representative birds of his homeland: 'the duri, the hassoun, the
sununu, the shahrur, the bulbul, the summan, and the hudhud,
small-talk companion to King Solomon himself.'

Even the names of the different kind of birds were charming.
When I read that list, I thought of the birds of my own past,
and of the koel's song in the summer.

Ehsaan was smiling. He raised the glass of wine in his hand.

—Kailash, please tell us, when you left home recently and
travelled to America, what did you bring with you?

—I was thinking of that question when reading
Shammas. I carried in my suitcase a copy of the *Illustrated
Weekly of India* with a photo-essay on Bihar. The photos are
in black-and-white. I recognize them as images from the place
where I have my roots.

—The magazine with the pictures, Ehsaan said, instead of
what someone in an earlier time might have done—the earth
from his native place in a jar, perhaps.

He looked at the others.

—I brought pictures of my parents and my dog, Peter said.

Others had probably done the same because they were nodding.

When no one else offered a response, Ehsaan said that
Palestinians who left their homeland and were never able to
return still keep the keys to the houses they had been forced to
abandon. The keys are useless now because the locks are gone.
But those keys are their portable homeland.

I had left home willingly but was still struck by how little
I had brought with me. It was as if I imagined I was going to
discover a new self. I thought of my own room in the university
apartment. The walls were bare—there was a window, but no
pictures—and the room smelled of the cheap synthetic sheets
I used. There was a lemon-yellow electric blanket on the bed.
Instead of my parents' photographs, I had carried in my suitcase
a magazine, my certificates, my degrees, a fading affidavit or
two. I had brought with me a few music cassettes in their

brittle plastic cases. Geeta Dutt, C. H. Atma, Mohammed Rafi, Hemant Kumar. In my apartment, I read for class while lying in bed, music playing on a two-in-one. For many years, often full of self-pity, I would think that Lata Mangeshkar was singing the anthem for people like me: *Tum na jaane kis jahan mein kho gaye...*

⌣

One day in class, my classmate, Siobhan, who seemed to be a current or past office-holder in all the progressive student organizations on campus, said that there was going to be a teach-in. War was imminent in the Persian Gulf. President Bush had sent the troops to Saudi Arabia and they were going to proceed to Kuwait to force Saddam to withdraw. There was a goateed speaker from Political Science who spoke a long time on the role of the oil economy in the war. The Iraqi invasion in Kuwait had actually benefitted the oil companies in the West. The rise in oil prices had earned them huge profits. This was true not only of the US but also companies based in other countries, all the way from Saudi Arabia to Venezuela.

Why then did the Bush administration go to war? Oil production from non-OPEC countries had declined in recent years, and the same story could be seen unfolding in the US. As Saudi Arabia, Kuwait and the United Emirates were of critical importance in the production of oil to serve our needs, Bush couldn't allow Iraq to dictate terms or control worldwide oil prices. In just the past few years, US reliance on Gulf oil had gone up fourfold, and if we understood this we would know why the US troops had been sent to the Middle East.

When the speaker finished, a group of students began to chant 'No Blood for Oil! No Blood for Oil!' Others were holding up signs. One said: 'A Kinder Gentler Bloodbath'. Two young women were holding the ends of a bedsheet on which they had spray-painted the words 'George Bush is Having a Wargasm'.

The writer Grace Paley, a tiny woman with a halo of silver hair, was asked to address the crowd. She spoke about a Marine named Jeff Patterson who, back in August, refused to join his unit. He sat down on the airstrip in Hawaii, unwilling to fight in a war he didn't believe in. He had joined the army to receive an education, but the time he spent at bases in Okinawa, South Korea and the Philippines changed his outlook. He was the first protestor from among American ranks; others were to join him later. Paley read out a statement from Patterson: 'I have, as an artillery controller, directed cannons on Oahu, rained burning white phosphorus and tons of high explosive on the big island, and blasted away at the island of Kaholawe... I can bend no further.' Before she ended, Paley said she agreed with what had been said about oil and war. The reality was even worse, she said. There was alternative energy for everything in normal, comfortable American life—television, air conditioners, light, heat, cars. There was only one enterprise that needed such massive infusion of energy that no alternative to oil would work—and that was war. A tank could move only seventeen feet on a gallon of gasoline. This war was a war to ensure that America could continue to make war.

Next it was Ehsaan's turn. Siobhan introduced him as her favourite professor. She said he had only recently spent a year teaching in Beirut. Ehsaan was wearing a tan sweater over a black turtleneck. His grey hair was cut short. He looked handsome. He smiled and said that as it was a teach-in he wouldn't waste time making jokes about Vice President Dan Quayle. Except we needed to be clear that in imperialist adventures the children of the rich didn't bear most of the ordeal. In other words, we should note that Quayle didn't enlist to fight in Vietnam, he joined the National Guard. Nearly sixty thousand Americans were killed in the Vietnam War, but of that number, fewer than a hundred were members of the National Guard. That was the reason why Quayle had joined the National Guard in Indiana.

Despite his cowardly record, Quayle had only the previous day spoken in New York, not two miles away from where we were meeting, in favour of an assault by the US. Ehsaan had questions for Quayle: Who will fight in our army? Who will be fighting in the Iraqi army? Who will get killed? He followed these questions by saying that, like Grace Paley, he too was going to read a letter written by a soldier. The letter had been written by an Indian soldier in the British Army during the First World War. The soldier was fighting in Mesopotamia, in what is present-day Iraq. He had written home in 1916 that a part of the 7th Brigade in which he was fighting was besieged and surrounded on all sides by the enemy. *Attempts have been made to rescue them, but without success. There was a fight on 6th March and heavy losses to us in the attempt to relieve them. Some of our men are in the besieged force, twenty in number. They have eaten their horses and mules. They have a quarter of a pound of flour each per diem. We are hopeful of being sent to join the relieving force.* Such precision about the pain and the suffering of comrades fighting in a war. A war, mind you, that has nothing to do with the private destinies and choices of these soldiers themselves. The whole truth is even more unbearable.

Ehsaan's voice rose higher. From records kept during the siege we learn that British officers amused themselves by designing menus featuring horseflesh. We also learn that Major Stewart's *devoted batman was killed while bringing his mule-steak lunch to his dugout*. No need to guess the race of the batman. He was killed because Churchill had acquired for the British government ninety per cent of the shares in a corporation called the Anglo-Persian Oil Company. It was necessary to control Basra; the lives of thousands of Indian soldiers be damned. If we are really interested in supporting our troops, which not incidentally are made up of a huge number of disadvantaged youth from minority communities, if we are interested in supporting these young men and women of colour, then let's not put them in harm's way to benefit a group of oil companies and the government that promotes their interests everywhere.

Loud applause at the end. I looked around for Nina but she wasn't there. My hands were cold and I liked the idea of smoking a cigarette with her. But I had an ethnography class in Schermerhorn in ten minutes and so I rushed away without shaking Ehsaan's hand.*

᷉

Nina and I met in a film seminar that first semester.† She had short-cropped hair, large brown eyes and impetuous lips. Her movements were full of allure; she was small-built and athletic: a dancer till her late teens. Even when she was not moving, just sitting in the dark watching the films that were screened for us in the small classroom, I was always aware of the outline of her features. Sometimes, instead of watching the film, I'd study

---

*A distinguished Dutch professor whose own research was conducted in Indonesia taught the ethnography course. He also had an interest in South Asia and the previous week he had screened a short documentary about a servant boy in a small town in India. I had found the documentary moving and certainly convincing. Growing up, I had witnessed the abuse of children employed as servants in homes all around me. But my own experience with servants was a bit different. Jeevan, a young, lower-caste man from our village, was the domestic help in the house when I was a boy. I must have been around four when Jeevan brought me to the bathroom door and asked me to peer inside. I hadn't noticed the crack in the wood before. And now I saw, as if in a film, my unmarried aunt, my father's younger sister, standing under the shower. I distinctly remember being puzzled, and perhaps embarrassed, by the patch of hair below her stomach. How had Jeevan known that I wouldn't tell my parents about this? This question didn't occur to me till I was in my late teens. I had forgotten the scene for years and cannot now recall what forced its return. I saw Jeevan in the village before I left for the US. He was a farmer now, prematurely aged, every part of his body shrunken except for the toenails on his cracked, bare feet. The soles of his feet had holes in them, as if a tiny screw had been put in and then taken out before repeating the process elsewhere, holes that Jeevan attributed to his standing for hours in the water in his paddy field. I photographed his feet and used the image in my first book, *Passport Photos* (Berkeley: University of California Press, 2000).
†If the reader in indiscriminate haste has rushed past the epigraph from Abraham Verghese on page 32, this would be a fine occasion to return to it. Even strong and genuine emotions can have their start in pure fantasy. Nina was a site of fantasy, yes, but she was also her own person, passionate and daring.

the light fluctuating on her face. One day, after the screening of Sidney Lumet's *Dog Day Afternoon*, I saw Nina bent over the water fountain. She raised her face, her mouth still wet.

I wanted to ask you something, I said to her. Nina laughed and asked if I wanted to know whether she was fertile. Although she was laughing, her look was calm and assessing. I, too, laughed. There was a great deal of nervousness in my laughter because I didn't know what to say. No, I told her, I only wanted to know whether she was going to register for Comp Lit 300 that would be taught the following semester.

—As a matter of fact, I am. How can I not enrol in a course that appears on the transcript as CLIT 300?

The following week in the film class we were discussing Nagisa Oshima's *In the Realm of the Senses*. The professor was a small Frenchwoman whose face and neck would get covered in hives if you asked uncomfortable questions.* An Italian girl was making a convoluted argument about Japanese cinema; she had recently watched a film about a nuclear explosion on Mount Fuji. Nina was sitting in a chair next to me. I don't know what possessed me but I passed a scrap of paper to her. On it I had written:

> *Wet moss between your thighs*
> *Semen*
> *Rains on Mt Fuji*

---

*I'm grateful to that professor for the useful advice she gave me later. I was ignorant of all conventions of academic paper-writing. At the end of the semester, after giving me a C, she pointed out very gently that I should buy an instruction manual. Many years later, when I was older and wiser, or at least more experienced, I came across a parody of that writing guide by Strunk and White. Written by a duo called Baker and Hansen. I thought their examples would have stuck with me if I had read them in college. Here were their own examples for what the original manual had provided under the rule 'Omit needless words':

*Used for the purpose of sexual pleasure. (wrong)*
*Used for sexual pleasure. (right)*

*His penis is a misshapen and uncircumcised one. (wrong)*
*His penis is misshapen and uncircumcised. (right)*

She surprised me by putting a small tongue out as if she was licking ice cream.

After I met Nina, I would buy magazines like *Cosmopolitan* at the supermarket if they had headlines like 'Ten Hottest Things You Can Say In Bed' or 'Seventy-Seven Sex Positions.' What did I learn from them? That I was supposed to say, *Is it okay with you if I take this slow?*

During a long ago winter afternoon, in Delhi, in my early teens, I had watched *Tootsie* at the Chanakya cinema hall. Dustin Hoffman, disguised as a woman, listens to the beautiful Jessica Lange complaining.

—You know what I wish? That a guy could be honest enough to walk up to me and say, 'I could lay a big line on you, but the simple truth is that I find you very interesting, and I'd like to make love to you.' Wouldn't that be a relief?

That had given me insight, except that it was short-lived. For, later in the movie, Hoffman, now without his disguise, sees Lange at a cocktail party. He tries out that speech on her and before he has even finished she has thrown a glass of wine in his face.

A better person would have learned to walk a fine line between the two conversations. Not me. I swung from one extreme to the other. Hence my hunger for instruction. When I met Nina I also bought *Romance for Dummies* by Dr Ruth. Dr Ruth encouraged you to make noise while having sex: *While you retain the right to remain silent, perhaps you could speak up a little before your final act.* Even a four-letter word. She said you never know how you'll react unless you give it a try at least one time. I enacted a silly pantomime when I came inside Nina that first time, not a war whoop exactly, more of a raised fist celebrating the revolutionary storming of the barricades. She, on the other hand, was silent, even pensive, though later that night she was affectionate, smiling, and this took away some of my foreboding. But here I'm getting ahead of myself.

In my department mailbox, just before Thanksgiving, there

appeared a red flyer.

'Do you like Walt Whitman? Yes, I like Walt Whitman. *Leaves of Grass.*'
Calling all foreign TAs. Come and learn to speak English by watching *Down By Law* (dir. Jim Jarmusch).
We will begin at 8 PM. 514 W 121st Street, Apt 3B. Door on the Left. Bell doesn't work. Don't let the cat out!
B.Y.O.B. 242-7311.
Host: Peter Koerner.

I took a bottle of wine for Peter. There was a naked woman on the label with the name Cycles Gladiator printed above her. The woman had a fleshy rump and long, fiery orange-red hair flying behind her. She was floating in the air, her hands on the handle of a bicycle outfitted with tiny, colourful wings. This would be to Peter's liking.

Maya from International Relations was already there, looking like the Rani of Awadh, a cat in her lap. Flowing silks and a sleepy animal with jewelled eyes. I recognized some of the others. There was Sean, the French graduate student and a black belt, who, I had heard, counted loudly (three-hundred-forty-three... three-hundred-forty-four...three-hundred-forty-five) when he was fucking. This information had come from Sean's housemate, an Irishman who had described himself, by way of comparison, as a 'semi-silent fucker'. Paulo, one of the Chilean anthropologists, was also someone I knew. He was there in the company of a woman with the semblance of a moustache.

I uncorked the bottle of wine I had brought. Then, I saw Nina stepping out of the bathroom, an air of privacy still attached to her. I went up to her hurriedly but she thought I only wanted to go to the bathroom, and stood back sideways, her back pressed against the wall to let me pass. We smiled at each other and I kept walking. Inside, I studied my face in the mirror. A wild thatch of black, curly hair. Round-rimmed glasses that failed

to hide thick eyebrows. The face looking back at me wasn't
ugly, but it was definitely ordinary. It didn't inspire confidence
that a woman in the room outside would look at it and think
she wanted to kiss it. I had been with Jennifer earlier in the
evening, we had eaten cheap Tibetan food together. But the
women in Peter's house, with whom I had sat in classes, were
still strangers to me.

When I came back I saw that Nina was sitting on a small
sofa with Paulo. I positioned myself on the armrest next to
Paulo and stayed silent because Nina and he were discussing
the music of Ornette Coleman. Others in the room were also
talking among themselves and drinking. Siobhan quoted a line
from a short story she had read in an American lit. class: 'To
see her in sunlight was to see Marxism die.' I hadn't heard the
writer's name before—and what was he really saying? Siobhan
was mocking the politics embedded in such desire. The people
bunched around her agreed with the analysis. One of them,
Marc, a poet who always carried a tiny tin of Altoids in his
hand, touched his hair and said, 'You can absolutely date this
brand of sexuality. It's an artifact of the Cold War!' But I liked
that line from the story even though I didn't understand what
it meant. I wish I had said it myself. Through the glass door
on the left I could see a small group was standing on the patio
outside—another feature of life in America, where you went
out into the fresh air to smoke. Inside, just before he put the
film on, Peter went up to Maya and kissed her on the cheek.
Maya touched Peter's face, and then made space for him on
the sofa. The cat left her lap and jumped away. For a moment,
or a little longer, I thought about what I had just seen. Maya's
undisguised affection for Peter and her plain, loving gesture in
front of everyone else. When had they fallen in love? It gave me
a little bit of a shock but it also made me feel guilty: I thought
of Jennifer and what she had said once about my not wanting
to touch her in public. Even if we had been lovers I wouldn't
have acted like Maya. I would not have rubbed noses and smiled
at her while our friends pretended not to notice.

The film was in black and white. An Italian man named Roberto was wandering in the night in New Orleans. Roberto carried a notebook with him and he diligently recorded all the American idioms he heard. He ended up in the Orleans Parish Prison, every surface in the film lit up with the dramatic lighting familiar to me from the Hindi films of the fifties or the sixties. Roberto attempted to speak like an American, except that he kept mangling his sentences.

—Jack, do you have some fire? This was Roberto asking his cellmate for a match because he wanted to light his cigarette.

Whenever I laughed, I looked at Nina. She was watching the screen with an amused expression. Roberto was charming; he had killed a man after an altercation at a game of cards, but he insisted that he was 'a good egg'. And he was! He had found a way to escape from prison. On the run, he lost his 'book of English', but he continued to entertain. He had memorized the American poets in translation, Whitman and others. I heard Frost's 'The Road Less Traveled' in Italian.

On the lam, Roberto found love. When he and his new girlfriend Nicoletta were looking into each other's eyes, someone standing behind me said they were speaking 'the language of love'. During these scenes I would sometimes think of Jennifer and at other times think of Nina. The film made me sentimental, lovesick, and Roberto's good luck gave me courage.

—Are you walking home? I asked Nina when she was leaving.

The sidewalks were darkened by the fallen autumn leaves. A shiny car passed slowly, music coming out of its open windows, and Nina said something about loving Prince. In a high falsetto, she sang, 'Cause nothing compares...' and then skipped ahead of me. I ran behind her.

—Do you have fire?

Nina was game. She pretended to give me a light, and I made as if to shake out a cigarette. When I cupped my hands around the pretend flame, her hands were nesting in mine. I found her touch thrilling. Even before I had reached her building, about five or six blocks from mine, I began to ask myself if I would ever kiss those hands. Her hands, her smooth arms. Her lips. Despite it not being very cold on the street my teeth began to chatter with excitement.

When we got to her street, Nina stood at the door and said, Do you want to come in?

—No, I said, a bit too quickly, and the hand I half-raised to say goodbye was almost reaching towards her. I turned away into the dark. Jennifer and I hadn't broken up yet, and that was part of the reason I had hesitated. The bigger reason was that I was a coward. I was disappointed that I hadn't had the courage to say yes but I was also secretly exulting. Nina's invitation was an augury for the future.

A week before the Christmas break, papers were to be submitted for all the classes. I could type them in my room or go to the library and use the word processors. I had only a little experience writing academic papers, and I feared that I was going to do badly. And what was I going to write about for Ehsaan?* I asked him about the letter he had read out at the teach-in. He gave me the title of a book by a British historian named David Omissi; in that book, I found other letters by Indian soldiers serving in the First World War, most of them in France. It would be best, I decided, if I could stitch together my commentary by taking excerpts from the letters I liked.

Fateh Mohamed had written in his letter to Punjab: *The*

---

*We had read E. M. Forster, Joseph Conrad, Frantz Fanon, Patricia Limerick, Assia Djebar, C. L. R. James and others. Ehsaan's one-paragraph description on the course syllabus read: 'This course views Western expansion into the Americas, Asia, and Africa as a development which shaped world history and civilization more decisively than any phenomenon other than capitalism. Beyond broadly surveying the course of Western expansion, our purpose is to explore its legacies to our time and modern civilization. Our focus is primarily on the outlook, cultures and mores, the ways of being and doing that, despite their enormous variety, colonial encounters spawned. Given this concern, the course shall rely primarily on historical narrative, literature, criticism, and cinema. Independently interested students are urged to inquire into art, an area we have not formally included.'

*cold for the last five or six days has been more intense than we have experienced during the two former winters. If one puts water into a vessel it is frozen in ten minutes. At the same time, there is a strong wind. If France had not been such a sympathetic country, existence under such conditions would be impossible. Through the kindness of these people [the French] we pay no regard to the cold. They themselves refrain from sitting near the fire-place and insist on our sitting there. Moreover, instead of water they give us* petit cidre, *which is the juice of apples to drink. Personally, except in the trenches, I have never drunk water.*

Too readily, I identified with what was in the letters: the desire to report on what was new but also to exaggerate, to make things extraordinary, to say that I eat meat every day or that I'm served juice and wine.* In most letters, however, the pathos was the plot. Consider the cry in another letter (less a letter than a single keening note) from Muhammad Akbar Khan to his home—*Is my parrot still alive or dead?*

A letter sent to Peshawar: *I have been in Hodson's Horse for the whole thirty-three years. During a railway journey when two people sit side by side for a couple of hours, one of them feels the absence of the other when he alights: how great then must be the anguish which I feel at the thought of having to sever myself from the regiment!* Such fine feeling! When I read the old soldier's letter I found myself thinking that this intense vibration of sentiment, the sense that the sender had about the sorrow of attachment, could only have come about through a long experience with separation and loneliness.

---

*There was such emphatic poetry present in the account of everyday reality. Let's read this letter that Kala Khan wrote to Iltaf Hussain in Patiala—*You enquire about the cold? At present I can only say that the earth is white, the sky is white, the trees are white, the stones are white, the mud is white, the water is white, one's spittle freezes into a solid white lump, the water is as hard as stones or bricks, the water in the rivers and canals is like thick plate glass. We are each provided with two pairs of strong, expensive boots. We have whale oil to rub in our feet, and for food we are provided with live Spanish sheep.*

At times, the soldiers seemed aware that the censor authorities would be reading their letters. They offered praise for the British king. They tried hard to reassure their loved ones. The soldiers were often careful in their phrasing of demands for goods that they could use to make themselves appear sick. Or high. One soldier wrote to say that the next time his relatives sent opium to France they should only say that it was cream to be rubbed into his beard. For their part, the censors withheld some letters or deleted parts of them. This was true also of the soldier's advice about the dispatch of opium.

Even when they were passed by the censors, several of the letters appeared unusual or transgressive to me, full of sexual boasting, and I was left unsure about what to make of them. A letter from Tura Baz Khan of the 40th Pathans from the Boulogne Depot in France: *[He encloses a cigarette card of Jane, Duchess of Gordon, After Sir Joshua Reynolds'.] This is the woman we get. We have recourse to her. I have sent you this [her picture] and if you like it, let me know, and I will send her. We get everything we want. [Letter withheld].*

A letter that I commented on at length in my paper had been sent by a soldier from the 20th Deccan Horse Regiment stationed in France; I didn't entirely understand the letter or its circumstances, but I was drawn by its quiet undercurrent of sadness and resignation. It was addressed to the headmaster of the soldier's village in Punjab and though it concerned a matter that was intimate, the language of the letter was formal, even abstract. For me, it was an example of a writer standing on the edge of grief.

*My idea is that, since it is now four years since I went to my home, my wife should, if she wishes it, be allowed to have connection according to Vedic rites with some other man, in order that children may be born to my house. If this is not done, then the family dignity will suffer. Indeed, this practice should now be followed in the case of all wives whose husbands have been absent for four years or more. It is permitted by Vedic rites, if the wives are willing. Everyone knows that that article, the consumption of which is increased while the production is stopped, will in time cease to exist.*

Other letters were easier to understand. Easier to understand, yes, but still difficult to accept. A brief unambiguous missive from Kabul Singh of the 31st Lancers: *Asil Singh Jat and Harbans have done a vile thing. They forcibly violated a French girl, nineteen years of age. It is a matter of great humiliation and regret that the good name of the 31st Lancers should have been sullied in this way.*

I got the paper back by mail instead of finding it in my department mailbox. In two places on the paper, Ehsaan had written *Good* in the margin. There was a paragraph of typed remarks on notepad paper stapled to the last page. Ehsaan had found my commentary on the letters 'a little thin'. There were various questions that I could have considered: What were the rules regarding desertion? How much did the soldiers earn? What was the imperial expenditure during the war? What were the customs as well as the laws regarding marriage? What was the punishment for rape? My eyes went down to the last line of the paragraph. I had escaped grievous bodily harm: he had given me a B.

*Part III*
_____
# Laura

umbrella made sense. I could really see him doing something like that." Walker is passionate about Hollinger's sculpture. "The first time I saw Steve's art work was the week I was getting married," she said. "I thought it was so amazing—so complex and sensitive and deep that I said to myself, If I meet this guy, I'm not going to get married!"

This was not the first time a Hollinger

The above clipping in my notebook is, I believe, from 2008. I don't know, or no longer remember, the individuals involved. I must've read it, and liked it, as a startling statement about the meeting of art and desire.

Also, in a child's hand, on a piece of paper torn from a sheet: 'Happy Fact: Otters hold hands when they sleep, so they don't float away from each other.'

*—Mr Kissinger, you're under arrest.*

This was to be said after dessert. Everything would be calm. Nothing out of the ordinary. Ehsaan believed that because they were academics, and had friends in common, they could get invited to a dinner where Kissinger was also a guest. People sipped cognac in such circles. Ehsaan would choose the moment to speak. He was articulate: his words commanded attention. He would get up and make the announcement about the arrest, addressing Kissinger directly.

Then Kissinger was to be taken to a meeting of anti-war activists. He would be questioned about war policies. The police by then would have started a massive manhunt, of course. The accused was to be moved from one hiding place to another, and, within a day or two, a statement would be issued that he had been arrested for crimes of war. The point was to educate the public. Put the war back on the front pages instead of endless stories about the breakup of the Beatles or Jim Morrison's allegedly lewd and lascivious behaviour. They would be clear about their

aims. Kissinger was to be released if the government stopped
B-52 raids in North Vietnam.

They had just been sitting around in a borrowed house in
Weston, Connecticut. A white single-storey house with a large
screened porch in the front. It belonged to Ehsaan's in-laws, who
were away in Europe at that time. He had cooked rice pulao and
chicken curry. Everyone was drinking chilled vin rosé and, when
that was gone, gin and tonic. Out of the ease of the evening, the
lingering light of the summer, and the flow of the conversation
among friends, had come the talk about making a citizen's arrest.

*Mr Kissinger, you're under arrest.* This phrase was noted more
than once in the indictment.

Ehsaan just laughed when I asked him about the Kissinger
trial. So many years had passed. But he had a purple mimeographed
article, pale with age, from the Bulletin of Atomic Scientists.
Noam Chomsky had given it to him, or maybe Howard Zinn,
he couldn't remember. At some point during the public trial of
Kissinger a member of their group would inform the American
public that the B-52 bombings had turned the rice fields of
Vietnam into a lunar landscape. The countryside was now useless
for crops, gouged by craters, some as large as 45 feet across and
30 feet deep. Placed end to end, these craters would form a ditch
30,000 miles long, a distance greater than the circumference of
the earth.

Ehsaan said that the idea first emerged at an anti-war rally at
St Gregory's Church in New York City. *Yes, Your Honour, ordinary
Americans had committed themselves to a plan of administering justice
because they felt that their government was acting in a lawless manner.*
At any large gathering a person would simply get up and say:
'We hereby arrest, in citizen's arrest, such-and-such people who
are government leaders.' Then 'subpoenas' would be 'issued.' It
was all symbolic, and involved no concrete action. The goal was
education. You would tell people that the task of filling the craters
in Vietnam would require moving 2.5 billion cubic yards of earth.
That unforeseen medical problems now ravaged the population
there. That people were living underground day and night, and

children were suffering from many disorders, including rickets
from living without sunlight.

The idea of arresting Kissinger was an escalation in the war
on war, a step-up from earlier actions like the burning of draft
records or the dumping of three buckets of human waste into the
Selective Service filing cabinet. But the idea didn't go any further,
because how would you get somebody like Henry Kissinger
without using some form of coercion? It seemed implausible.
Ehsaan and his guests spent twenty minutes discussing this plan
that evening but abandoned it even before the ice had melted
in the glasses from which they were drinking.

Except that, a few months later, in November 1970, when
J. Edgar Hoover spoke in a Senate Appropriations Committee
hearing, he mentioned this conspiracy and, for good measure,
a plan to blow up underground electrical conduits and steam
pipes serving the Washington, D.C. area. It was pure fabrication,
Ehsaan would say later. Along with Ehsaan, the others named by
Hoover were two Catholic priests and two nuns who had been
active in the peace movement. After having made the public
accusation, Hoover now threw hundreds of his agents into the
investigation of anti-war activities. A little over a month later, FBI
agents knocked on doors to serve federal grand jury subpoenas
to scores of people. There was going to be a trial.

—Everything about the way the government put the case
together and pursued it was exaggerated and comical. We had
reasoned, over the caprese, that Kissinger was the right person
to arrest. He was a bachelor, with many girlfriends. I guessed
he wouldn't want too many bodyguards around.

For his part, after Hoover's announcement, Kissinger
speculated that 'sex starved nuns' were behind the plot to kidnap
him. President Nixon gave the go-ahead by saying that he would
let the Justice Department carry out its prosecution unimpeded.
Ehsaan said that they phoned William Kunstler, and after a
hurried meeting, the famed counsellor released a statement on
their behalf: 'Mr. Hoover is overgenerous. We have neither the
facilities nor personnel to conduct such an enterprise. Nor do

we have access to unallocated funds like the government does....'
Their struggle was to impart a sense of reality into a scenario
made feverish by Hoover's paranoid imagination. That is why the
lead defence counsel, Ramsey Clark, in his opening statement
on the first day of the trial, reminded the jury, 'Of course we
know that Henry Kissinger wasn't kidnapped. He is alive and
well in Peking today.'

The trial was held in Harrisburg, during the first three months
of 1972. *Your Honour, there would have been no indictment, and
no trial, had it not been for a letter that was written after that
summer meeting in Weston, Connecticut. A love letter, no less. This is
the juncture where I wish to note, once and for all, that the plot of
history advances through the acts of lovers. Oh, the wisdom of love.
The superiority of love and its many follies. I also wish to add that
these details were later to be faithfully communicated to Nina when
she and I fell in love. The discovery of these details I think was a part
of the excitement of being in love with her. Do you understand what
I am getting at here, Your Honour? I beg for the Court's forbearance.*
Present at that planning dinner in Weston, Connecticut, on the
night of 17 August 1970, had been a young woman named
Laura Campbell. Laura had just started teaching Art History at
a Catholic college in New York. She was also a nun. And she
was falling in love with a man to whom she wrote letters each
week in prison. He was a priest who had waited for the police
to come and arrest him after he had poured blood on draft
records to protest the war.

The priest's name was Francis Hull. He was serving a six-year
sentence in Lewisburg, Pennsylvania, for his anti-war activities;
he was also a participant in the civil rights movement and a
critic of the isolated stance of the church in black communities.
Father Hull had said, 'I have faith in the Almighty who will
save our souls. I am just trying to save the lives of the young
blacks being sent to Vietnam.'

Father Hull also had faith in a fellow convict, Douglas Adams.
Adams was on a student release programme and would go each
day to Bucknell University to take classes. While on campus, he

would hand over to a librarian named Mary any letters from Hull that he had smuggled out in his notebooks. The letters were for Campbell, mostly, but also, on occasion, for other activists. Mary, in turn, gave Adams the letters she had received in the mail from Laura. Neither Francis Hull nor Laura Campbell knew that Adams would carefully open each letter and make a photocopy that he would take back with him to prison in a manila envelope. This was because after he had read the first letter from Laura to Francis, and dutifully made a copy, he had approached the FBI and become an informant.

Ehsaan hadn't even laid eyes on Adams until the trial began and Adams, flanked by US marshals, stepped into the courtroom. He was a thickset man in a lavender shirt standing stiffly on the sea of slime that was the court carpet. He was the main witness for the government. Adams would not look at any of the defendants. In his deposition, he made the claim that Ehsaan had called him twice, at a laundromat, to discuss plans to kidnap Kissinger. Ehsaan told the press that this was 'a complete falsehood'. Admittedly, Adams didn't have any qualities that would have incited Ehsaan's interest or trust. Adams had served for a short time in the US military in Korea, and then passed bad cheques and stolen a car. Back in America, after escaping from a military stockade, he had once again used forged cheques in Las Vegas and then Atlantic City. His father, in conversation with a journalist, said that his son had not spoken the truth even once in his life.

Yet, Adams was a kind of a charmer. At Bucknell, he told the young women he befriended that he was very active in the anti-war movement and was probably under surveillance by the authorities. He claimed close friendship with Francis Hull, the mention of whose name stirred people's curiosity and admiration. Adams started dating two female students. He proposed to one of them, a blonde named Jane, but she had doubts about marrying him. To put her in a better frame of mind, Adams went ahead and bought her a bus ticket so that she could travel to New York City for the first time in her life, where she was to meet Sister

Laura and open her heart to her. This was a plan suggested by
Adams. En route, Jane opened a letter from Adams that he had
said she should wait to read till she was on the bus. The greeting
he had used, as well as the words he had employed to sign off,
had been borrowed from what he had seen in Laura's letters to
Francis. He had also written that if he sometimes appeared distant
in his manner it was because someone close to him had once
ratted him out to the FBI. Adams told Jane in the letter that
he had proposed to her because he had cancer and he wanted
her to give him six months of happiness.

Let us pause here for a moment. The contempt that Ehsaan
and others felt towards Adams, that feeling, slightly exaggerated,
is in my heart too: in a memory that is not mine, I see Adams
stepping into the courtroom flanked by armed marshals who
tower protectively above him and I hiss in anger. Adams looks
nervous because in all the stories we have read liars look around
apprehensively while still managing to avoid meeting anyone's
eyes. Ehsaan will not even look at him, but I do. My interest
in Adams borders on sympathy. He claimed that he was close
to Hull, he thought the women he wanted to date would be
impressed; I was to do the same with Nina, bringing back to her
stories of my encounters with Ehsaan. Adams stole words from
Hull and Laura, and used them in the letters he wrote to Jane. I
don't want to be Adams in his plaid shirt and oversized glasses,
and I don't want to sweat like him, but I am him. *Let me explain
with an example, Your Honour.* In Ehsaan's class the previous
semester I had read Stuart Hall who was born in Jamaica and
spent most of his life in England where he gained a following
as an enormously influential cultural theorist. In his essay, Hall
said that people like him who came to England in the fifties had
actually been there for centuries. He was talking about slavery and
sugar plantations. 'I am the sugar at the bottom of the English
cup of tea.'* Symbolically, Hall was saying, the people from the

---

*Stuart Hall, 'Old and New Identities, Old and New Ethnicities.' Xeroxed
copy of an article in typescript sent to Ehsaan by his old friend Hall. The

from the darker nations had a long history in the West. The symbol of English identity was the cup of tea, but where did the tea come from? 'Because they don't grow it in Lancashire, you know. Not a single tea plantation exists within the United Kingdom. Where does it come from? Ceylon, India. That is the outside history that is inside the history of the English. There is no English history without that other history.' Powerful stuff and delivered in Hall's inimitable way. In a poem I was to write for Nina a few months later, I shamelessly put as my closing line: *I'm the sugar at the bottom of your coffee, I'm the colour in your cup of tea.* End of pause.

Laura Campbell and Francis Hull had hit upon a strategy. They were afraid that a guard could discover their letters if he checked the pages of the notebooks where Adams used to hide them. So, they would always begin as if they were putting together a college essay. Laura Campbell titled the letter that formed the basis for the indictment 'Reflections on Technological Advancement—On the Anniversary of Man's First Landing on the Moon.' The first paragraph read:

> Is it possible to reverse the trend of technological advancement—of any advancement? Seems we all have the tendency (& in difficult circumstances almost the need) to look back to days when life was better, air was cleaner, and, with their difficulties, human relationships were easier & more 'beautiful.' Confession—I do that a lot. But it seems clear that it's not possible to reverse it, to go back. Despite the dangers & difficulties, one must apply a moral consciousness to here & now & all that means & commit one's life to shaping out a future of hope & life. Without knowing what that may mean in terms of proximity to loved ones one still tries to say 'yes' at times more weakly than others.

piece was published a few months later in Anthony D. King, ed., *Culture, Globalization and the World System* (New York: Palgrave Macmillan, 1991). See pp. 48-49.

The second paragraph began with the words 'What were our thoughts last year as man first walked the moon?' but was quickly followed by a line that dipped into the personal, recording Campbell's pleasure at their last meeting. 'The best part was seeing you in the old fighting spirit and to know first hand that beyond physical confinement, they had no control over you.' And then came the part that had given J. Edgar Hoover cause to launch an investigation:

This is in utter confidence & should not be committed to paper & I would want you not even to say a word of it to anyone until we have a fuller grasp of it. I say it to you for two reasons. The first obviously is to get your thinking on it, the second to give you some confidence that people are thinking seriously of escalating resistance. Ehsaan called us up to Connecticut last night. He outlined a plan for an action which would say—escalate seriousness—& we discussed pros and cons for several hours. It needs much more thought & careful selection of personnel. To kidnap—in our terminology make a citizen's arrest of—someone like Henry Kissinger. To issue a set of demands, e.g. cessation of use of B52s over N. Vietnam, Laos, Cambodia, & release of political prisoners. Hold him for about a week during which time big wigs of the liberal ilk would be brought to him—also kidnapped if necessary (which, for the most part it would be)—& hold a trial or grand jury affair out of which an indictment would be brought. There is no pretense of these demands being met & he would be released after this with a word that we're non-violent as opposed to them who would let a man be killed—one of their own—so that they could go on killing. The liberals would also be released as would a film of the whole proceedings in which, hopefully, Kissinger would be far more honest than he is on his own turf. The impact of such a thing would be phenomenal.

Ehsaan would come and stand behind me, reading the files over my shoulder. I was his teaching assistant that semester, this would have been the year 1991, I'm quite certain, and I was assigned to organize the papers in his study at home. He saw me reading Sister Laura Campbell's letter. He was silent for a while and then, leaning over me, underlined with the nail of his right thumb the words 'should not be committed to paper.' He laughed a shrill laugh and turned away to answer a phone call. His voice came from the next room.

—Jonathan, how are you? We will discuss that but first I must tell you: I have found a cheese that will appeal to you...

I returned to the papers spread out before me.

Three days later, during that summer of 1970, Adams had brought Francis Hull's reply to the librarian. The response bore the title 'The Use and Effectiveness of Group Therapy in the Federal Penal System'. The opening line: 'An emphasis on relationship seems to have sponsored a growing tendency on the part of the penal administrators to have inmates in more personal contact with one another and with staff members.' Immediately followed by a few lines about how keenly Hull had savoured Sister Laura's visit: 'the best part of the afternoon was your glowing person'. Then, as if a discussion was being conducted in a public meeting, he dived into a critical assessment of kidnapping Kissinger to whom he referred throughout the letter as 'Brain Child'. A couple of lines that allowed Hoover to include the charge about sabotaging the heating system in Washington, D.C.: 'Why not coordinate it with the one against capitol utilities—you should talk more thoroughly with the chargé about this, or with Little Shane or Big Joe German. To disrupt them. And then grab the Brain Child. This would be escalation enough.' Hull had expanded on the notion of 'effective propaganda and the movement' for the length of two paragraphs. At the end, he had added, 'Will you permit me a little compliment, Sister? The big difference rests largely with your coming in. Will you permit me another observation? My affinity for you was not wholly personal—I would have been a fool to ignore what you had to offer to revolution. Re spirit—you insisted on your freedom, you had incomparable generosity and you loved the Book of Jesus. And when this odyssey is over, I will learn from you, receiving the education that results from a marriage of minds and souls.'

Among the nine folders related to the trial in the study was a clipping that described Ehsaan as 'a slim, debonair 40-year-old with excellent manners and a dazzling smile'. The main story was about Ehsaan raising funds for the defence. Ehsaan had received two thousand letters of support and two that were unfavourable. The most touching letter, the report said, was from a black Vietnam veteran, a former student of Ehsaan's, who thanked him for 'being nice to me and treating me like a human being'. This vet had enclosed a $3,000 check, his entire discharge pay—'because now that my government has done this to you, you need all the help you can get.' The vet had originally intended to use the money as a down payment on a house. Ehsaan returned the check, the report said, suggesting that a hundred dollars would be 'a fairer contribution'.

In another clipping it was noted that a marshal inside the courtroom referred to Ehsaan as 'that camel driver'. One of the Harrisburg citizens in the court's elevator told the reporter: 'that Pakistani should be shishkabobed for bringing the country more trouble than it already has.' This could have prompted outrage or indignation in my postcolonial heart but what interested me more was the following description in another report, this time by a male reporter, in what gets called 'a newspaper of public record': 'Sister Laura frequently wore mini skirts and with her long shapely legs, her smooth complexion, oval face and almond-shaped blue eyes, she looked younger than her thirty-two years.' When I read that, I thought of Hull writing to Campbell, 'Will you permit me a little compliment, Sister?' And I saw Ehsaan, near a giant sunlit window in the courtroom, I saw him with his dark handsome face and his aforementioned dazzling smile, lavishing attention and words on the mini skirt-wearing nun.

Ehsaan came back from talking on the phone and I turned to the page where he had put his finger on the phrase. His leg was hurting again; I saw him grimace when he sat down. I had a question for him.

—Why did she put all that in the letter?

—The first thing you are taught as a guerrilla in Algeria is the following motto: *Quand tu es en prison, tu ne demandes que des oranges.* When you are in prison, you ask only for oranges... It takes a lot of revolutionary discipline to resist the temptation of asking for more than oranges.

When Ehsaan had been the age I was then, he had gone to Tunisia as a graduate student at Princeton to do research for his doctorate. In nearby Algeria, revolution had caught fire. It was said that Ehsaan had travelled to Algeria and fought in the war against the French. Had he? No one knew for certain. A couple of people remarked to me later that Ehsaan wasn't averse to myth-making. I myself never got the chance to ask him and, years later, sitting in a restaurant one rainy evening on Broadway, when I asked his widow that question, she quietly said that she didn't know. I had liked her honesty, especially when I pressed her to explain why Ehsaan had chosen to stay in the US and not return to Pakistan when his studies were over. She laughed and said, In Pakistan women wore the hijab. Here they showed their legs.

But back in Ehsaan's office that day, I had looked up from the photocopied letter written in the neat, right-sloping handwriting of Laura Campbell.

—It must have been terrible for them...for these letters to be read out in court.

—Oh, it was appalling, Ehsaan said. They were lovely people, with great dignity. It went on for hours. They just stared at the floor.

The defence lawyer had cross-examined the government witnesses. He didn't believe Adams had been left with even a shred of credibility. They didn't need to carry out the charade any longer. The charges were preposterous. He simply got up and said, *These defendants will always seek peace. Your Honour, the defence rests*. The jury voted ten to two on acquittal for all charges. In the months that followed, both Hull and Campbell quit their religious orders. They got married and opened a community house in a black neighbourhood in Baltimore.

—I went to their wedding, Ehsaan said. They now have two children. You should visit them. They will welcome you.

—During the trial, they must have had a chance to see each other in court every day? That must have been a relief.

—They never hid their affection for each other in court. They always embraced when they came together. It shocked some people. I liked them for that... And that is how one must understand what Laura did in her letter. She was sharing a secret with her lover—that is all. They had kept him in solitary confinement because of his hunger strike in Danbury prison. She was giving him hope. I have to tell you, they often struck me as naïve, but they were also the most honest people I had met.

⌒

Years have passed. It is a hot June day and I am at a Starbucks at a rest stop on the New Jersey Turnpike. People come here with their gas tanks empty and their bladders full. In the newspaper someone has left on the table there is mention of a priest who had used bolt cutters to cut a hole in a chain-link fence and then stepped atop the silo of a Minuteman III nuclear missile with an anti-nuke banner wrapped around his body. It is not Francis Hull. But lower in the report, there is mention of Laura Campbell, and then the phrase 'the widow of Francis Hull'. So, like Ehsaan, Hull is also gone. Campbell must be in her late sixties now. I call directory information, and, a few minutes later, I am asking Laura Campbell for permission to visit.

—Would you like lunch? This is the simple, straightforward question she asks me on the phone.

She is tall, grey-haired. Wearing a t-shirt that says 'ROTC Off All Campuses'. Her denim trousers are splattered with paint. The small house behind her serves as a meeting place for activists: on Fridays, which it is today, they distribute food and clothes in the morning. But it is past noon now and on the table set outside the house are scattered the leftovers: an out-of-season woollen jacket, a mustard-coloured sweater, old socks, neatly paired. At the far end, I can see a nearly empty container of soup and alongside it an aluminium tray with dry breadcrumbs. All around us are tombstones. I ask Laura if it would be possible for her to show me Hull's grave before we have lunch. She introduces me first to a donkey they have in their stable. She pats the donkey, whose name is Vinnie, and rubs her mane. Then we go among the sassafras trees to look for her three pet goats. Planted amidst the thousand dead, Irish working-class folk from early in the nineteenth century, many of them new immigrants, are walnut and maple trees. Also elm and oak. The goats have as their companion and guard a tall llama named Paz. I pet the goats and try to do the same with the llama but Sister Laura stops me.

—They're not used to touch. Their tongues don't distend, so they have never been licked by their mother. But they are very sensitive, very intelligent, oh yes.

A large black marble gravestone with a Celtic cross on it marks Francis Hull's resting place and Laura slowly runs her hand across the top of the stone. It is a tender gesture. She points out the plum and fig trees close by, and the lettuce bushes and the lines of carrot. When we go inside and sit down for lunch, she holds my hand as she closes her eyes and prays. The meal is simple, pasta, cold cuts, fresh salad. In the car, I had thought I'd ask her questions about Ehsaan and Francis Hull, but I realize that I'm just happy to be in her company.

—All the news-reports I had read about the trial mentioned your prettiness and your love for Father Hull. Was that love a part of what you thought of as the revolution?

I feel a bit prurient asking her this, but she doesn't hesitate.

—You want what is good in your life also to be enjoyed by others.

*These defendants will always seek love. Your Honour, the defence rests.*

⌒

CLIT 300 was titled 'Brecht and His Friends'. During that semester, I saw Nina in classes twice a week. I flirted with her more confidently because I saw that she didn't take me seriously. Once, I stepped into the classroom and saw her seated in a circle of four or five others. I noticed right away that her outfit, a pale raw-silk vest over a sleeveless cotton shirt, had been made in India. She probably bought it from a place like Bloomingdale's but as far as I was concerned they might well have been a gift from me. Stepping close behind her, I felt the fabric of her vest with my fingertips.

—Nice. I see that my cousin did a good job on his wooden weaving machine.

I didn't check to see if the others were amused or full of contempt. Probably both. All that mattered was that Nina was smiling.

—Your cousin? The one who lost his arm in the war?

—The very same. As a matter of fact, just last month, he was brought to London—to present a bolt of the finest silk to the Queen at the Festival of India. A thank-you for having ruled over us.

—Well, I thank your cousin for his nimble fingers. I prefer his wooden machine to all the mills of northern England.

*Your Honour, by the standards of a court of law, we were full of lies. But how liberating were those lies! They gave me so much pleasure!*

I laughed at her remark. I didn't want the banter to end.

—The mills are now closed, I said, and I hear they are all full of regret.

—Yes, serve the English fuckers right. May they suffer from gout and be forced to take the air in Brighton.

Nina was sitting down and, laughing, I put my palm on the back of her neck. She lowered her head as if I had just announced that I was going to give her a massage. And that is what I proceeded to do, making slow circles at the base of her skull with my thumbs, eyes fixed on the point where her hair was the shortest. I was conscious that the talk in the room had grown quiet but I wasn't going to stop. When Nina murmured her thanks I brushed the small bones on the back of her neck with my fingers bunched together. Her skin felt cool. I was flooded with a sense of peace.

This was the first time I had touched Nina. By pressing against the back of her chair, I could hide my erection. I was trying to breathe normally and stay quiet, but silence seemed to weight the moment with a significance and I didn't dare contribute further to it. I began to blabber.

—Madam, I say this not to brag, but to make myself accountable: I come from a long line of mystic masseurs.

—Your immense promise is evident to me, Mr Biswas.

The professor, David Lamb, walked in. Quiet, precise, wearing glasses that a decade later would be called Franzenesque. Lamb noticed what I was doing. I bet he would have liked to get into bed with Nina. It would no doubt happen very naturally with him. The two shared so much, conversation between them would flow without the need to pretend or exaggerate. They would sit at one of the restaurants uptown, drinking wine with cheese and olives, exchanging jokes about a performance they had both seen separately at the Papp Theater. One of them would mention dinner, and the other would readily agree. When night came, it would only simplify rather than complicate things. And, in the morning, Lamb would pick up his stylish glasses from the side table and look at her smiling at him. When she sat up, he'd say something funny and she would bend down and kiss him on that impressive nose. He saw us, my hands upon her neck, and said nothing.

I removed myself to the remaining seat that was across from Nina. If she was at all conscious that we had engaged in an intimate act she didn't reveal it. Our eyes didn't meet during the rest of the class. I would think of Nina's lowered head and exposed neck when, weeks later, I found a book called *The Art of Sensual Massage* among the seven or eight books stacked in her bathroom. A blue circle on the cover said 'Over One Million Copies Sold'. Even today I can step into a natural health food-store and the sight of candles or bottles of almond oil will bring back the dreamy, low-lit aura of limbs tensing and then easing under the pressure of my fingers. There is a particular smell I can catch in my nostrils, faintly floral mixed with something more warm and earthy, which is for me the smell of anticipation, or, more accurately, the scent of the soon-to-be-fulfilled promise of sex.*

ꓽ

Just the other day someone sent me a photograph of a CNG yellow-and-green autorickshaw in Delhi. At the back, on its yellow canopy were the words 'Asli Jat' in Hindi. That was understandable. But below the words in Hindi, were the words in English:

NOBODY REMAINS VIRGIN
LIFE FUCKS EVERYONE

When I was growing up in India, the common signs in English

---

*The book that Nina and I were to have most fun with was one that claimed to help women achieve orgasm. The book wasn't Nina's. We found it in a café in Gardiner, Montana. Hippies, white people with their hair in dreadlocks, ran the café. The book sat on a shelf next to *Catch-22*, a guide to Antarctica, and if I remember right, a new-looking copy of *Blood Meridian*, and several other novels whose spines are now blurred in my memory. The books were there for customers to peruse while they waited for their avocado sandwiches with homemade goat cheese and alfalfa sprouts. In the book on orgasms, Nina found a passage to her liking and showed it to me. I whipped out my notebook, as sensitive and artistic men are supposed to do on such occasions, but then decided to steal the book instead. Tempo is important during sexual activity, the author had noted, before citing the kind of anthropological knowledge that fascinated Nina: According to Dr Sofie Lazarsfeld in *Woman's Experience of the Male*, 'We are reminded of the popular custom in Thuringia. There a couple will not marry until the boy and girl have sawn through a log together. If the rhythm of their movements agrees, the marriage takes place; otherwise the association is broken off.'

on public transport were variations of O.K. TATA, HORN PLEASE, USE DIPPER AT NIGHT. When did Delhi's autorickshaw drivers become a part of Macaulay's English-speaking army dispensing metaphorical wisdom about getting fucked? This particular four-letter word—short and packed with consonants, yet malleable and open to a range of inflections. I'll tell you a little later of a discovery I made, that there was a whole sermon on it by an Indian guru.

EVENINGS AT 7.
MON      ALCOHOLICS ANONYMOUS
TUES     ABUSED SPOUSES
WED      EATING DISORDERS
THU      SAY NO TO DRUGS
FRI      TEEN SUICIDE WATCH
SAT      SOUP KITCHEN
SUNDAY   SERMON 9 A.M. 'AMERICA'S JOYOUS FUTURE'

That was the postcard I pinned to the door of the office for the English department's teaching assistants.* The card showed a notice board of the sort you see at schools and churches, with white plastic alphabets inserted into holes in the black board. (The keen pleasure of embracing shallow stereotypes! I was a foreigner. Still am, after more than twenty years.) An arrow drawn on the postcard with a felt pen pointed to THU. Office Hrs, 4-6 PM and my name next to it.

Six of us used the office. Nina's desk was in the same room. And Pushkin's, as well as Ricardo's, and Larry Blofeld's. Closest to my desk was my friend Peter's. Near my postcard on the door

---

*Nearly all the graduate students in the department were teaching assistants: our tuition fees were waived because we were more than willing to serve as anxious, often unconventional, perhaps overqualified, certainly underpaid, but also otherwise unemployable, conscripts in the army maintained by academia. Like many others before me for the past hundred and fifty years, I couldn't have made it out of India without this readiness on my part to be an indentured labourer.

were his office hours (Koerner: T-Thu 1-2 PM and by appt).
Partly out of solidarity and partly to taunt me, he had tacked on
a print of a 5x7 photo showing a sign outside a church.

STAYING IN BED
SHOUTING, OH GOD!
DOES NOT CONSTITUTE
GOING TO CHURCH

I could have pasted above my own desk a picture of the Taj
Mahal on the wall. This was certainly true during the early days,
when I wouldn't have thought twice about stealthily tearing out
an Air India ad from a magazine in the university library. The
record should state clearly, however, that the first thing I tore
out was a reproduction in *The Atlantic* of an early painting by
Picasso. *Your Honour, Picasso had painted it after first making love.*
*The brown back of a thin male sunk into the flesh of a shapely woman*
*with commodious thighs. What caught my eye was the woman's slim*
*and languid arm, with its high elbow, holding Picasso in place.* Then,
when I began reading writers I hadn't read in India I tacked their
pictures in place of the notice from the church. Brecht, Baldwin.
This was still during my first year in America. One day I found
a postcard in Greenwich Village that showed a piece of graffiti
on a wall. Where had the photograph been taken? There was
no indication. It quoted an exchange between a reporter and
Mahatma Gandhi: .

—Mr. Gandhi, what do you think of Western
civilization?
—I think it would be a good idea.

This new postcard had pride of place on the wall: when a visiting
student spoke to me, he or she could look past my head and
read the postcard. It was like an imagined thought-bubble, a
witty statement that I wanted to adopt as my line on stage.
This was my private version of 'To be or not to be' or 'Friends,
Romans, Countrymen'. But then one day, a flyer appeared in my
mailbox. The opening words were: *If God is dead, then you lose the*

*most important word in your language. And you need a substitu...* *Instead of God, Fuck has become the most important word in our language.* The words were from a speech by Osho, who was also known as Bhagwan Rajneesh. All kinds of flyers, pamphlets, announcements were put in our mailboxes every day. The difference was that an Indian had written these words. Therefore, I treated them as my own. I made copies for all my friends and officemates. The following day, or the day after that, there was a tape in my mailbox. Both the flyer and the tape had come from a Bengali grad student, Biman, who otherwise kept himself busy with work on his thesis on Naguib Mahfouz. I listened to the tape with great interest. Osho spoke with what in this country was called a *pronounced accent*. For me, his voice was like the voice of my relatives and friends, even the word 'English' uttered with a sibilant hiss. Osho's whole lecture was a disquisition on the word 'fuck'. The guru's lecture was repeatedly interrupted by laughter from his American audience. This filled me with elation. I ignored the awful shallowness. An Indian was holding forth on the English language, offering a sermon from below, an unholy discourse on how sex was the new divine, and all the white people couldn't have enough of it!

Fuck, we belonged!

—First thing, when you wake up, if you repeat the mantra five times 'Fuck you' it clears your throat too.

That was Osho speaking. I played the tape on the boom box in the office.

Osho started as a teacher in a small town in Madhya Pradesh but later became an international guru. People gave up their lives, and their property, to flock to his ashram in Pune. I had heard that Osho told people to free their minds and that, inevitably, there were orgies at his ashram. Sometime in the eighties he moved his ashram to Oregon. My father had a friend from college who was a psychologist from Chapra; he read Osho's books and wanted to follow him to America. One evening, when I was a teenager, this man arrived at our house in Patna wearing a saffron kurta. He asked my mother for some sindoor so that he could put a red mark on his forehead. Did my mother have a necklace of rudraskha beads? She did! He wet the tip of his fingers at the sink and touched his curls. He was going to a spiritual meeting, he had hopes of impressing a linguist who had come from America. I had always thought my father's friend was good-looking, he had a lazy charisma, and now, as I listened to Osho's tape, the memory of my father's friend came back to me. Some months later, he died in a car accident; he never got a chance to travel to America. But Osho, from a similar place, from a similar caste, had made it. He was a role model.

—One of the most interesting words in the English language today is 'Fuck'. It is a magical word.

This was Osho again, speaking out from the tape.

And then there was a weird, quite exact and also quite inaccurate, in fact plain wrong, listing of the usages of that word. Osho, in the manner of a schoolteacher, named the grammatical category and then provided an example. And each item was followed by uncontrollable laughter from his devotees. I heard the laughter and imagined half-naked hippies, who had flocked to the huge ranch in Oregon, laughing with tears running down their cheeks.

> —Transitive verb: John fucked Mary.
> —Intransitive verb: Mary was fucked by John.
> —Noun: Mary is a fine fuck.
> —Adjective: Mary is fucking beautiful.
> —Ignorance: Fucked if I know.
> —Trouble: I guess I'm fucked now.
> —Fraud: I got fucked at the used-car lot.
> —Aggression: Fuck you.
> —Displeasure: What the fuck is going on here?
> —Difficulty: I can't understand this fucking job.

It was weird and incoherent, but my friends were laughing. Here was an example of what Americans meant when they said: *It is so bad that it is good.* Every now and then, we would press the Play button and listen. For weeks, my officemates tried to speak like Osho.

It was funny because it was Osho, the small-town Indian accent mixed with the ready report on American idioms. That was part of the humour. As was the fact that here was a spiritual leader holding forth on the word fuck. And then there was that part too, which was surely present in the reaction of my friends, about how banal it was in the end. They were laughing at the fact that something quite stupid was actually succeeding. It was fun. (For e.g., *Surprise: Fuck, you scared the shit*—pronounced by Osho as *sit—out of me.*)

Rajneesh, for that was Osho's original name, had been a professor in his early days. A professor of philosophy. He gave up teaching after he became the 'Sex Guru' and began to gather followers from all over the world. Before Manmohan Singh and other political leaders engineered a liberal reform of the Indian economy, at least twenty years earlier than them, Rajneesh was preaching that socialism would only socialize poverty. What India needed was not more Gandhis, but more capitalists.

—But your Osho is a Jain. He comes from a family of merchants. He might speak of God, but he is a man after money.

This was my father, in his own small-town way, talking about Osho with his psychologist friend one day.

Osho had no use for scholars. He had no use for religion either. But although he read little, he had made it a point to read the Bible. He read it, he said, like a detective story. It had everything, the Bible—love, life, murder, suspense. It was sensational. He said that his thinking about scholars was the same as that of Mullah Nasruddin. This was the story he narrated: A man came to Mullah Nasruddin and said, Nasruddin, have you heard? The great scholar of the town has died and twenty rupees are needed to bury him. Mullah Nasruddin gave the man a hundred-rupee note and said, Take it, and while you're doing it, why not bury five scholars?

The orgies at Osho's ashram had been reported even in the *US News & World Report*. My officemate, Peter, claimed he had read about them as a teenager in Germany; he had an aunt in Cologne who abandoned her studies, got Chinese tattoos on her stomach, and dreamed of joining an ashram. After Osho was deported from the US, twenty-one countries denied him entry. He had gone back to India and died recently. That, as they say in America, was a downer. In Oregon, there had been arrests and all kinds of charges by the police. His long-time secretary, Ma Anand Sheela, a woman born in India but married to an American, was arrested on charges of attempted murder. Asked by journalists in Australia about the fears people had about the Osho cult taking over that country, Ma Anand Sheela said, 'Tough titties.'

*Tough titties!*

I asked Larry Blofeld, my officemate who was writing a novel, what that phrase meant.* He smiled and flexed his pectorals.

Larry had a great tolerance for my failings. I once discussed Faulkner with him, and even if I were asking a question about a character in *Absalom, Absalom!*, for example, Larry would answer my query only by making some connection to India. Even if the only connection he could make was to Indian food served in a restaurant he regularly visited. If he couldn't make such a connection, he would slip into barely disguised mockery.

Now, in response to my question, he leaned back and said, *Tough titty, said the kitty, when the milk went dry.* Ever heard

---

*Larry's novel was titled *Pop*. Not about a father, as I had first assumed, but about popular culture. Young people dropping out of college to become singers. It began with a young man driving down from Chicago to the university in St. Louis with his girlfriend. I knew this because I once asked Larry to read me the opening page. It was a magical thing for me, the fact that someone I knew had written a novel. Larry took out his manuscript from a folder with an elastic band around it. His protagonist Blake was at the wheel. This was the line I asked Larry to repeat so that I could write it down: 'Illinois is a large state and during the four hours or so they were on I-55, across the distance that stretched roughly between the block from where Al Capone directed his operations and the small house in which President Ronald Reagan was born, Jessica twice removed her seat-belt to blow him.'

that? It's not such a hot phrase in New Delhi?

I didn't say anything and just smiled politely.

—Tell me, how far is India? Larry asked.

I shrugged.

—Okay, answer this question for me, please. What's closer to New York? India or the moon? I'll give you a hint. You can see the moon.

Bile rose in my throat. I was aware of the effort I was making to keep smiling.

Larry raised his eyebrows. He was asking if I had anything to say.

No, Larry. As Osho would say, Fuck you.

⌇

One evening students rushed into the university library, screaming, and threw fake blood over each other. The red liquid spilled on the library floor and on some books open on the desks. The students were enacting a scene from the war in the Gulf. A few 'medics' carried out the 'wounded and dying'. The leader of the group, Marc Rosenblum, said that the students at Mosul University, where the US had bombed the cafeteria, 'didn't have the opportunity to get pissed off because their books had been damaged'. I was in my room and missed out on the whole thing.

I also missed out on a 'kiss-in' that Siobhan and her friends in ACT UP had organized in lieu of a teach-in. The event was reported in *The Spectator* with a somewhat obvious picture of two female students kissing while Senator Jesse Helms scowled at them from a poster held up in the background. People gathered on the steps of the library nearly each day with banners to protest the war. I often saw Nina among the protesters. I would arrive there and scan the crowd for a beret and a Palestinian scarf. Also, dark shades and often a cigarette in her hand. That was Nina. I dreamed of walking up to her and kissing her hard. I'd run into her in the TA office but I found the public vibe more inviting. She intimidated me. The war was discussed everywhere. I tried to attend the protests but I also had to deal with my own courses and the class I was teaching. It was too much. I would be eating a quick lunch in the café in Pulitzer Hall and catch on the television screen the press briefings that the military conducted. I had missed the show on PBS where both Ehsaan and Said had appeared. To add to everything, there was always the worry about money. If during a particular month I sent a hundred or two hundred dollars to Lotan Mamaji's family in Ara, it put pressure on me to scrounge and save. In my sleep I would have dreams that were filled with a vague anxiety: I was leaning over a bridge in my village, trying to spit into the river below, but my mouth was dry and nothing came out. In the blank water beneath me, small fishes swam.

Soon it wasn't so cold anymore. The war ended; the protests had made no difference. Dick Cheney said on television that the Iraqi Army was conducting 'the Mother of all Retreats'. The scene outside my window changed. Dirty snow that had stayed seemingly for months under the dumpster and mailboxes melted. A dogwood tree in the park put out tight buds that became beautiful red flowers. I could see turtles in the green pond. And there were daffodils! *Your Honour, is there an immigrant from India or Jamaica or Kenya who isn't thrilled to see the first daffodils of spring? The honest person forced to memorize Wordsworth's 'Daffodils' without having a clue about what those flowers looked like can celebrate spring with the kind of joy that the native-born can never know. This is how we know we have arrived!*

I had just had lunch and was on my way to the library. I told myself that I could read later, when darkness had fallen, and that right now, given how bright and warm it was outside, I should perhaps find a friend to have a beer with. Larry was probably in the TA room, slaving over a critical work on Bellow. He could easily be persuaded to put on his Ray-Bans and sit outside in the sun at Max Café. In the office, I saw that the overhead lights were off but Nina was there, sitting at her desk, her face bathed in white under her table lamp. A green frog jumped out of my chest and plopped down in the little pool of light beneath Nina's chin. Or, that is how it felt. My heart had turned into a frog and escaped from my body. It now lay pulsing under the eye of a woman I loved from a distance.

—Comrade Nina!

In response, an amused shake of the head. A balanced mix of enthusiasm and indifference.

—Comrade IRS to you, my friend. I'm trying to do my taxes.

Taxes! With a dramatic flourish I extracted from my backpack a yellow folder I had been carrying for a week: my W-2 statement, a dozen receipts from the university bookstore, the bus and hotel receipts from the graduate student conference on Rushdie in Buffalo. My fear of Nina made me bold.

—Nina, I beg you. Please stop. Let's do our taxes together.

—Why would I want to do anything so painful with you?

—Comrade IRS, let's have a beer then. But let's also do our taxes together. I cannot make head or tail of those forms.

She agreed that it was glorious outside, gathered her papers and switched off her lamp.

In the TA office, the light that filtered in through the window was weak, half-nocturnal. For a moment, Nina stood still, thinking. A fish suspended in water. A thin blue sweater hung loosely from her shoulders. Something clicked in her mind, and she darted towards the door, all brisk efficiency.

—Do you have the forms?

—No!

We stopped at the campus post-office to pick up the tax-return forms. Every chair and sofa at Max Café accommodated an affluent law-school student, so Nina decided we could go to the tiny park near her apartment instead. Nina grabbed a blanket and a cooler from her place. A short trudge up a hill till we came to small stone tower built to commemorate the death of sailors at sea. Was it on that first visit, or later, that she told me that all those vessels that had gone down were slave ships? No mention on the plaque of the hundreds crammed together under the grated hatchways, men and women and small children drowned with the manacles still bound around their legs and necks.

Nina spread out the blanket on the grass. In the cooler that

I had carried I found three bottles of beer and, in a silver-foil bag, spoons and a pint of ice cream. In the distance, maybe three hundred yards away, visible through the black trees that were still bare, was the highway. Nina lay down on her stomach, pen in hand, the pages of Form 1040NR spread out in front of her. *Name and address*, she said, and without waiting for me to reply, began to write. But my mind wandered.

*Filing Status*
*Exemptions*
*Adjusted Gross Income*
*Line of Your Spine*
*Your Legs*
*Oh, Nina's Legs*

I readily responded to her questions, mostly by making up my answers, and like a shrewd lawyer she accepted what I told her.

—Don't fuck with the state, Nina warned. She looked up, her dark glasses hiding her eyes. I don't want to see you deported, she said.

Did she mean it in the way I hoped? Later, she would say yes, but in this and other instances, I kept an open mind. *The only point worth considering, Your Honour, is that it was the solemn enactment of the fundamental duty of the citizen, paying taxes, which brought the two of us closer together.* While she showed her agility with numbers, I smelled the grass and imagined pulling her skirt down the length of her smooth legs. Her breasts were pressed against the hard ground. I wanted to cup them and hold them gently, patiently, while she quickly multiplied one thousand ninety-four point one nine by six.

She brought her calculations to a close. It turned out that $187 was to be refunded to me. I signed my name at the bottom of the form.

—Thank you, I said, thank you.

She pushed her shades up on her head.

—What are you going to do with your dollars?

—Can I take you out for dinner?

We went to La Cucaracha. With the first sip of my margarita, a fine calmness descended on me. I wasn't acting cocky and, to be honest, my mind wasn't entirely free of doubt. Still, I wasn't worried about Nina and me anymore. There was little anxiety. In fact, there were moments when I felt certain that this woman who was laughing and mocking me as she ate tortilla chips was waiting for me to kiss her.

—You are in some terrible situation on a ship, let's say. A field trip gone horribly wrong. And the only way you can escape is if you slept with one of your professors. The question is: who would you *not* sleep with, like never, never, not in a million years to save your fucking life?

—Bonnie Clark, I said after a pause.

—That was too easy. Let me change the question: who would you absolutely want to sleep with, even if you were doing this only because the pirates who had captured you were going to kill you otherwise?

*I would sleep with you. Only you. But more important, can't time just stop? I want this minute to last forever.*

—I'm not afraid of death, I said instead.

—Why can't a dog tell a lie? Is it because he is too honest, or is it because he is too sly? Poor Wittgenstein!

I had not read Wittgenstein. But David Lamb, our professor from CLIT 300, had read Wittgenstein, and Hegel, and Kant, and Stanley Cavell. Lamb had once said at a party that whenever he suffered from insomnia he read Derrida. *Not because he makes me go to sleep but because he makes staying up a pleasure.* As I thought of Lamb, a sliver of ice lodged itself in my heart. My earlier assurance ebbed, and I felt stranded on the shore, watching the boat slowly receding. My father had grown up in a hut. I knew in my heart that I was closer to a family of peasants than I was to a couple of intellectuals sitting in a restaurant in New York. Our dinner of skirt steak and jumbo shrimp was nearly over, and now because I was uncertain why we had been laughing only a minute ago, a sense of fatalism began to overtake me. The fickle human heart, prone to despair. How quickly the boredom sets in.

Perhaps Nina noticed a change.

—Okay, truth-teller, she said, it is time to get you off this ship and into your bed.

We got into Nina's hatchback and she said she shouldn't have drunk so much. I was relieved when I saw that Nina didn't turn onto her street, that she was going to drive me back to my place first. The tension eased. Now that I didn't have to contemplate whether or not I was going to be asked to come up to her apartment, I could relax again. But to deal with this disappointment, I wanted a cigarette.

—You know what I'd like right now? I said cheerfully.

—A blowjob?

I laughed too loudly, and she laughed too.

When she dropped me off, Nina said she needed to use the bathroom. I heard the noise of the flush in the toilet. And I moved away down the corridor, to open the front door for her. Instead, as soon as she came near me, I said, Don't leave.

My hand went up to her cheek.

—*Finally.*

She made those quotation marks in the air with two fingers of both hands when she said that. She wasn't done.

—She said, Jesus, is the paint dry yet?

A person who is laughing is difficult to kiss, so I hesitated a moment. She put a finger on my mouth and leaned in closer, a serious expression on her face. The soft crush of her lips on mine released a fury of desire in me. We kissed for a long time, standing in that hallway, Nina's back pressed against the wall.

*I am from a land of famines, Your Honour, and I displayed such hunger, such astonishing greed.* Eager to touch every part of her, I turned Nina around so that her back was to me. She raised her arms, her palms flat against the wall. I was the blind man. Her breasts were in my hands. *One afternoon in Delhi, Noni had gone with Deepali from Sociology to Surajkund. They came back late. What did he most like about her? Noni said that Deepali's breasts were like kabootars in his hands, two soft, startled pigeons fluttering under his fingers. Your Honour, this is the truth of my American*

*Dream: to possess the life of a Sikh from Patiala.* At least, that is what the dream was till I met Nina and she took me, almost daily, to other neighbourhoods. During my adolescence, I used to make guilty entries in my journal. I never once wrote down the word 'masturbation'; I only recorded that I was 'distracted'.* *In my teens, I had been innocent of even something like a Victoria's Secret catalogue. Your Honour, Nina made such self-consciousness a thing of the past. Nina, once we became lovers, rid me of my guilt.* She'd examine the pictures in the catalogue and ask me which model I wanted to fuck. Where do you want to do it, the wooden deck visible towards the top of the picture, or right here on the sandy beach where she has planted her red toenails?

All through that afternoon, while she had helped me with my taxes, I had gazed at Nina's legs criss-crossed on the woollen blanket. Now, crouching down in the hallway, beside my bike that I had bought from a Chinese electrical engineering student for twenty bucks, I was kissing the back of Nina's knees. I kissed her and licked her, pushing my tongue everywhere I could. In touching her, I was touching the sea, I was walking on soft sand, I was tasting the salt of my infinite longing. I heard her sigh when I moved my hands up to her crotch. Then she said, Let's go to your bed.

*I apologize, your Honour. Even at that moment, I could almost hear my mind repeating clichés—such a long journey.* Not from hallway to bed, but from the long wanting to the moment of fulfilment. This is what sex with Nina had meant to me: keen desire and struggle, and, just when it seemed that the goal was still so far, success. This ache that I had nursed so long, as if for

---

*Not very sophisticated as a system of notation, I know. Unlike Victor Hugo who concealed his many sexual activities from his longtime mistress Juliette Drouet by adopting a varied system in his notebook. Here is James Salter on Hugo: 'Along with a woman's name or initials, he might mark an *N* that stood for naked; something else for caresses; *Suisses*, for breasts; and so forth, a kind of ascending order. For everything, the full act, he wrote *toda*, all. There was something noted for almost every day.' James Salter, *The Art of Fiction* (Charlottesville: University of Virginia Press, 2016).

a lifetime, ended with Nina naked under me. A pair of white thighs opening, legs wrapped around my torso and then spread wide. Her head was inching closer to the wall behind her, and putting my hand protectively on her hair, I moved deeper into her. Her moans soon turned, with a half-gasp, into the phrase that the article in *Cosmopolitan* had said every man wants to hear, I'm going to come.

*Part IV*

## Wolf Number Three

'They know I'm a foreigner. It makes me a little uneasy.'

—James Salter, A Sport and a Pastime

There had been a complaint. So even before the new academic year began, my second year in America, all foreign teaching assistants were required to attend a workshop. My officemates and I were to teach Freshman Composition, but graduate students from other departments had different teaching responsibilities. At the workshop, there were free doughnuts and coffee. Far too many Chinese and Indians filled the room. Pushkin was there because attendance was mandatory. Otherwise, he wouldn't deign to come to such things. He had a volume of Nirala's poetry with him; he said he was translating it for a London publisher. Pushkin was from Gwalior, from a Brahmin family close to Nehru. He was the son of a politician who had written a book of poems in Hindi. I didn't know this then but in a few years Pushkin would surprise Ehsaan by being invited to have dinner with Kissinger after he had published an article on Afghanistan in the *New York Review of Books*.

His full name was Pushkin Krishnagrahi. He didn't offer an easy entry into his world but he gave thrilling glimpses of it through some of the things he said.* For instance, he once explained he was unimpressed by a particular author because 'literary reputations in the United States are merely a function of real estate'. He was rangy and wore his hair long. He had a beard. His seriousness was a part of his get-up. He presented his seriousness first at conferences and academic festivals. Yet, even Pushkin was there in the room. Nina, however, was not.

---

*I've had many reasons to admire Pushkin but I've never admired him without some reservations. Somewhat recently, an obituary for a British writer reported on the following conversation: 'Once, in a restaurant, he looked across the room towards a reasonably famous novelist. "That crowd are all so watchful and withheld," he said. "I wonder what they've got to be so withheld about?"' When I read those lines, I thought of my old friend Pushkin, but not only of him. No, I thought of the quiet, judgemental editor I knew in New York and also several of my English department colleagues from all over the country I used to run into at the MLA.

Nina, who was American. A native speaker. I wanted to see her very badly.

And right then, at that orientation for the foreign TAs, a woman named Donna handed out photocopies of an article from the campus newspaper, *The Spectator*. A girl was sitting on the grass in front of Farrow Hall. Under the picture it said, 'Melanie Olson, Astronomy major, dropped a Math course because she had trouble understanding her foreign TA'. The girl was wearing a denim skirt and the photographer had taken the shot with the camera tilted up from the ground. Blades of grass shot up in the foreground.

Peter was seated next to me. He put his finger on the photograph and spoke in a half-whisper.

—Actually, she said she likes taking it in the ass but her foreign TA couldn't seem to understand her.

Peter wore thick glasses and smelled of cigarettes and sweat. On the other side of him sat Maya. She was trading barbs with Donna.

Maya spoke in a fake British accent. She had lined her dark smoky eyes with kohl, and her neck and arms sported delicate silver jewellery. She was from Delhi. I could see her spending afternoons in air-conditioned rooms in South Extension or Greater Kailash: lush green potted plants, and cushions on low wooden diwans arranged creatively in patterns of gold, magenta, and red.

—I'm not here to rid American undergraduates of their provincialism, Maya said to Donna. That is emphatically not a part of my job description.

Her Chilean friend from Anthropology, Paulo, enthusiastically bobbed his head and beat his hand on the table. Donna pulled her jacket over her stomach and said that there would be time for discussion at the end of the workshop. Maya said that Bush was bombing Iraq. Perhaps this could be the subject of their later discussion.

Peter raised his rounded chin towards Maya, and said quietly, Do you know this annoying woman sitting next to me?

His faint show of sarcasm hid a fascination with Maya. Within three weeks of their first meeting, during the previous semester, they had become lovers. It was one of the things that I would always think about when I thought about love: acerbic and fragrant Maya in love with the acerbic and slovenly Peter. Did they fall in love because, in a sense, they spoke the same language, their poisonous tongues entwined in a beautiful, private dance? Except that when they were by themselves, they seemed quiet and subdued, not at all given to angry pronouncements about the world. Instead, they were attentive to each other, solicitous, generous with their gestures of affection. It seemed they were very happy just to sit in each other's company. Mugs of coffee beside them, I'd see them reading under the red and white awning of the Hungarian Pastry Shop, or standing outside West End bar smoking endless cigarettes.

Putting all the participants in pairs, Donna said we were now to engage in role-play.

—You are a teacher who is talking to a student who has missed class because he or she has had to deal with an emergency.

There were titters. Donna held up three ringed fingers. She read from a chart that said:

> *Please pay attention to*
> *A. making eye contact,*
> *B. clarity of expression,*
> *C. showing a friendly attitude.*

Before taking turns playing teacher and student we were to talk to our partners for five minutes. My partner was one of the Chinese students, and the sticker on her chest said Cai Yan. I had seen her before talking to Maya, and guessed she was in International Relations. I felt an inward dread that I wouldn't understand what she said, but she was calm and spoke clearly. Her manner made me self-conscious and I tried to speak less hurriedly.

Cai Yan's parents lived in Quanzhou. Her mother was a schoolteacher. Her older brother was a well-known pianist in

Shanghai. Her father had been a bureaucrat but had resigned some years ago and owned a factory in nearby Guangdong. I asked her what the factory manufactured. She had so far maintained a slightly imperturbable smile but now she gave a short laugh.

—Black Dragon Brand Rollerblades.

—Indian names always mean something. Is that true of Chinese names too? What does Cai Yan mean?

—My name… I think it means a bird in spring, or a spring swallow.

Cai Yan was slim and elegant. The jacket she wore had small buttons shaped like horseshoes. Her hair was black and covered her head like a fine helmet.

She said there had been a fire in the laundromat she had been using over the weekend. She had been able to save her clothes, but she had been unable to go back in again. The fire had spread so quickly. (When she said 'utility' had she actually meant 'futility'? Or when I heard 'breeze,' isn't it likely she had said 'breathe' as in 'I found it difficult to breathe'? Did my speech also confound her in the same way? I felt that both of us were playing a guessing game a little bit. But, there was no mistaking the word 'fire'.) Her bag with several library books and also her journal were inside and nothing had remained but charred pages and wet black ash when the fire had been doused. I listened to her carefully, and felt alarmed and sorry. She said that the fire was the reason why she hadn't been able to complete her homework. That is why she had also missed class. You see, it was an emergency. Oh! She saw my expression and raised her eyebrows at the look of confusion on my face. I laughed when I understood that this was a story but she didn't alter her Mona Lisa smile. Apparently she was unwilling to be amused by the stupidity of others.

Donna had wanted us to play the part of the affable teacher, listening patiently to a student's brittle fabrications. I had made an error and assumed at first that Cai Yan was describing what had actually happened to her. When it was my turn, I started with the truth. I told Cai Yan that when I was in my teens in

India, the walls of the huts close to my village had graffiti on them with slogans like *Chairman Mao is our Chairman*. We could be on a bus on the highway and it would be held up in traffic for half an hour because of a march denouncing the massacre of protesting peasants. Thin, kurta-clad young men and women singing on the highway: *The East is Red! The sun rises! China produces Mao Tse-tung!*

—Dong Fang Hong, Cai Yan said, with a trace of excitement. That is the name of that song.

She said she had sung it in school.

As Donna had instructed, I maintained eye contact with my partner and exhibited a pleasant and friendly manner. I began to show off.

—I asked, Do you know Lin Biao?

Even in the eighties, with Mao and Zhou En-Lai already long dead, and the reformist Deng in power, China meant something different in India. There were still communist groups in the villages around my hometown that were fighting for a peasant revolution. Mao was their god. Often in the trains going past Ara, there would be a motley crowd of young men and older folk who would sing songs about the social change about to come with the blessings of Mao. Everyone in those groups had the same look of zealous certainty on their bearded faces, and their singing needed no further accompaniment than the sound of the train and a tambourine.

The name that I had thrown at Cai Yan, Lin Biao, was that of a legendary associate of Mao's. Lin Biao was later accused of political treason and died while attempting to flee in an airplane. I knew his name because I would read in the papers that the Maoists in the Bihar countryside were following the 'Lin Biao line'. This meant the belief that one day the villages would rebel and overwhelm the passive, decadent cities. For Cai Yan's ear, I invoked danger. In my late teens, I would be sitting at breakfast with toast and scrambled eggs, a novel by Somerset Maugham beside my plate, and a crowd would surge at the mouth of the street. I added colour. I said that the radicals, waving red flags,

would sometimes allow me to leave for my classes. When I came
back, there would be three cows standing in the garden outside.
In the bedroom in which my parents slept, a new family would
be sleeping after having chopped up the bed for use as firewood.

She listened seriously but without any curiosity.

—I was exaggerating, I said.

—I know, she said. She spoke softly, even serenely. There
was no smugness in her.

But I was wrong to think that she hadn't been curious. As
I realized much later, the mention of Lin Biao's name was a
mistake. I had invoked it on a whim, but to Cai Yan it meant
nostalgia. Nostalgia not for the China of her childhood but for
the poor villages of my past. In such fleeting connections are
destinies shaped. Before two years of our graduate study were
over, Cai Yan would talk to Ehsaan and decide she would write
about Maoist struggles in various parts of India.* By the time
that happened my romance with Nina would have gone the way
of subscriber trunk dialling and mimeograph machines.

ʃ

---

*I have in my notebook, this advice on writing about place, advice presented
in the black and white shades of noir lighting, apparently for men only—
although Cai Yan, as a woman, called into question the fungibility of all
these categories:

Chandler always prided himself on being, as he said, the "first to write about Southern California in a realistic way," going on to note that "to write about a place you have to love it or hate it or do both by turns, which is usually the way you love a woman."

Hanif Kureishi's *The Buddha of Suburbia* was published the same year that I came to the US and I discovered it a year later when I read the novel in one of my courses. Probably the one called 'Black Britain'. The book presented an England strung out on what one character in *Buddha* called 'race, class, fucking, and farce'. I embraced this eclectic attention. (*Race & Class* incidentally was the name of a serious journal—Ehsaan was on their editorial board—but Kureishi wanted to mix it up with *Fucking & Farce*. Mind and body, together!) Then I watched a video of *Sammie and Rosie Get Laid* in the library. Kureishi had written the screenplay. Shashi Kapoor played Rafi Rahman. A handsome Pakistani politician who is charged with having introduced martial law in his country and other attendant abuses like torture and maiming. One episode in the film affected me the most. Rahman goes to meet Alice, the woman he had loved when he was a student in London. In Alice, Rafi had found his white woman. She had loved him. He had made promises to return, but never did. Alice, played with a kind of luminous fragility by Claire Bloom, takes Rafi to her cellar and shows the clothes she had packed, the books, the shoes, the bottles of perfume. She shows him the diaries from 1954, 1955, 1956, inscribed with letters to 'My Darling Rafi'. But Rafi has no response for Alice when she says to him bitterly: 'I waited for you, for years! Every day I thought of you! Until I began to heal up. What I wanted was a true marriage. But you wanted power. Now you must be content with having introduced flogging for minor offences, nuclear capability and partridge-shooting into your country.' I thought of Jennifer as I sat alone in the library carrel watching this scene. Would she ever say that she had waited for me?*

---

*Alice reminded me of Jennifer and no one else. That memory, and the accompanying feeling, was special to her. I read somewhere that Bobby Fischer could run into someone and say, about a game they had played fifteen years earlier, 'You should have moved your bishop to e7.' I'm very bad at chess but the remark spoke to me because I'm aware I sit outside a cave with a hoard of precise memories. Each half-eaten meal, filet mignon

While writing a paper on Kureishi I came across a remark
he had made to an interviewer: 'I like to write about sex as a
focus of social, psychological, emotional, political energy—it's
so central to people's lives, who you fuck, how much you love
them, the dance that goes around it, all the seduction, betrayal,
loyalty, failure, loneliness.' This appeared like a credo I wanted to
adopt. Not so much about writing, but about sex being central
to our lives. Still, I wasn't very confident and took the quote,
which I had copied down on an index card, to my friend Peter.
He sucked on his cigarette and nodded his head when I read
out Kureishi's words to him. Right on, he said, and then asked
if I wanted a beer.

We sipped our beers. The light of the setting sun flooded the
room. Peter got up and put on a music tape, one that he used
to play in our shared office, Keith Jarrett's The Köln Concert.
When he sat down with a fresh beer bottle, I thought Peter
looked thoughtful, maybe even sad.

—Sex is a difficult thing, he said.

I stayed silent.

—It's important, of course, as Kureishi says. I guess I'm saying

---

abandoned on the table in a Spanish restaurant, each darkened window
and accompanying hangover, each sunrise, each sunset, Patsy Cline on a
juke-box in a grimy rural bar in Montana, each touch, its temperature,
each empty bottle of wine thrown in the trash but now locked in that cave
behind me, belongs to a particular moment and a particular woman I'm in
love with at that moment in the past.

A memory, from several years before I left India, Gulzar's song from
the film *Ijaazat*: 'Mera kuchh samaan'. My translation can never convey the
elation, and then comfort, I found in the song's inventory even years after I
first heard it: 'My few things are still with you / Those wet monsoon days
/ That single night wrapped in my letter / Erase that night / Please return
some of my things…' The image of the lovers struggling in the rain under
one shared umbrella—and, after love has ended, the woman recalls bringing
her lover back half-wet, half-dry. Her desire is still beside the bed, return it
to me, she says. As I write this down, I realize that the appeal here was of
loving as a nostalgic act: all the beauty is in the remembering, it is all in the
past and therefore safe.

it's a huge and complicated thing and it's not always possible to get to everything hiding underneath.

Peter had so much heart, and such honesty always. Still, he surprised me by telling me about Maya. He said he stayed up late one night at Maya's place. It might have been TA work. Then, in the dark, he felt his way to the bed where Maya was already asleep, and accidentally bumped into a package left on the floor. At the sound, Maya screamed and getting up from the bed rushed into her closet. Peter couldn't understand what was going on. In fact, he said to me, he was perhaps screaming too. He was scared of what had happened, and quickly put on the light.

—It's only me, it's only me.

Maya said nothing in response. Peter said that Maya always slept naked in bed and she looked especially vulnerable coming out of the closet. He got into bed next to her. He had been scared, Peter thought now, because he was seeing Maya suddenly as someone alien. She went back to sleep or that is what he thought but then Maya sighed and adjusted her head on his shoulder.

—Sorry, she said quietly to him. It has to do with something that happened in my childhood.

Peter waited in the dark. She didn't say another word. The next morning he mentioned what had happened but Maya wouldn't say anything more. He took the hint and never brought it up again but just the previous week, after Maya was angry with Peter about his staying quiet for hours not speaking to anyone, Maya told him about her past. She said that when she was in high school in Delhi, her parents were in Moscow for two years. Her dad had a position in the Indian embassy. Maya was left behind to complete her school year in Delhi. She stayed with her uncle in Jor Bagh. This man wasn't really her uncle, he was her father's closest friend from college, a successful lawyer and on the governing board of the Delhi cricket association. He came home from the club late and raped her every night except when she had her period.

—Every night. Forget rape. Just think, every night. How do you wrap your head around such a thing? She was sixteen. I didn't even ask her how long she stayed in that house.

⌣

I didn't mention any of this to Nina perhaps because I almost instinctively felt that she would think it was wrong of Peter to tell me about Maya. After all, Maya wasn't my friend. I was tempted to tell her about my conversation with Peter when we came back from watching *Thelma & Louise* but in the end I said nothing.

The film had been playing for several weeks at the movie theatre near 84th Street on Broadway. A light drizzle was falling. In the early afternoon Nina and I walked over to the theatre and settled down with popcorn and giant sodas. Thelma's ridiculous husband reminded me of a cousin of mine in Dhanbad. I had seen him hold his hands out and wait for his wife to button his sleeves and strap his watch on his wrist.

When the two women stopped at the roadhouse, I felt the tension growing within me. Thelma was drinking and dancing with a man named Harlan. Later, just as Harlan was about to rape Thelma in the parking lot, Louise stepped into the frame with a gun. A minute later, when Louise shot him, Nina let go of my hand and surprised me by clapping. I clapped too, and then a few others in the theatre joined in, although at least one person, a man from a row behind us, asked us to quiet down.

There were funny moments in the film but it wrung the sadness out of us. Thelma, played by Geena Davis, undergoes a huge change (she gets radicalized, as Ehsaan would say), and Louise, Susan Sarandon's character, is strong and clear-headed and entirely without any illusions. While watching the movie I knew that Nina would later ask me which scene was my favourite. I had very much liked Thelma's resolve at the end when she says, 'I can't go back... I mean, I just couldn't live.' Or earlier, her saying to the cop before locking him in the trunk of his squad car that he should be nice to his wife. 'My husband wasn't sweet to me. See how I turned out.' In another scene, Louise was a bit dismissive of her boyfriend Jimmy's affection. She tells

Thelma, 'He just loves the chase, that's all.' It made me think of
something Jennifer had once said about me, but I wasn't going
to tell this to Nina.

The popcorn and the soda had robbed our appetite for dinner.
We sat on the steps outside Nina's building with a couple of
Coronas.

—Did you immediately know why Louise didn't want to
drive through Texas?

—I didn't, I said.

An old woman walked past us on the sidewalk with her
tiny dog on a leash.

—Did you? I asked.

—It was the most powerful thing about the movie. The past
that lies there under the surface.

When I heard Nina say this, I thought of Peter and what
he had told me about Maya. I didn't have the courage to say
anything about Maya. Instead I said, I liked that song about
the woman who realizes that she's never going to ride through
Paris in a sports car…

—Marianne Faithfull, Nina said. The song is about a suicide.
You should listen to another song of hers called 'Broken English'.
I have it upstairs.

This was the moment during the evening, with the street
darkening as we sat on the steps, when I began telling Nina about
the teenage daughter of my father's first cousin. Suneeta lived
in the village where my father had grown up. Her father was a
farmer like everyone else in the family, but he was also a drunk.
He got into scraps and often beat his wife, a tall woman who
people said was very strong herself. Their house was separated
from my grandmother's by a narrow dirt lane. Deepak, Suneeta's
elder brother, had taken after his father. When he was a boy,
he would follow me all day when I visited the village, eager to
bring me fruit or jump into the village pond if I asked him to.
But he was now grown up. My grandmother complained that
Deepak stole her grain. Like his father, he would climb the
khajur tree and drink the toddy straight from the pots that the

tappers had hung there.

Suneeta was tall like her mother. Her skin was fair and she had light-brown eyes. Once, my mother had my father stop the car as we entered the village because she had seen Suneeta out at the village's edge grazing the two goats and a buffalo her family owned.

—Don't you go to school, child? My mother asked Suneeta.

—Masterji beats me.

—Why does he beat you?

—I didn't bring the kilo of rice he wants from all the students.

A few more years passed and Suneeta was a teenager. She was shy with me and I had only exchanged a few words with her, but my grandmother had complaints about her too. Suneeta sneaked into her small kitchen garden and stole the spinach. I remember her in a cheap, orange cotton sari, her hair slightly unkempt, looking attractive and just a little bit dissolute. The news of her death came as a shock. At first, the story in the family was that the girl had been trapped in love by an older, wily man, a distant relative of ours. I was told that Suneeta would go into the mango grove behind my grandmother's house to meet her lover. He lived in the village too, and was married, and this man had killed her. This story, like all stories in my family, hid something darker. Later, I learned that one night Suneeta had gone into the house of a distant relative of ours to steal and was caught. The man kept her imprisoned in a room for a couple of days and raped her. Another friend of his also joined in. When word got out, Deepak and his father walked into that house and slit Suneeta's throat. When the police arrived from a nearby town, things were so handled that it was the rapists who were charged with the murder. They were now in prison and would die there. I was told that Deepak didn't even return home; he disappeared from the village and was working as a daily-wage labourer on a railway line in Assam. A few people believed that he had come back and was a rickshaw puller in Patna. When I next went to the village, Suneeta's mother held my hand and cried for the children she had lost.

Night had fallen now. After a while, Nina had a question.

—Did she approve of what Deepak had done?

—I didn't pry for details.

—I don't mean, did you ask her if he was able to behead her in a single motion.

—I know what you mean.

—I guess I'm saying—

—Well, I was finding it difficult to talk to her. She was holding my hand and crying. I was also distressed because, every few seconds, she kept lifting my hand to her eyes, using it to wipe her tears.

⌒

Nina enrolled in a course taught by Ehsaan called 'Flags and Rags'. She hadn't been in Ehsaan's class during the first semester I studied with him. That fall, Nina was taking a course in Marxism and deconstruction with an Indian professor and another course in Victorian literature. The class on Victorian novelists was taught by a star in her field whom I had once met at a party—the Victorianist sat on the floor in the kitchen, drunk, snot running down her nose, while her husband entertained the nervous students in the living room with his stories about teaching in Africa. 'Flags and Rags' was structured as a critique of nationalism. I was in that class with her and Cai Yan and several others. We read Gramsci and Tagore because Ehsaan's heroes were failed revolutionaries and poets. Nina liked the syllabus, she liked Ehsaan too, but she often joked that she had signed up because of a mistake. She had at first thought the course was about fashion and it was called 'Fags and Rags'.

We started going to a bar on Thursday nights. Starting at nine, anyone could take the microphone and recite poetry. Five people in the audience chosen at random used scorecards to mark poems on a scale of one to ten. One night, a slim man, clean-shaven and bald, reading a poem about queer love and clear rage. Then someone with Bobby Kennedy's face printed on her trousers reading her poem about her lover, and an Indian woman in the

audience shouting that she wanted a ten for that one. 'I love
poems which have nipples in them.' The emcee tilting his bearded
face and saying *Let's have a tete-a-tete about that, ha-ha.* A young
black woman in a baseball shirt with 'Crooklyn' written on the
back softly reciting a lament about the many moons of unwanted
pregnancies and deaths in poor homes. That first time, on the
late-night subway bringing us back uptown to our apartments,
I put my mouth close to Nina's ear. As if I was standing in the
bar speaking into the microphone, I improvised words that were
delivered to the backbeat of the train's moving wheels: I read in a
book, baby, that this is the hour of the immigrant worker – after
the milkman and just before the dustman. / With his immigrant
love, his love-poem is a stammer at your doorstep at dawn, /
a terrible, trapped-up hope in this hour of becoming. / It has
nothing of the certainties of those who give names to bottles
of wines in the languages of Europe. / A woman just into her
twenties, from Shanghai, alone at an underground train station
/ in the middle of New York at night / after working overtime
in a garment factory, / looks at her hands for a long moment /
in the bluish light of the station.

   Such discoveries during that semester. For my birthday, Nina
gave me a book of poems by radical Latin American poets. I
wrote poems about every part of Nina's body. My poetic interest
widened and I had soon compiled a set of political poems that
began with a rousing line I had stolen from Joseph Heller: 'Even
that fat little fuck Henry Kissinger was writing a book!'*

   *Tongues untied, Your Honour. The language of liberation that
came through language itself. And then the liberation of the body.* In
the cabinet where I store my passport there is a yellow ticket
from Billy Bragg's 'Rumor of War' concert. The ticket was stapled
by Nina to a card on which she had copied down a line that
Antonio Gramsci had written in a letter to his future wife: 'How
many times have I wondered if it is really possible to forge links

---

*Joseph Heller, *Good as Gold* (New York: Simon and Schuster, 1976). See p.
328.

with a mass of people when one has never had strong feelings for anyone: if it is possible to have a collectivity when one has not been deeply loved oneself by individual human creatures?"*

The Billy Bragg concert was at the nearby Beacon. Nina and I walked there together, holding hands on the warm summer night. It was a small theatre and it was packed. Bragg wore a black t-shirt and black jeans, the guitar hanging from his shoulder. His songs were against war and against greed. It seemed to me that if he kept singing any longer, all the punks in the front row who were dancing by simply bouncing up and down would start tonguing each other. Nina and I went drinking afterwards, and when we were walking back to her apartment, she sang Bragg's line over and over again: 'I dreamed I saw Phil Ochs last night.' When we got back, she didn't lead me to her bed where we often made love and slept with our legs entangled three or four times a week; instead, carrying a blanket in one hand and a small flashlight in another, she led me to the roof. We were in the dark on the top but all around us were the lights of the city.†
On our right, spanning the darkness, the towers of the George Washington Bridge. The illuminated bits of Cliffside Park in distant Jersey afloat in the waters of the Hudson. Nearby the red glow of a sign for a parking garage.

The narrow beam of the light that had climbed up the stairs, three or four steps at a time, has now jumped across twenty-odd

---

*Antonio Gramsci, *Selections from Cultural Writings*. David Forgacs and Geoffrey Nowell-Smith, eds., William Boelhower, trans., (Cambridge, MA: Harvard University Press, 1991). See p. 147.
†This immense solitude in the middle of the city. I'm reminded now of another clipping in my notebook. 'A flourishing slum' is written on the top and the following section pasted below: 'Parapa then fixed a man-sized plank to the hutment wall, so that while his father and brother made love to their wives below, he could stay chastely on the shelf. Still, he sometimes sleeps outside, beside an open sewer, in the blissful quietude of the street.' (A Google search reveals that this clipping is from *The Economist*, 19 December 2007. I conducted this search because I wanted to find out why I had written 'A flourishing slum' on the top of the page. It is the title that was used in the magazine.)

years. It comes to rest beside Nina and switches off. She is lying
on the blanket on her stomach. She has spread some clear gel
in her hand and put it on my cock.

—Higher, she says.

I haven't done it this way. It excites me but I'm also, quite
honestly, afraid that it might hurt her. I feel the tightness of her
muscle and its release, and she is soon pushing back, making a
sound that makes me want to thrust back.

—Do you want me to come harder?

Somewhere among her moans a murmured yes, and the
fingers of her right hand touching the back of her own neck.
By then was I standing or kneeling? I came in a rush and her
back arched, and she bucked again and again.

—I love you, I love you, Nina said. And then, Let's go down
and catch the end of *Saturday Night Live*.

That semester, in his seminar, David Lamb used a book whose
title, *The Tremulous Private Body*, would come back to me after
Nina and I had finished making love. She would be holding me
and I'd feel her body rocked by a passing shudder. During that
moment, she'd clutch me tighter and when the moment had
passed, she would turn away and promptly go to sleep. I once
mentioned *The Tremulous Private Body* to her and she immediately
began to mock Lamb. I liked this. It took away my feelings of
fascination and jealousy. A week or two earlier Lamb had wanted
a book report from us on another book he was teaching, *Roland
Barthes by Roland Barthes*. Barthes had quoted a letter from a
man in Morocco identified only as Jilali. Jilali's letter was about
what he himself called 'a disturbing subject': 'I have a younger
brother, a student in the third-form AS, a very musical boy (the
guitar) and a very loving one; but poverty conceals and hides
him in this terrible world (he suffers in the present, "as your
poet says") and I am asking you, dear Roland, to find him a job
in your kind country as soon as you can, since he leads a life
filled with anxiety and concern; now you know the situation of
young Moroccans, and his indeed astounds me and denies me all
radiant smiles…' Barthes described the language of the letter as

'sumptuous', 'brilliant', and 'literal and nonetheless immediately literary'. Everyone in Lamb's seminar focused on what Barthes had called 'the pleasures of language' that spoke, '*at the same time* truth and desire: all of Jilali's desire (the guitar, love), all of the political truth of Morocco.' I penned a mini-essay on utopian discourse. But Nina's book report was considerably shorter. She xeroxed a section of the letter quoted in *Roland Barthes by Roland Barthes* and then distributed copies to everyone in the class. Nina had used a felt pen to write across the page the following question for us: 'Did that bastard Barthes give Jilali's brother a job?'*

I was deeply in love with Nina but it is possible that an objective viewer would have thought that I was obsessed with her. Maybe Nina thought this too, although she never said it. For several weeks during that first summer, she was gone. She was staying at her parents' summer home. Her parents lived in Pittsburgh but they spent the summers in Cape Elizabeth, Maine, where they had a cabin. During her childhood, Nina had spent summers in Rome, which is where her father was from—Nina's parents met in Rome when her mother had travelled there as junior from Dartmouth on her study abroad programme. But for many years now the family had summered in Maine. Nina told me that they didn't have a phone in the cottage; so I waited for her letters. The letters arrived every few days, though not as often as I wanted, in envelopes that had pictures stuck on them and, once, a section of a map showing the beach and the ocean. Inside were messages that were crumbs that fed a hunger and left me famished. *I'm aware, Your Honour, of the language I'm using but may I proceed to the bench to present evidence? This is Nina in a letter stamped 29 June 1991: What I have to say about what you*

---

*The affectations of graduate student life: love expressed in the idiom of required reading in the doctoral seminars. A reader of the *Village Voice* on Valentine's Day that year (1991) would have encountered in the personals, in the section captioned *Public Display of Affection*, the following message for Nina that had cost me thirty dollars: 'Hey babe: Let's snuggle in bed and read the poetry of the future or even the missionary-position Marxist writing you so greatly admire. XOXO'

*have called your situation is this. I want your constant hand on my
back, your unwaged agricultural labour in the fields of my nightly
dreams, I want your back pressed into my front, your warm Brazil
and shy Tierra del Fuego. I want your cumspattered shirts and your
baby, baby.*

Another time she wrote: *Today I've got something which I've
never had before, which is laryngitis. I can scarcely make a sound.
Today I could whisper sweet filth in your ear. Have you ever wanted
to fuck a mute, honey?*

Filth!

Your Honour, I have entered the body of America. I have
spoken filth in the ear of one of your fair citizens when I was
inside her.

Your Honour, this was something new for me.

She was hospitable in the extreme, meeting me with laughter.
Her laughter alone saved me from my self-ridicule. Or what I
imagined as the world's ridicule. Your Honour, when I was on the
phone with her I spoke in a high British accent, having stooped
to using words used by Prince Charles in his conversation with
Camilla Parker Bowles. (I was a boy in school when Charles
kissed Diana on the balcony of Buckingham Palace. A decade
was to pass before I read of his long, continuing affair with the
aforementioned Parker Bowles who had approached him at a polo
match with an unforgettable proposition: My great-grandmother
was the mistress of your great-grandfather—so how about it?)
Such has been my pathetic, unsentimental education! I have relied
in my games of seduction on words plucked from the airwaves
by a scanner and published by British tabloids for laughs:

Charles: The trouble is I need you several times a week. Oh,
God. I'll just live inside your trousers or something. It would
be much easier...

Camilla: (in a falsetto) What are you going to turn into, a
pair of knickers?

Charles: Or, God forbid, a Tampax.

Camilla: (shrieking) Oh, darling!

No one had ever talked to me like Nina did. Before she left

for Maine, she gave me a leather bracelet with a silver clasp in
the middle. I thanked her with a kiss.

—Try not to let any woman touch it while you're having
sex, she said.

I had often thought of other women. Did she know this? I
might have laughed nervously.

—Do I have dibs on your sperm?

—Yes, I said. I was unsure what dibs meant but I didn't care.
My sperm, I said, and the scented mangoes from my mango
orchards, all the fruits of my toil too, the tree of my childhood,
the furnished apartment of my soul.

These florid speeches. Was she mocking my feverish syntax
when she sent me her occasional letters written with great
rhetorical flourish? More than once I thought we were like two
porn artists hamming it up for the camera. This was not the
greatest danger. The biggest challenge to love is not when you
pretend you are in a porn film: no, no, it's when you believe that
you are in a bad Hindi film, delivering reassuring saccharine
platitudes to each other. Nina lived her life in a B. R. Chopra
movie for a while and then made her escape.

What was Nina's natural mode of talking? When you phoned
her, the answering machine picked up the call. She never answered.
Instead, you got Laurie Anderson's voice saying, 'Hi, I'm not
home right now...?' A series of electronic beeps, punctuated
by a detached repetition of clichés, a language removed from
sentimentalism. It was intelligent and all incredibly hip even if
a little removed and maybe cold.

But this is wrong, of course. Back in April, on my birthday,
we had been drinking beer and I said I wanted to see a fish
tattooed on her arm. Some weeks later, on her own birthday, she
had acquired a tattoo. The new oil on her arm formed a pool in
which hung a single fish. Nina owned two eight-pound dumb-
bells that she used to strengthen her muscles. She watched the
fish as, weight in hand, she flexed her arm.

—Will you marry me?

I asked her this impulsively, as I watched her exercising. I laughed when I said that, but the words still hurt in my throat.

—You want to do it for the Green Card?

She was smiling. The dumb-bell rose and fell in a precise arc.

—Yes, when they ask me over at Immigration, did you marry her for love, I'll say, Yeah, I love the way she climbs on top and fucks me. Nina, I'll say, lick my mouth and show them how wet it is when you are done with me.

I might have babbled on. There was always just that hint of seriousness between us that made me nervous and talkative. I recognized, not for the first time in my life, that as far as women were concerned I preferred taking the low road of indelicate candour. *But I was also, Your Honour, exploring language. I was the poet of my own sexual liberation.*

After the dumb-bells and a run, Nina and I ate a simple dinner of rice and beans in her kitchen. The television was on in the next room. Maybe it was something said in the news, Nina turned to me and asked whether the Immigration and Naturalization Service had a uniform.

—Yes, I said.

—Do you ever imagine having sex with the Border Patrol? You know, the way porn in Israel has sometimes much to do with the Nazis.

I was aware that Nina had been in long relationships with others before me, one with a man who was much older than her, a designer of yachts. Then she had dated, for two years, a man named Jonathan who was a labour organizer. Compared to her, I was inexperienced. She knew that I had been friendly with someone at the university and was perhaps sleeping with her. But I had told her nothing because Nina had never enquired. When Nina put to me this fairly innocent question about the Border Patrol, I asked myself anxiously if she liked to imagine having sex with someone else. The thought of loving Nina forever, and only her, passed through my mind, as it often did, in some kind of quick, sad, dulling way. And, characteristically, what emerged from my mouth was more insincere banter propped up with academic jargon.

—You're asking me do I want to be fucked by the state?

—Well, have you watched *Night Porter*?

I hadn't. Nina said it was a story about a former SS officer, now a night porter in a hotel in Vienna, and a woman who was a survivor from the same camp. The officer and the prisoner had been lovers in the camp. I interrupted Nina.

—No, I would like to fuck Susan Sontag. Or maybe Susan Sarandon.

Nina considered the point. I wanted very badly to be in love with intelligent, well-read women. And Nina was exactly that. I had fallen in love with her, and with her prose. Her perfume and her lips too. No, with her prose and her lipstick. Even plain words seemed so potent. Once, I came out of the shower and she was lying naked in bed, a lovely creature stretched on the dark sheet: on the inside of her thigh, in dark red lipstick, she had written *Here*.*

ᴊ

I came home from the library and checked the tiny tin mailbox before entering the apartment. There was a postcard from Maine with a picture of a cowboy stuck on it. The photo had probably been cut from a trashy magazine. On the other side, Nina had written: *Just saw a program on TV about American cowboys. There was one small bit that was interesting. These rodeo wrestlers hold a steer by the horns and bite its (very) sensitive lower lip to bring the animal down to the ground.*

I felt an onrush of blood, a sudden heat and an upheaval. This is the effect that many of Nina's letters had on me. At other times, I was left uncertain. Mystery surrounded her words. One day she wrote that she had fallen asleep in the dentist's chair and she had a dream about us. We were seated in front of a hypnotist who was putting her to sleep. The two of us were

---

*After Katherine Mansfield's death from tuberculosis, Virginia Woolf noted in her diary on 28 January 1923: '…our friendship had so much that was writing in it.'

holding hands. Even as she was drifting off to sleep, she was telegraphing a message with her fingers. She was saying that she loved me, she was asking for my help. *Help me!* I found this appeal indecipherable. And then Nina had added: *I'm not at my parents' place right now but I'm going to drive down there tomorrow. If you are a good one you'll soon mail me a letter tasting of pears and licorice and your own sweet self.*

Not at her parents' place? Where was she, and why hadn't she called? I sent her a card. I was like a man waiting for the bus on a long strip of empty road, uncertain whether the bus ever came on that route. In the food co-op that evening, while purchasing my groceries, I also picked up pear and licorice. But there was no call from Nina. Finally, four days later, a postcard arrived. I couldn't tell where it had been posted. In Nina's neat, angular hand, the following message: *I heard on the radio today that Columbus's men, unfamiliar with the migration patterns of American birds, regularly mistook the mid-Atlantic presence of feathered companions (en route to Africa) for signs of landfall. Continually disappointed. Where are you? I tried your office and your house. White featherless biped (f) seeks warm-blooded tropical creature (m) for new world adventures and more.*

It helped that she had mentioned the radio; her story appeared anchored in some sort of reality. But how could she have missed me? If I wasn't at the office, I was to be found in my apartment, reading all the books that Ehsaan wanted me to read. The truth was that I had grown suspicious of Nina and there were often occasions when I didn't even know whether what she had written was true. Then, I'd feel guilty and simply wonder whether I had misjudged her.* At other times, I questioned her judgement.

---

*I told Nina that last Christmas, I was thinking of her while sitting alone in the dark at a movie theatre watching *Pretty Woman.* I was weighed down by self-pity. My remark was a demand for sympathy. But Nina wasn't much concerned. She said, *Ugh... Couldn't you have found another movie? That film represented the dream of Reaganomics: that the recession could be brought to an end by giving a blowjob.*

How could I not love her! She gave me a map of the world in which we lived!

After I was rejected for a journalism internship, she wrote: *I'm sorry that you didn't get the job. Is it at all liberating, I wonder. It's come to be that I can't imagine anyone really likes to go to work. The Great Depression was such a fertile period, you know. The things that were invented in that decade include the TV, the helicopter, nylon stockings, the jet plane, and that thing that is a jet plane in nylon tights, Superman. Think of the many classics of literature that were written during that time!*

Was she right? I was so taken by the drama surrounding the messages that I don't think I got the chance to really understand what she was actually saying in any letter of hers. *Such drama!* On some days, two or even three letters. She would write, *I'm so happy to be tearing up the letter I had begun.* And I'd spend the day wondering what it was that she had written or not written. And then I would find another one, *It's your world, I'm just livin' in it.* (I checked Nina's horoscope in *Mirabella* when I was at a hair salon. This is what I read and, naturally, tore the page out to take home with me and stick in my journal: 'If you thought you had your fill of personal and professional dramas, forget it. The fireworks are *far* from over. You, and sexy Virgo Richard Gere, have spent a considerable amount of emotional energy this year trying to figure out the state of your love life. Now it's time to move on. The lunar eclipse on June 8 will make you even more intense and sensitive to others' whims. Surprising events around the solar eclipse on June 23 will clear the air, and you will be ready, willing, and able to do battle for the best reason of all: true happiness.' *Clear the air! Clear the air!*) It doesn't matter if I can't remember what our fights were about: it was always in a way about the same thing. She was often in another city, she would say she would call, and didn't; her small lies, which she said were the results of her nervousness from my continually testing her, drove me to the brink of madness.* She sent me letters. All

---

*I have now looked in all the four notebooks I have from that period but I can't find a sheet I had torn from a magazine: it was a 'found text' that a man had left behind in his airplane seat, with the names of two women on

her letters were so beautifully crafted—which only added to my suspicion. The mention of any other name in a letter she had sent me would take away all the pleasure of receiving any words of affection from her. I discovered jealousy was a disease whose first symptoms were a sudden darkening of the universe followed by a sudden onset of a faint prickling on the surface of the skin, especially the face, before a hammering commenced in the heart.

I always complained to Nina that she didn't love me enough, and I didn't realize for a long time that in doing this I had already lost the game. It was all futile really. There could never be a cure. I had become attached to a story that started one night: I got up in the middle of the night and the thought came to me out of nowhere that Nina wasn't in Maine. She was in Pittsburgh with her ex, Jonathan. As soon as the thought came to me, I knew with deep certainty that it was true. I said this to her when we next spoke on the phone, and she surprised me by accepting my charge, only adding that while the details were correct I had drawn the wrong conclusion. Jonathan's mother was dying, first her kidneys had failed and then her other organs went kaput.

—This is a woman who has been very kind to me, particularly during one long sickness. I wanted to do the right thing by her, but wasn't at all sure that you would understand. I'm sorry. In retrospect, I should have been honest with you.

I accepted this explanation but my doubts lay in repose only for a short while. I had been naïve. I had been blind to the fact that Nina was still in a relationship with Jonathan when I stepped into the picture, and then I treated the discovery of this fact as a revolutionary breakthrough in the way in which knowledge was to be forever organized. I'm certain I was tedious. More than

---

top of the page and the attributes, both positive and negative, listed under each name. 'Great cook', 'honest', 'good in bed', 'bad breath', 'kind to my parents', and the like. How many times I had drawn a list about Nina! And sometimes matched them with another name next to hers! 'Gracious', 'sexy', 'smells nice', 'little lies', 'careless', 'forgets to mail letters', 'good Scotch', 'doesn't cook', 'smokes too much', 'distant', 'beautiful laugh', etc. No mention of 'love'.

once, Nina protested against my absurd complaints.

—I'm boxed into a historical corner. One that I cannot seem to get out of, even when I'd give anything to be able to do that.

—I love you and am not always sure you love me.

—I sometimes think that if you really loved me you'd let me out of this mess.

—Are you saying you want to end this?

—No, I'm just saying that if you could ever let the test be over, I could stop failing.

Whenever we had a conversation like this, I felt immediately chastened. There was another thing. I fumed, I accused, but Nina never. She didn't raise her voice. In fact, I don't think she regarded blunt statements at all as truths. If you weren't being decent, were you being truthful? When I was bitter, I would think it was a class thing, this obligation to be polite. At other times, I felt like a heel.

Sometimes after we fought, I would come back into the apartment and hear her voice on my answering machine. When this happened, I relented quickly and called her back. But there were times when I didn't care. The stab of guilt I had experienced earlier was no longer there; its place had been taken by rage. I was too angry that she hadn't written, or hadn't called, or been out late with friends.


When she returned from her vacation, Nina said we could go on a trip together. She came to my apartment. We fucked with a mix of efficiency and impatience, we ate Chinese takeout, and then we fucked again as if we were getting rid of the memories of early summer. Or, that's what I thought later as I watched Nina lather her hair with shampoo when we stood under the shower together. The Aveda bottle said Black Mulva but, of course, she called it Black Vulva. No one I had seen in my life, except maybe two half-naked men once beside a village-road near Hajipur, bathing next to a water-pump after a day's labour in the fields, rubbed soap on their limbs more vigorously than Nina.

She manufactured a skin of foam and was scarcely recognizable when she transformed herself into an unworldly creature with suds in her hair and froth covering even her face. I heard this creature asking me where I wanted to go.

—Grand Canyon.

In her silence I knew I had said the wrong thing.

—No, but there's Las Vegas close by.

It was now my turn to remain silent.

Florida was too close. Hawaii too far away.

—Can you land somewhere in the middle of the country and then drive through Yellowstone?

If we were going to drive, Nina wanted to go to California instead.

—We will drive down Highway 1 with the Pacific outside the car window. You'll love it.

Water had washed away all the soap bubbles from her hair and face: she appeared beautiful and gleaming, scrubbed clean, with dark glittering eyes and a peachy mouth.

I liked the idea of the drive with the ocean outside but all I had seen of this country were cities on the east and the west coast. What would I have known of India if I had visited only Bombay and Calcutta? I wanted to drive through parts of the US, its vast middle, and then roam in the wilderness. I suspected we weren't going to the Grand Canyon because of some past association.

—We'll land somewhere and just drive through Yellowstone, I said.

The ticket we bought was for mid-July. When the date drew close we went to the Countee Cullen Library on 136th Street and checked out a batch of books on tape: Norman Mailer's *The Executioner's Song* (because it was the thickest and had the largest number of tapes in it); *The Great Gatsby*; a three-in-one set of Toni Morrison's works, *Sula*, *Song of Solomon*, and *Beloved*; also Alice Munro (*Selected Stories*, read by, yes, Susan Sarandon), a book by Elmore Leonard, and Nabokov's *Lolita*. Nina didn't think we'd have that much time but she didn't protest. She chose a book called *Middle Passage*, which I'm quite sure we never listened to.

Next step: a trip to AAA to get a TripTik made for the drive. From Cheyenne, Wyoming to Missoula, Montana.

—Yes, madam, thank you, the route should pass through Yellowstone, yes.

The heavily perfumed woman, of sixty or thereabouts, held three differently-coloured markers between the fingers of her left hand. She would select one of them and highlight a highway so that the yellow would light up like a runway through the flat green of the paper. Our trip was going to take three or four days. Nina felt we should give ourselves a week; we were flying into Cheyenne and then flying out of Missoula. These names, till now unfamiliar, came to possess magic.

～

We were graduate students; we used words like 'research'. So, on our second day in Yellowstone, we found ourselves using that word. When we discovered that even though it was still summer, there was snow in some of the areas, and that we should have brought jackets and sweaters, we began to tell each other that we hadn't done the right research. Here we were in a forest of fir, the setting sun having slipped behind the horizon of rock, and the cold hung like desolation among the lodgepole pines stripped by summer wildfires. It was evening and nearly dark, but we weren't worried. On the contrary, all the uncertainty and the cold outside added an edge of excitement to our drive. We were going to find a motel among the three places marked as X's on our map. It appeared that we still had anywhere between thirty and seventy or eighty miles to go. We should have bought a travel-guide. Instead, we had concentrated on finding the right books to bring on our trip. The book-on-tape in the car's cassette-player right then, as we drove with our dashboard light lit up in green, white and red as if it was Christmas, was a thriller about an airline stewardess smuggling cash. A voice said in the dark: *They watched Jackie Burke come off the Bahamas shuttle in her tan Islands Air uniform, then watched her walk through Customs and Immigration*

*without opening her bag, a brown nylon case she pulled along behind*
*her on wheels, the kind flight attendants used.*

I leaned forward in the passenger seat and switched the voice
off. The tension in the story was making me jangly. It affected
my nerves and I sought release.

—I read a story once by Milan Kundera. This woman pretends
she is a hitchhiker when she gets into her boyfriend's car. It is
an erotic story but a very messed up one...

—Did you tell me your name, sir?

Nina was smiling a little bit.

It was not very dark, but there was no one else around. Nina
stopped the car on the side of the road. I got out to stretch my
legs. When I was back at the door Nina slid into the passenger
seat and then turned back, facing the road we had driven on.
She said she didn't want her skirt on. I was eager and felt her
wetness with one hand—and, as I remember this, or think I
remember, I cannot help asking if Nina, wherever she may be
now, also remembers the same things from our relationship. (I
took a picture of her in New York City under the sign of a bar
named Chameleon. That's you, I had said. Such cruelty. She must
remember that.) I want to believe that she remembers how the
sound of our breathing filled the car. In the distance, through
the rear windshield, I could see a point of light travelling high
up on the mountain: a car's light appeared and disappeared as
if I were watching the flight of a firefly. When I entered her
from behind, even in that cramped space, does she remember
thrusting her ass back into me with tiny, ecstatic jolts? In the
story that I have formed in my head, though this could be from
another time, I remember that when I made a caressing gesture,
gently touching Nina's breast, she pushed my hand away and
said, *Fuck me.*

⌒

On the screen of memory, the light resembling the flight of a
firefly is replaced by the gibbous moon. It is summer and the
moon is my companion on a train ride back to Patna from

Delhi. The other passengers in my compartment are sleeping; I'm reading a novel by Lawrence Durrell, a writer who was born in Jamshedpur, only a few hours away from Patna.* The book has been recommended to me by a woman I've met at college in Delhi. She is an undergraduate too, studying literature, and her parents are professors at a college nearby. I think of her as modern—which I'm not—because she has acted on stage and travelled abroad. She has a tall forehead and light-coloured eyes. We have drunk tea together and smoked cigarettes outside the college canteen but we aren't lovers. We are too shy or too young to have even held hands. I have in my bag the address she has given me for her aunt's home in Baroda where she'll be visiting that summer; I've been asked to write letters to her and I'm already writing one in my head as I turn to look at the moon. There isn't now, nor will there be in the future, any real intimacy between us. What do we know of love? No one in my family has married outside our caste. Love is the province ruled by kids with cars and memberships in clubs; the young men I see around me bathed in cologne, peeling wads of Wrigley's chewing gum before going up to say hello to a woman. I have taken the young woman's notes from a lecture to a student in the dorm who claims to be an expert at handwriting analysis. I realize it is a bit like going to an astrologer. He looks at her closed letters and describes her as 'emotionally reserved and suspicious of others'. Looking at my notebook he traces in the air the long tails beneath my letters and says, with a hint of indecision, that those loops 'represent a vivid imagination but might also mean that you are mired in sensuousness'. If there's been any romance it has been entirely in my vivid imagination! But I've acted with exorbitant passion in one respect. On the night before our exams, another student brought to me the

---

*Durrell's novel has an enigmatic epigraph from one of Sigmund Freud's letters: 'I am accustoming myself to the idea of regarding every sexual act as a process in which four persons are involved. We shall have a lot to discuss about that.'

question papers that would be unsealed the next day. I didn't ask him how he got his hands on the leaked papers; without thinking twice, I got into an autorickshaw and went to the woman's house. She was surprised to see me, and to discover that I knew where she lived, and she was more surprised still to find out the reason why I was standing at her door. I didn't study that night. I was nervous and eager to know whether I had given the woman I liked so much the correct information. The test papers turned out to be authentic and she laughed when I confessed that I had performed badly. I hadn't done the work. Our friendship didn't grow although we exchanged a few letters in which we enclosed some wan attempts at poetry. A year before I left India, I read in the newspaper that she had been awarded a prestigious fellowship that would allow her to write about Tagore at the University College in London. Then I heard from someone that she had become a lesbian, and this news, which I received in New York, pleased me. Both of us had stepped out of the protective armour of our earlier weak transgressions. And tonight, when I picked up that volume of Durrell's to confirm what I remembered of the epigraph, I turned the pages to recall the story, so removed from me now and distant in so many ways, and my eyes found the following words: *There are only three things to be done with a woman,' said Clea once. 'You can love her, suffer for her, or turn her into literature.' I was experiencing a failure in all these domains of feeling.*

ᶜ

Gallatin National Forest. Our cabin had a heater but the cold seemed to seep through invisible cracks and pooled near our feet. A little before dawn, I felt Nina stirring and then saw that her eyes were open. She complained about the cold and said she wanted pancakes. Pancakes and coffee brewed over a wood-fire. I huddled closer to her.

The Gujarati man at the reception said we would have to wait an hour to get breakfast, but if we drove north, we could see wolves at this time. Where would we find them? We had discovered the lodge with much difficulty. But the man was assuring.

—Turn left when you come out of the gate. Drive north for half an hour, and you'll see them crossing the road or in the grass leading to the river.

—Okay, so the wolves are out at this time. What about pancakes? Isn't there an International House of Pancakes out there somewhere?

—You'd have to drive to Bozeman for that. They will be open when you reach them because it'll take you four hours to get there.

Of course, we didn't go. We fed each other chocolate and drank bad coffee, lying in bed, listening to the dry, detached voice of Jeremy Irons reading *Lolita* on the tiny cassette player that Nina used to record interviews. *To any other type of tourist accommodation I soon grew to prefer the Functional Motel—clean, neat, safe nooks, ideal places for sleep, argument, reconciliation, insatiable, illicit love.* We looked around the cold room, its pink wall and the framed picture of a young grizzly stepping into a frothy stream, and we laughed. As if by agreement, Nina hunched herself under the blanket and crawled up until she was lying on top of me. She sat up and made small, deft adjustments so that we fitted well together. Jeremy Irons was saying, *I have never seen such smooth amiable roads as those that now radiated before us, across the crazy quilt of forty-eight states. Voraciously we consumed those long highways, in rapt silence we glided over their glossy black dance floors.*

⸫

Six months later, I thought of Nina's face in the motel room that morning when I heard mention of wolves on the radio. It was my father's birthday and I was going to call him in India. But first I was waiting for Nina to call me from her conference in Boston. I didn't want her to get a busy signal if she called. On important days, I called my parents. Half a world away, the phone rang in Patna. As I've mentioned, my parents didn't have a phone at the time. Nowadays every milkman has a mobile phone in his front shirt-pocket. *Your Honour, I'm describing another time. Calls used to be expensive, and it could take an hour to get a connection. When I called the neighbour's number, someone would run out to get my father. I usually hung up and then called AT&T to complain that the line had got disconnected. The operator would apologize and then call for me without charge. As far as I was concerned, immigration was the original sin. Someone owed me something. This half-expressed thought had found a home in my heart. It provided me an exaggerated sense of identity, and granted me permission to do anything I wanted. I'm not trying to justify anything; I only intend to explain.*\*

I had never spoken to my family about Nina. My father's questions when I was on a visit to India were like the following: 'Can you tell me why Americans are more punctual as a people?' Or, 'Is there any way of explaining why Indians spit so much?' For her part, Nina had never asked me much about my parents. This surprised me a bit. Not just my parents, I don't think even India interested her. I remember her saying once that if she ever visited India, she would be sure to skip the Taj Mahal. In Grand Central, we had seen a tourism ad for India: in the sky above the marble dome of the Taj, a monument to Shah Jahan's love for Noor Jahan, were the words: *And to think these days men get away with giving flowers and chocolates to their wives.* Nina wasn't very impressed.

—Don't you think it's somewhat perverse—beautiful monuments built for women when they are completely dead?

She chuckled when she said that. To show that she meant well, she kissed me on the ear.

A few months after we had been together, I decided to introduce India to her by showing her one or two films by Satyajit Ray, starting with *Pather Panchali*; but then I grew nervous, fearing that she would get bored. Another evening we went to Blockbuster to find a video. Nina was standing behind me in the store, her breast pressed against my back. I told her I

---

\*I have the following quote in my notebook: 'I carry a brick on my shoulder, in order that the world may know what my house was like.' —Bertolt Brecht

wanted to watch a movie neither of us had seen before. I picked *The Silence of the Lambs*. She said that she had always wanted to see that movie. I liked it from the very first scene. Ten minutes into the movie, I put the new VCR on pause to say to her, in my best Anthony Hopkins impersonation, *I'll have you with a little Chianti and some fava beans*. Her dark eyes brightened and she made an eager swallowing sound with her tongue. I reached across and kissed her because, unlike Jodie Foster, she had a full, insolent mouth. Later, while we were still watching the movie, she made a comment that told me right away that she had seen it before. I didn't ask her about it. I had stopped doing that now, but I kept a private count of the times she lied to me. *Insidious intent on my part, yes, Your Honour. This was a small obsession. The way in which a country will stamp your passport every time you enter and leave. An exercise in record-keeping.*

A week later, I woke up in the middle of the night and grew conscious of a memory that I had forgotten. I recalled Nina telling me once while we were out on a walk that she had a History professor as an undergrad whom she now called Hannibal Lecter. After she had graduated, she had gone to thank the man in his office. And the professor, reserved and more than twenty years her senior, had left his chair and come to her. He had stuck his tongue into her mouth and sucked hard for a moment and then just as abruptly withdrawn and sunk back sheepishly into his chair.

I was now sitting waiting for Nina's call from Boston and the story crossed my mind—a thin cloud moving across the face of the sun—about that night we had watched *The Silence of the Lambs*. In a self-pitying way I told myself that I had come so far from my roots: there was nothing of my day-to-day affairs that I could share with my parents. I wondered what I would say to my father on his birthday when he picked up the phone in Patna. I was sitting close to the phone. Nina hadn't called even though she had said she would. The conference in Boston was titled 'Moving Image'. The coffee I was drinking was a Sumatran brand called Mandheling that she liked. We had bought it together, not that it really mattered. I didn't even like drinking coffee, but there I was, with a cup in front of me, waiting, pretending to listen to the radio. That is what mattered, that I drank coffee now. I also let people smoke in my car because then Nina's doing the same wouldn't bother me as much. I switched on National Public Radio most mornings because she liked to wake up to it and I told myself that this way we'd have more things to say to each other.

*Immigrant, Montana.* Those were the words I suddenly heard on the radio. The name of a place. NPR's Liane Hansen said that federal officers had killed a wolf at a ranch near Immigrant, Montana. I was instantly back in Yellowstone with Nina, listening to tapes as we drove through the forest. Her mock-fear of bears when she took off her clothes. And the wolves. That morning in the motel, they were only half an hour north of us!

—Wolf Number Three, Hansen said with a slight smack of her lips, had developed a taste for sheep.

A man from the National Park Service said that Number Three had killed at least one sheep, maybe three, and then he was moved sixty air miles away, but he came back and another sheep was attacked.

—Three made a mistake, we gave him a second chance, he made a second mistake; we removed him from the population.

I felt like laughing. In the quietness of my apartment, I heard this man trying to sound like Harvey Keitel. I realized I was doing what Nina always did—talking back to the radio.

—This is NPR! When did you hire Quentin Tarantino?

I yearned for Nina. Now I felt I understood why she listened to the radio: it was as if she was walking alone down a crowded street and the world reached her in the form of scraps of overheard conversation and shouts. I wanted my voice in her ear. It was my father's birthday, he was now sixty-five, and his weak heart was killing him. He would not live long. So I told myself that on this special day the least I could do was love my girlfriend. If Nina were around—or even if she would simply call me that day—I'd say to her 'I love you'. I wanted to see her laughing when she heard me say that I liked Wolf Number Three and his preference for unbrainy sheep over vixen. I had this image of the wolf running through sixty miles of undergrowth, across frozen lakes he had never seen before, never pausing because his eyes were hungry for home, for the sight of the familiar fence and the sheep ranged inside.

—Honey, I hope he got to pull one down by the throat, the sheep's head thrown back and the blood warm near his mouth, before some stupid, solemn jerk with a hard-on nailed him with a three thousand-dollar rifle.

*Part V*

# Agnes Smedley

*In a magazine I found a list of 237 reasons why people have sex, from a poll conducted by University of Texas psychologists Cindy Meston and David Buss. The list started with 'I was bored' and ended with 'I wanted to change the topic of conversation'. In between were others like 'I was feeling lonely' and 'I wanted the person to love me'. And, 'I wanted to burn calories'.*

Nina didn't forget the wolves.

    Months after we had broken up I looked inside my mailbox and found a postcard showing Old Faithful with a small news clipping stuck on it. Nina's handwriting was recognizable in the address she had written, but she had written nothing else.

> The reintroduction of wolves
> to Yellowstone National Park has
> failed to stop elk from eating
> quaking aspens, disappointing
> scientists who had hoped that the
> wolves would do so by creating a
> 'landscape of fear'.

That was the last note I received from Nina after she told me that she no longer had the stomach for any more fights. When she said she was going to just walk away, I began to apologize. We were outside my apartment on Morningside Drive, standing on the broad sidewalk. The day was cool, the locust tree had put out white flowers, and fresh leaves covered its branches. A garbage truck was idling on the corner. The breeze carried a faint stench, I remember this clearly. A graduate student in Art History, who had had beers with me, saw our serious faces and decided not to interrupt. Nina looked sad but she had made up her mind. She left me admiring the strength of her decision. I had nothing to back my despair. So many times I had told Nina that I wanted our relationship to end, and she had fought back; now, it was she who was telling me it was over but it was clear that nothing I said would make a difference.

    —I love you. You know I love you.

    —Try to find someone who loves you, and love her back.

    She was right about that, but she was wrong about the wolves. Just the other day I watched a video called 'How Wolves Change Rivers'. The introduction of wolves in Yellowstone changed the ecology in unexpected ways. The wolves didn't just kill the deer.

Their presence meant that deer and elk avoided certain areas like valleys and gorges. Vegetation returned to these parts and so too did other forms of life like birds and beavers. As a result of the banks being stabilized, because of new grass, there was reduced erosion and the rivers stopped changing course. On the brief video, the presenter, George Monbiot, spoke about this as a miracle. He spoke in a voice that was gushing, often breathless, wholeheartedly enthusiastic, even optimistic.

I wonder whether Nina has watched the video. Because of the lies. I don't mean Monbiot, with his fast-flowing words. Instead, I'm talking about my lies. Once, after we had been arguing for an hour, Nina had said she had read my journal. My anger vanished, replaced by panic.

—Kailash, she said, I found it depressing to just read those pages. How do you even manage to live the life they describe?

She usually called me AK but used my formal name when she was upset. Which pages had she read? I kept quiet.

—I always knew about the girl from the coffee place.

When we had been fighting, fighting and then making up the same day or three days later, then, in between those days, or maybe after dinner, or in the morning, I would try to wrangle a bit of intimacy with someone else. There was Amy from the organic coffee place down the block from the university; after my first fight with Nina, I had gone to watch *Reservoir Dogs* with Amy. For much of the movie, I had my hand between Amy's thighs. I'm sure I put this detail down in my journal. (I had probably also noted what Amy had said to me after we had first slept together. She said that a friend of hers had acted in a porn film in which she had given a blow job to a dog. A German shepherd. I put this in a poem. Peter used to go to the café where Amy worked. He heard me read the poem and his only comment was that Amy was describing not her friend's experience but her own.) There was a second Amy too, a photographer at the student newspaper, who was going through a breakup. I had kissed her in the dark room while working on my own prints. It didn't matter who you fucked in the dark. One face became

transposed on another; anyone's body could be Nina's. Had Nina
read about her too? I had written about the night I spent with
Trish from Comp. Lit. She rode a motorcycle; Trish was the only
grad student in our cohort who had slept with a professor, a man
who taught Lacan. Trish had delivered a conference paper about
phone sex. She wore tiny black skirts and I had admired her in
the couple of classes we had taken together because she appeared
fearless. There was very little emotion in Trish's brief encounter
with me, however, and she had barely concealed her boredom,
even her contempt, when I started talking about Nina in bed.
If she had read my terse but accurate description, Nina didn't
say anything. It was clearly too depressing to even talk about it.

When we broke up, I made an entry in the journal about a
young visiting assistant professor who had been hired to teach
screenwriting for that semester. She was French-Algerian and
had a boyfriend back in Lyon who was away teaching in Dubai
for a year. My journal records that I told Fadela about Nina, and
she was frank about her boyfriend. When we went to Kinko's
to make a photocopy of her book manuscript we kissed in the
store for twenty minutes.

‌                              ⌐

More than two decades have passed since that last morning on
Morningside Drive. Not even work has brought us together again,
although at airports, for some reason, I look around to see if Nina
is there. *Airports, Your Honour, are the places where immigrants feel
most at home. And also most uneasy.* The closest I came to a sense
of her, except for the sudden dreams that appear in my sleep and
catch me unawares, her lips on mine, her hot tears on my shoulder,
was when I rented a car in Denver and drove north through
Yellowstone Park. I had gone to Denver on behalf of an Indian
newspaper to report on the Democratic National Convention
when Barack Obama accepted his party's nomination. Hope was
in the air. But even the expression of hope can very quickly appear
routine, as in the ritual of the roll call, when the different states
offered their electoral votes to each nominee. 'Madam Secretary,

Maine, the sun comes out in Maine the first in the nation....'
'Illinois, home of Abraham Lincoln.' 'Mississippi, home of the
blues.' 'Ladies and gentlemen, fellow Democrats and friends, we
bring you greetings from the great state of Georgia, the thirteenth
state in our union, birthplace of Dr. Martin Luther King Jr...
where we look to the future with an optimistic gaze...we, the
empire state of the South, the jewel of the South, the great state
of Georgia....' *No, Your Honour, I mean no disrespect. I only mention
this to communicate my interest in the democratic process and in the
sweet, folksy music of American speech. And I wouldn't put too fine a
point on the manner in which, even in that moment, when the votes
were announced, the bland and cheerful tribute to homeliness barely
hid the preceding battles over political real estate.* But that was in
Denver. After a day and half on the road, in the tiny pale green
Mazda, I was at the mouth of Yellowstone National Park.

It was three o'clock at night and I drove past the unmanned
ticket booth. The car's lights grazed bushes of sedge and boulders
beside which grew small yellow flowers. Near a turn, three elk
appeared right in front of me, as if they had conjured themselves
out of the darkness. Like ladies of the night, stepping on high
heels, the animals gingerly crossed the asphalt and disappeared
into the pines on the other side. I rolled down the window.
The air was cool and I saw above the dark outline of the hill
to the right a small moon. Over the sound of the car, I heard
the nearby howling of the wolves. In another half an hour, when
the first tattered signs of day appeared in the east, I could make
out that the dark shapes that looked like boulders in the field
were bison. And when it became lighter, closer to the river, were
visible the grey wolves trotting amidst the solitary pine and the
rows of cactus. Number Three, where have you gone!

Immigrant, Montana, was a small town with an old saloon
and two stores that rented canoes and fly-fishing equipment.
For a souvenir, I bought a fly, an iridescent form speckled with
blue and grey; under its belly was a shining hook. Black granite
mountains rose high on the other side of the Yellowstone river.
The river flowed a short distance away from US Highway 89 that

cut through town. When I walked down towards the water, small grasshoppers leapt out of my way. The river water shimmered in the sunlight, and it was difficult to see the trout. The sun and the infinite blue sky, everything was beautiful, and yet this place could well have been a ghost town. It was a name that I had long carried in my imagination; it now belonged to the past. For all these years it was a name that brought together, like the two hands of a clock meeting at the right hour, the two most deeply-felt needs of mine, the desire for love and the hankering for home. There was nothing here for me.

Last summer, I was at a writers' colony in Maine. The town in which Nina's parents had a cabin was only fifteen minutes away. I looked up their name in the phone book and was surprised to not find anything. But an online search quickly yielded results. There was an obituary in the *Cape Courier*, the local paper. Nina's mother had died due to heart failure. The first paragraph gave the date and cause of death. The short paragraph that followed made me certain that Nina had written it. *For Mrs. Robin, the day imposed a simple rigor that had to be met with an aesthetic offering; her instincts were democratic, and she aimed for elegance and economy. She cast an equal, but critical, eye, on the layout of the morning newspaper, the township's budget allocation for the area schools, the arrangement of flowers on the desk in her study. She was an artist and an activist. Over the past year, during her convalescence, she wrote many letters to editors of newspapers on matters of concern like rent control and graduated income tax; when she had energy left from such endeavours, she painted lovely watercolours of the kestrels and bohemian waxwings that sat on the branches of scrub pine and juniper behind her house. She spoke amiably to the ringed plover and red-necked stints she encountered during her strolls on the beach, and came home to play a wicked game of rummy. Mrs. Robin is survived by her husband, Joseph, her daughter Nina, and her twin grandchildren, Rebecca and Adam.* Suddenly, in that familiar land called language, the painful past was alive again.

I was looking among my papers just now for a particular postcard from Nina. I didn't find it but look—here's a detail from that reproduction I had torn out of a magazine during my first days in this country. 'The Lovers' by Picasso, 1904. 'The drawing was done after Picasso first made love to Fernande.' (He would have been twenty-two at that time. Had he really not made love to anyone else before? I think I unconsciously decided this was his first time because I was older than him at that time.)*

---

*The torn sheet with Picasso's drawing. Proof against any argument that my report on desire is a recent preoccupation. It is true that I have published nothing over the past ten years, but I have notes. E.g., a clipping in my notebook has the following two bits of information: 1. Scientists could not say why some Australian women felt sad after otherwise satisfactory sex. 2. Mares are more likely to intentionally miscarry when they have mated with foreign stallions. ('Findings', *Harper's* magazine, June 2011, p. 88.)

Also, scribbled on an earlier page, the following observation: 'Prairie dogs kiss more often if humans are watching' ('Findings', *Harper's* magazine, April 2011).

*Your Honour, was it fair on my part to wonder who was the researcher at* Harper's *magazine during those months in 2011 when I was paying attention*

A couple of days or maybe a week after our breakup, I had seen Nina at the Riverside Church where a teach-in was being held to discuss the acquittal of the cops who had beaten Rodney King. I was seated in the last row but had a clear view of Nina as she stood with her back to the wall. She had joined her palms together as if she were praying. How many times had I held those hands! I could go up to her and kiss her fingers, if she would let me. After ten minutes, I got up and left the meeting. It was too sad to keep looking at Nina.

In the days that followed I felt that I had failed not only in love but also in life. I fretted and moped because others around me were doing far more interesting things. Peter had gone to Hamburg with Maya; from Germany, they were going to travel to France. Maya's parents were flying from Delhi to Paris, and they would come down to the south of France, to a village near Avignon, where Peter's uncle, a gay man and a successful painter, owned a farmhouse and several acres of land. Peter and Maya were getting married there. We had all been invited, but no one could afford it. (Except Pushkin, but he had indicated that there was a conflict.) Larry Blofeld was working as a teacher at a summer camp for teenagers among the Californian redwoods. His novel was going to be published in a year. Kurt Vonnegut had given him a blurb. Ricardo was preparing a paper on cities and slums. Cai Yan was interviewing an Indian sociologist in London who had once been a member of the Naxalite underground in Bihar. Even Nina, despite the distractions of our troubled relationship,

---

*to that section? Such an avid interest in the quiddities of sex! Young journalist, where are you now? Did you find in love the satisfaction you wanted? In March 2011, for instance, the 'Findings' section reported the following: 'The sexual arousal of men is dampened by sniffing the tears of a woman.' 'Young straight American couples who agree to be monogamous often aren't.' 'Apologies are disappointing.' Such are the gifts of the Internet, Your Honour, a basic Google search revealed that the journalist in question, now an editor at Harper's, had been born in Delhi! Onward!*

*Dear editor, may your curiosity and interest in the world be rewarded a thousandfold!*

was making progress with her project on those she called the daughters of Mother Jones—Grace Lee Boggs, Audre Lorde, and Angela Davis.

Pushkin Krishnagrahi had received a grant for a translation project that was now nearly complete. He was translating from Hindi into English the story of a fifty-eight-year-old low-caste man who had spent his life as a manual scavenger on the outskirts of Delhi, carrying shit on his head or on a cart, shit collected from row upon row of old houses. When I read the section that Pushkin showed me, I felt envy. Pushkin was already the writer I wanted to be. And, in translating the testimony of the untouchable man, he had done good work, not just because it was time well spent, but because the story, even in translation, carried the hurt of the real. As a young reviewer in Delhi, Pushkin had railed against left academics and activists; in a surprise turn, which of course made sense, after coming to New York he had become the voice of the oppressed.

I had once known a man named Prabhunath whose father had been a minister in the Charan Singh cabinet. This fellow Prabhunath was a landlord in Palamu and he had said to me that the lower-caste people would always remain under the upper-castes.

—You see, balls. He was pointing at his crotch. Balls will always hang under the cock, he said.

People like Prabhunath belonged to an older India. That particular India was alive in news reports that came to us about young couples lynched for marrying across caste lines or a Dalit beaten to death after drinking water from a well for Brahmins. Unlike Prabhunath, Pushkin was a member of the new India. He was a Brahmin, and his place in the world owed a lot to his past, but he had disavowed his origins and was now at home anywhere in the world. He wouldn't talk of a Hindi writer from Jaipur without also mentioning Jorge Luis Borges and Buenos Aires or Nâzim Hikmet and the Sea of Marmara.* When it came

---

*I liked Pushkin for saying things like 'You know I can see why Pico Iyer says "one reason why Melbourne looks ever more like Houston is that both

to romance, he probably thought it would be provincial to sleep with someone who was taking classes with you. He was more adventurous. I heard he was dating an opera singer in London. She was famous for her radical views. The previous winter she had gone to South Africa to sing for Nelson Mandela. If you caught Pushkin walking across campus on a Thursday night, he would, always very humbly, turn down your invitation for a drink. He was going to wait till he was in the air, he might add a bit later. He was on his way to LaGuardia where he was going to catch the late Virgin Atlantic flight to London.

I must sound bitter. I have good reason. One night, during a conversation that went exactly along those lines, I asked Pushkin why he wasn't going to France for the wedding of our friends. Pushkin said he had already said yes to the organizers of a literary festival in London. Usually, he was parsimonious with information but now and then he threw me a crumb. He was going to moderate a discussion on the representation of violence. Who was going to participate in that discussion? Oh, it was going to be the writer J. M. Coetzee and the philosopher Judith Butler. Pushkin then asked me politely what I was planning to do that night. The desi taxi drivers were going on strike the next day in New York and I was meeting one of them to perhaps file a little report for a newspaper in Delhi. Pushkin nodded and we soon went our different ways.

That night, after making me wait half an hour, Imran pulled up in his cab at the corner of Amsterdam and 121st. We sat talking in the car for a bit and then he started driving. He took a fare down to Wall Street. From there we went to the East Village to drop off another customer. It would be midnight soon.

---

of them are filling up with Vietnamese pho cafes.'" It gave me a sense of what it meant to possess a global identity. It was something I wanted for myself too. But when I was getting drunk in Delhi with my friend Shankar, a journalist at *The Telegraph*, he had harsh words about Pushkin. Shankar said that Pushkin was just a jet-setter. He quoted from a piece he had just read to underline his point. 'He isn't global at all. He's just from another planet. It's called the First World.'

Imran asked me if I'd like to watch dancers and I said yes. We
drove uptown for another fifteen minutes. Heavy curtains at the
front door and then in the darkness, the glow of bodies: young
women, completely naked, stood like mannequins in a row behind
glass walls. Imran led me inside toward the music that flowed
out into the semi-dark in an intensely pleasurable stream. Here
customers, mostly men but also women, sat around tables. On
both sides were wooden benches where women were performing
lap dances. Waitresses milled about carrying trays with drinks.
On one table, two Indian men, young and stylish, were smoking
cigars. A beautiful black woman, her breasts bare but wearing a
golden thong, came up to Imran and me. We exchanged hellos.
Imran offered her a drink. She wanted a Cosmo, she said, and I
asked for a gin and tonic. A moment later I thought of Pushkin.
It was his favourite drink. He must be having his drink by now.
In a little while, Imran was going to pay the black girl twenty-
five dollars to do a little lap dance for me. She would put a hand
lightly on the back of my chair and dance, her mouth close to
mine, her breath smelling faintly of a mint-flavoured gum, and
then she'd pull herself higher, coming closer, so that she brushed
her nipples against my cheek. All the while, she never stopped
making conversation, asking me to name my favourite restaurants,
as she turned one breast and then the other towards me. I said I
couldn't recall the names just then and she laughed and, taking
my hand, pushed it down under her thong, snapping the band
on my fingertips. I turned my head away from Imran and saw
just five feet away an old man, maybe seventy years old, staring
impassively in front of him as a girl sat on his lap. That night,
when Imran brought me back to my apartment, I was aware
that I hadn't even asked him enough questions to be able to
write a newspaper report about the strike. Instead, I had visited a
nightclub. Anyone wanting to become a writer couldn't say no to
experience. As I was falling asleep it occurred to me that I, unlike
Pushkin, was doing no writing. I didn't dwell on that thought.
I was mostly thinking of the thin black girl in the bar with the
fragrant breasts who had said her name was Zaire. I was never

going to see her again but the scent of her body clung to me.
In the dark of my room I shut my eyes and saw the glitter on
her skin. I wanted to make love to her. She had said, *Remember
I'm Zaire, just like the country, come and visit me again real soon.*

To remove the 'Incomplete' from my transcript after my second
semester, I had to write another paper for Ehsaan. We had read
Fanon in his class. In one of the chapters Fanon had written
about love between a black man and a white woman. I asked
Ehsaan if I could write about desire. I was thinking of what Nina
had once asked me about the movie *Night Porter*. The messiness
of love. The complications of desire, especially forbidden desire.
Love *despite*, or *in spite of*, love beyond and across dividing lines.
That must have been at the back of my mind when I thought of
that movie's presentation of love between the Nazi officer and
the woman in the concentration camp.* Was there a film in the
postcolonial context that I could focus on? Ehsaan said yes. He
mentioned the films made about love during the Partition. Then,
he stopped.

—Are you familiar with the name Agnes Smedley?

I hadn't heard of Agnes Smedley. She had died in 1950, and
although I didn't know it then, she would change the course of
my life.

Early in the century, in March 1918, a trial was held in
New York City—*United States of America vs. Virendranath
Chattopadhyaya and Agnes Smedley.* Chattopadhyaya, or Chatto
as he was called, was a nationalist who had arrived from Calcutta
under the pretext of pursuing graduate study in Physics. He was
from a famous, well-educated family; the poet Sarojini Naidu was
his sister. Smedley had been born in a poor family in Missouri
and she was training to be a teacher. After hearing a lecture

---

*It would be years before I would discover that the words that appeared in the
opening paragraph of Roger Ebert's dismissive one-star review of *Night Porter*
included the following: 'nasty', 'lubricious', 'despicable', 'obscene' and 'trash'.

at Columbia University by the great Indian leader Lajpat Rai, she offered help. He asked her to type a manuscript about his experiences in the US in return for private classes on Indian history. Smedley admired Rai immensely but didn't follow his moderate politics; after his departure, she fell in step with the Bengali revolutionaries who were looking for allies in their battle with the British. Virendranath Chattopadhyaya was one of them. The trial in which Chatto and Smedley were charged with treason was based on the discovery, the previous March, of thousands of dollars in cash as well as machine guns and ammunition in a Houston Street warehouse in Manhattan. The money and the weapons had been supplied by the German military attaché. The defendants were accused of smuggling arms supplied by the Germans to aid radicals fighting for independence in British India.

While in prison, Smedley wrote stories about the prostitutes, alcoholics, lunatics, and thieves who surrounded her. She had been familiar with poverty in her childhood and youth. Perhaps because of her past, and also because of her politics, her portraits of those she met in prison were a not-so-subtle denunciation of the immense class divide in American society. And later, upon her release, after she had witnessed for another decade the struggles of the Indian revolutionaries in exile, she also wrote an autobiographical novel. Ehsaan wanted me to study Agnes Smedley's literary outpourings and conduct research on the trials of the Indian radicals on both coasts. Maybe my thesis, Ehsaan suggested, could grow out of this project.

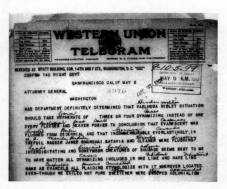

**Department of Justice**

## TELEGRAM RECEIVED.

San Francisco, Cal., Dec., 19, 1917

Attorney General:-

Slip of paper with following message in code was attached to
code message from Berlin to Chakrabarty. This appears to be in
same one, three, ought, four, ought, code as some of the Luxburg
messages. Can this be deciphered in Washington?

one, three, ought, four, ought.  two, two, eight, ought, seven.
nine, four, seven, eight.  three, two, eight, seven, one.  seven,
six, nine, ought.  two, three, six, seven, seven.  one, six, two,
two, ought.  one, three, five, eight, one.  one, three, two, ought,
four.  five, five, ought, three.  two, three, eight, six, seven.
nine, three, four, six.  one, four, ought, five, ought.  one, two,
one, two, seven.  one, six, five, three, four.  two, two, seven,
eight, nine.  five, four, two, one.  one, one, ought, seven, seven.
nine, five, five, seven.  one, eight, three, seven, nine.  one,
eight, two, three, six.  five, two, ought, six.  four, one, eight,
eight.  one, one, nine, four, seven.  nine, six, six, ought.
one, eight, four, seven, two.  one, four, one, four, four.  two,
nine, three, nine.  nine, five, ought, nine.  one, one, three,
seven, two.  one, one, three, one, ought.  one, seven, four, six.
three, six, seven, ought.  nine, seven, five, five, six.  two, two,
six, three.  six, four, five, five.  nine, five, three, ough.
one, six, two, four, eight.  one, eight, three eight, ought,  three,
three, four, eight, seven.

PRESTON, U.S. ATTORNEY.

9-10-3-512
MAR 22 1918 A.M.
WARREN

Chatto was held in prison for eight months and Smedley
for seven to eight weeks. When he was released, Chatto was a
physical wreck, unable to walk even a few steps without Smedley's
help. In January 1919, they travelled together to France to take

part in the Paris Peace Conference, and later, in 1921, to Russia
to attend the Comintern gathering. They didn't find an audience
with Lenin and had to leave disappointed. Assured of German
support, they travelled to Weimar Berlin to escape British spies.
Berlin was staggering under inflation. Smedley found out to her
dismay that six weeks' wages could get a working person only a
pair of boots. The economic crisis also forced Chatto to give up
his plans of founding an organization in Germany that would
build support for India. By the fall of 1923, the inflation in Berlin
had reached its peak. Smedley wrote in a letter that she had been
mutely observing people dying a slow death. There was a small
church on her street, and she'd watch funeral processions arrive
and leave. Workers used all of their wages for just a couple of
loaves of bread, some potatoes, and margarine. Meat and fruit was
beyond their reach. She could not find sugar in any of the stores.

When Smedley first met Chatto, she thought he looked
fierce but also ugly with dark, glittering eyes set in a pockmarked
face. He was a short and thin man, in his early forties but with
already grey hair. In the reminiscences of a well-known Danish
novelist, Agnes Smedley was described as bright and vivacious,
full of vigour, fond of wearing costumes and dancing. But despite
their physical differences Smedley and Chatto were attracted to
each other and went on to get married. They discussed politics
with great excitement and she later said that he was the first
man to whom she hadn't lied that her father was a physician.

I was soon immersed in the account of their relationship.
Smedley had grown up poor, her education had been haphazard,
and her childhood had been harsh. Chatto, on the other hand,
was from a distinguished Brahmin family. He was a polyglot
who had been educated at Cambridge, and had lived a luxurious
life. Neither his education nor his family's wealth saved him
from pettiness. In more than one letter, Smedley discussed her
problems. In one she wrote that Chatto was 'suspicious as hell
of every man near me'. There was also some professional jealousy.
Smedley published an article about Indian immigrants in *The
Nation*, and Chatto commented disapprovingly that she was

'showing off'. Smedley had other complaints. All the time that she was in Berlin, the small home that she shared with Chatto was continually overrun by guests. Smedley wrote, *Moslems and Hindus of every caste streamed through as though a railway station or a hotel. Students came directly from their boats, carting all their bedding and cooking utensils.* Smedley didn't really know how to cook, but she was now expected to do just that. In the margins of the same letter, she wrote: *I cook until the very walls of our home seem to be permeated with the odor of curry.*

When she had been only twenty-two and working as a teacher in Missouri, Smedley married an Irish socialist. (This was less than a decade before she met Chatto.) Her husband was a union organizer and journalist. He lived in St. Louis and travelled a great deal; this suited Smedley because she didn't want to be tied down to a domestic life. She was squeamish about sex. She was opposed to the idea that the mere act of marriage should require that a woman suddenly welcome a physical relationship with a male; she also detested the prospect of becoming a vessel for bearing children on a regular basis, which had been the fate of her own mother who had succumbed to madness after giving birth to her seventh child.

To make matters worse, only four months into her marriage, Smedley found out that she was pregnant. Abortion was illegal and she had to go to Kansas City for the operation. On the train ride back, Smedley was in pain and she sweated and moaned in distress, and, according to her biographer, Smedley's husband asked her to stay quiet and sit up straight in her seat because of the looks she was attracting. Smedley refused to speak to him for several weeks. Six months later, she wrote to her husband, *I take the blame. I do not want to be married; marriage is too terrible and I should never have entered it. I was wrong—for you loved me and I do not know what love means. I want my name back, also.*

A shift came in 1917 when Smedley met the legendary birth control pioneer, Margaret Sanger. Sanger had launched a public education campaign. Her attempt to popularize contraception was aimed at liberating women, to encourage them to think about

sexual behaviour as not only appropriate but also pleasurable.
Smedley was twenty-five by now. Quite soon after the divorce
was finalized she plunged into an affair with a journalist named
David Lee Willoughby. The affair left her feeling unsatisfied and
lonely, and she tried to quell these feelings by entering into short-
lived relationships with other men. One of the biographies I read
had this to say: 'A pessary might allow Smedley to be as sexually
predatory as any man. Her inability to trust anyone sufficiently
to permit real intimacy, though, denied her the happiness she
sought. If she were to feel, as she wished, that her life had
meaning, she needed more meaningful work.' This search for
meaningful activity led Smedley to active engagement with the
Indian freedom struggle and her meeting with the man who
would be the centre of her life for so many years.

There was one disturbing detour, however. Smedley had an
encounter with M. N. Roy, a well-known communist leader, an
encounter that hurt Smedley and cast a pall on her relationship
with Chatto. In late March 1917, after a meeting of a group
of Indian and Irish revolutionaries at the Hotel Mayflower in
New York City, Roy asked Smedley to accompany him to the
Grand Central Station where he was to meet two men who were
bringing letters from Moscow. It was cold outside and Roy needed
to fetch his coat from his room. Smedley accompanied him to
the fifth-floor room. Roy came out of the bathroom where he
had gone to wash his face and found Smedley near the radiator
warming her hands. He turned her around and kissed her. For a
moment or a little longer, Smedley told a friend later, she liked the
pressure of Roy's lips on hers. But then an older unease suddenly
bloomed inside her and she tried to get out of the embrace.
Roy was adamant, however, and pinned her down on the bed.
Many years later, when Smedley felt that her relationship with
Chatto had drawn her into an abyss of self-loathing, and that
each day brought with it the threat of a nervous breakdown, a
psychiatrist suggested that she write a memoir. She sat down to
work on a thinly disguised autobiographical novel, *Daughter of
Earth*. For the first time, the episode with Roy found its fullest

mention in its pages, and Smedley also revealed how what had happened in the hotel room lingered in her life with Chatto. Within the space of three pages in *Daughter of Earth*, Smedley moves from the love that an Indian revolutionary felt for the narrator, to their quick marriage a week after their first meeting, to the husband's enquiry of whether Roy was one of the men that Smedley had been intimate with earlier in her life. On the night of her hurried wedding, Smedley's protagonist wakes up to find her Indian husband staring at her, speechless, with a strange, drawn face. He finally asks her a question—*Tell me what men said to you... The men you lived with.*

I began working on my thesis for Ehsaan. For a few pages, I would see the world with Smedley's eyes, and then, with a feeling of uneasy identification, with her husband's.* I saw myself as if in a mirror, my face night-lit with jealous rage, standing beside Nina's bed. I was asking her about Jonathan. So many times I had contemplated her past. I imagined her sitting on the deck of a yacht off the coast of Maine. The yacht was owned by a former lover of hers. The two of them were sipping white wine and eating grilled lobster. I returned to such scenes in my mind as I read more about Chatto. There were other aspects

---

*That sexual tension, born out of jealousy, was so vivid. I was familiar with it. But there were other things that I also recognized in Chatto, particularly when I read what Jawaharlal Nehru, in *An Autobiography* (1936), remembered of Virendranath Chattopadhyaya: 'Popularly known as Chatto he was a very able and a very delightful person. He was always hard up, his clothes were very much the worse for wear and often he found it difficult to raise the wherewithal for a meal. But his humour and lightheartedness never left him. He had been some years senior to me during my educational days in England. He was at Oxford when I was at Harrow. Since those days he had not returned to India, and, sometimes, a fit of homesickness came to him, when he longed to be back. All his home-ties had long been severed, and it is quite certain that if he came to India he would feel unhappy and out of joint. But in spite of the passage of many years and long wandering, the pull of the home remains. No exile can escape the malady of his tribe, that consumption of the soul, as Mazzini called it.' *Your Honour, I'm in pain, I suffer from the consumption of the soul.*

of Smedley's story that also affected me deeply. Earlier in her book, her heroine described receiving a letter from jail: *I read and re-read a letter lying before me. It was from my brother George. I could tell no one of its contents, for I feared that none of the people I lived with would understand. They idealized the working class, and I feared they might not understand the things that grew in poverty and ignorance. They would say my brother would have been justified had he stolen bread, when hungry, but he should not have stolen a horse. Even I, who loved him so dearly, felt this.* These words had come from a great distance and found a place close to my heart. What Smedley had written about the unfeeling hypocrisy of those who idealized the working class also applied to the people sitting around me at the seminar table in Ehsaan's classes. But, more than that, her words took me back to my own relatives in Bihar. Their small worlds, their plain poverty, and the ordinary complications of their difficult lives. Ehsaan had once told us that he did not see a light bulb, hear a radio, or ride a car until he was eight or nine years old and he did not fly in an airplane until he was twenty-one. I shared a bit of that past with him and wanted to write out of that experience. Was this only nostalgia on my part? I had left home and the immensity of that departure sought recognition in my new life. I think that was the main thing. What I was learning in America was new and illuminating but it became valuable only when it was linked to my past.

⌣

Ehsaan told me to read a short story by Somerset Maugham called 'Giulia Lazzari' because it had a connection to Agnes Smedley. The story is narrated by a dapper fellow named Ashenden. He is a British novelist working as a spy in Europe for his country. Now he is on a mission to arrest Chandra Lal, an Indian revolutionary in Berlin. Chandra is a lawyer by training and bitterly opposed to British rule in India. Although he receives funds from German agents, he doesn't use the money on himself. He is hard-working, principled, and abstemious; he keeps his word. In all these respects, Chandra resembled the man who was his model, Agnes Smedley's husband, Virendranath Chattopadhyaya. The eponymous character was Italian, a performer of Spanish dances, and a prostitute.

More than the discussion of politics in the story, the smaller personal details arrested my attention. Here were the two Englishmen in the Maugham story discussing Chandra's looks. Looking at the Indian's photograph, the narrator observed, 'It showed a fat-faced, swarthy man, with full lips and a fleshy nose; his hair was black, thick, and straight, and his very large eyes even in the photograph were liquid and cow-like. He looked ill-at-ease in European clothes.' Ashenden's superior expressed surprise that Lazzari could have fallen for Chandra.* He said, 'You wouldn't have thought there was anything very attractive in that greasy little nigger. God, how they run to fat!' I went back to the description that Smedley had offered of the Chatto character in her novel, *Daughter of Earth*: 'He was thin, with a light brown skin, and his hair was black and very glossy. His eyes, shaded by heavy eyebrows, made me think of a black Indian night when the stars hang from an intensely purple heaven. Over the eyes was an intangible veil of sadness—how could a man with such an intense face have sad eyes! He was perhaps in his early thirties.' I wasn't thinking just of myself, dear reader, and how a white woman might regard me. I was thinking of Ehsaan and his charm. He was my idol. I had not forgotten a news report from the Kissinger trial. A reporter, who was female, had written:

_____

*Your Honour, the sting of such judgement but also the comfort! The comfort of knowing that if I too was being judged in this way, then I wasn't alone. Let the record state that Nina and I had once made love in a small patch of grass near the university's Administration Building one afternoon. It was the fourth of July. The US flag flapped above us. I was aware of all kinds of negative judgement, Your Honour. How could she have fallen for me? I suffered under an invisible indictment. And, in response, it was as if I was saying to Nina, I kiss you with my alien tongue, your body taking me in against Article 274 of the Immigration and Nationality Laws that presses on bodies penalties for encouraging or inducing an alien to come to, enter, or reside in the United States.

'Ehsaan is an exquisitely polite man with dazzling white teeth and large divergent eyes which give him an abstracted look.'

In the paper I submitted to Ehsaan, I adopted a more academic tone. I pointed out that the tale written by Maugham invested the British with control and cunning. The qualities of those who inhabited the fringes of this colonial narrative, the swarthy-skinned inhabitants of a world that was unstable and filled with need, were questionable. Chandra and his ilk were suspect, and their judgement, if not their moral nature, was deficient. These characters might have some fleeting nobility, or passion, and even pathos, but they didn't have the gift of narrative. Their words didn't have coherence, and their lives didn't have the unity that comes from the power to tell a story. There was also the crucial question of love. Ashenden had asked Lazzari if she really loved Chandra, the man he wanted to catch. Lazzari replied: 'He's the only man who's ever been kind to me.' In Smedley's novel, her protagonist said to her Indian lover: 'I have loved no one but you.' (*Did I think of the women I have loved when I read those words? Yes, I did. Did I find myself judged? I surely did.*)

In what I wrote for Ehsaan I do not remember whether I examined the congruences or the differences between Maugham's Chandra and Smedley's Chatto. In Maugham's story, Ashenden uses Lazzari to lure Chandra to a port town. Upon discovering that he has been trapped, Chandra swallows poison and dies. It is more likely that I only pointed out that the real-life Chandra Lal eluded the British rulers in a different way than Maugham had imagined. But his end was tragic too. Chatto had been active during the last years of his life in communist Russia. The British still ruled India and would not permit his return. He was arrested on 15 July 1937 during Stalin's purge. His name appears on a death-list signed by Stalin on 31 August that year. He was probably executed on 2 September 1937.

⁓

There was a party at Ehsaan's house. I went to pick up Peter as planned but when I rang his bell Maya came to the door. Her face was puffy. She said that Peter wasn't well. *What happened? Was his illness serious? But in that case he could have told me this himself! He could have called!* Over the months that followed this conversation became routine, following a pattern; and for too long, until it was too late, I only thought that Peter was withdrawing from us because he was falling deeper and deeper in love with Maya.

The invitation to the party had come from Prakash Mathan, an older student. He was completing his doctorate in International Relations, something about the informal sectors of lending in the Brazilian and Russian economies. Prakash wore beautiful silk shirts. He had come to America as a boy from Kerala with his mother after she found a job as a nurse in Houston. His father had worked as a car mechanic in India. At the party, while Ehsaan cooked, Prakash served drinks. Prakash was mixing Manhattans for us when Cai Yan asked him to tell me a story he had told her earlier about Ehsaan. Prakash raised his eyes and asked, Which one?

That was another thing about Ehsaan, there were always stories. The previous week he had me over for lunch at his house. The lunch was for a Pakistani friend of his, a doctor at Columbia Medical, whom he had known for many years. He had cooked keema, baigan bharta, and his trademark dal, with a tadka of onion and garlic fried in oil floating on the surface. The doctor was in her late thirties, pretty, and stylishly dressed. Her husband was an American, a well-regarded scientist.

—Did Harvey tell you about his first scientific experiment? Ehsaan asked the doctor about her husband.

The doctor had probably already heard about the experiment, probably from Ehsaan himself, but she smiled and shook her head.

—This was when Harvey was four years old and living in Brooklyn. He was in the backyard and decided that he was going to pee right there. To his surprise, a worm emerged from the little puddle he was making. He promptly concluded that worms came from your urine. He was a scientist. In order to prove his hypothesis, he went back the next day and repeated the experiment. To his satisfaction, another worm appeared from the puddle just as before. Here was reproducible proof! He told me he held on to this scientific belief till he was nine years old.

Now, at Ehsaan's party, Prakash embarked on the story that Cai Yan wanted him to tell me. We were standing in Ehsaan's balcony with our drinks. Prakash was balancing his drink and a cigarette in the same hand.

When Ehsaan was in his twenties in Pakistan, some years after he had migrated there from Bihar, he received a Rotary fellowship to study abroad. He knew he wanted to visit four places when he left the subcontinent. Three of those four places he visited en route to the United States. Now Prakash put his free hand to use, holding up one finger after another:

1. He went to the Highgate Cemetery in London to pay homage to Karl Marx;
2. He also visited 221B Baker Street, for its well-known literary landmark;
3. And he made sure he got the opportunity to wander through the British Museum, where his reaction was, Return the loot!

The fourth place he wanted to visit was in the United States, in Chicago, and it was the site of the Haymarket Riot in 1886. Ehsaan wanted to go there because, as a boy, he had been taken to May Day celebrations in India. He wanted to lay flowers at the Haymarket monument to honour the striking workers who had marched in the first May Day parade. But several years were to pass before he could visit Chicago. He had, by then, been in and out of the country, doing research and political work for several years in Tunisia. In 1967, ten years after he first arrived in the United States, Ehsaan found himself in Chicago. He left his hotel and bought a bouquet of flowers; however, when he got to Haymarket, he could not find the monument. He asked several people but none seemed to know about the landmark struggle for an eight-hour working day. Finally, someone pointed it out to him. It was the statue of a policeman who had preserved law and order on that day long ago. Ehsaan brought the flowers back and gave them to a young woman he liked at the conference he was attending.

I clapped my hands.

—Wait, wait, there is more, Cai Yan said.

—Well, here's the thing, Prakash said. All this happens and just a year later Ehsaan gets a fellowship in Chicago. This is at the Adlai Stevenson Institute. And he is giving a speech at an anti-war meeting. He recounts the story about his search for the Haymarket monument. He tells the audience how shocked he was that the historical memory of workers' resistance, recognized and celebrated around the world, hasn't been honoured in its own place of origin. Not long after, two FBI agents show up at his door. They want to know what he had said at the sit-in about Haymarket and who had been in the audience. It turned out that the Weathermen had just blown up the offending statue of the Chicago policeman.

—Let's call him here, Cai Yan said.

All three of us turned to look at Ehsaan who was chatting with an old man with a Moses-like beard.

—Would you like a real drink, Prakash called out.

Ehsaan heard the question, excused himself and walked over to where we were standing.

—Prakash told us the story of how you got to see the four great sights. Including Haymarket, Cai Yan said.

—Did he tell you that I got a visit from the FBI after I had spoken about Haymarket?

—What did you say to them? I asked.

Ehsaan was a master of pauses.

—They first asked me if I was a citizen of the United States. This was in 1968. I said, No. They said, Don't you feel that as a guest in this country you should not be going about criticizing the host country's government? I said, I hear your point, but I do want you to know that while I am not a citizen, I am a taxpayer. And

I thought it was a fundamental principle of American democracy that there is no taxation without representation. I have not been represented in this war in Vietnam. And my people, Asian people, are being bombed right now. Surprisingly, the FBI agents looked deeply moved. They blushed at my throwing this argument at them. They were speechless.

He was smiling. A couple other students had joined us to catch the end of the story. One of them asked Ehsaan how he understood what had happened with the FBI agents that day.

—Well, at that time, I understood something about the importance of having some correspondence between American liberal traditions and our own rhetoric and tactics.

It is a tenet of graduate student life to debate such pronouncements. The more serious-minded amongst us, Pushkin perhaps, had maybe taken a lesson from this, a lesson about aligning pronouncements with practice. But what was to remain with me after all those years was the example of Ehsaan seeking Marx and Sherlock Holmes together in London. It was as if someone from my town had expressed the ambition to read everything by Mahatma Gandhi and watch every Dilip Kumar film! Or better still, a friend showing devotion to the revolutionary life of Bhagat Singh and also taking joy in reciting the batting and bowling figures of Ranjitsinhji.

From Ehsaan we sought narrative. We didn't always care how much of it was non-fiction or fiction. Ehsaan lived—and narrated—his life along the blurry Line of Control between the two genres. Others responded in kind.

For instance.

Standing in a kitchen in Amsterdam, where he headed the Transnational Institute, Ehsaan narrated the story of his childhood to the great writer John Berger. Later, Berger gave a fictional name to the Ehsaan character in his book *Photocopies*.

When Partition took place, Ehsaan was only thirteen years old and living near Gaya in Bihar. His older brothers took Ehsaan in a train to Delhi where they were put in a refugee camp where there had been an outbreak of cholera. Ehsaan's family was to board a plane for Lahore but there had been a mistake. They were a seat short. Ehsaan stayed behind. His brother gave him a rifle and some money. He was to wait for the next available flight to Lahore. No plane came and Ehsaan was forced to join a long column of refugees leaving for the border.

Although he was young, Ehsaan soon found himself being counted among those who were the guards. It so happened that on the third day he saw armed men running towards them across the irrigated fields. Ehsaan had hunted deer in his village in Bihar. He dropped to the ground, took aim calmly, and killed four of the attackers. People looked at him with respect. In the column there was a man who was an opium-eater. Ehsaan had seen him as a beggar in the refugee camp but now, unable to feed his addiction, the man had begun to act normal. He was walking with a more upright gait. Then, something happened that brought Ehsaan closer to the addict.

There were young women among the refugees and the sight of them often disturbed and excited Ehsaan. They caught him gazing at them sometimes, and he often caught himself furtively admiring the shape of their lips. He imagined their breasts brushing his cheeks. There was among them one that he especially liked. She wore a white tunic decorated with white flowers that were small, like pinprick stars. Once, during a stop to eat, Ehsaan saw the young woman step into a mango grove, and then he saw a man get up and walk in the same direction. Among the trees, the man began to touch the woman despite her protests, and, in that instant, without thinking about it, Ehsaan raised his gun and shot the man.

The woman began to scream. She was crying, 'Murderer, murderer.' In his confusion, Ehsaan fled. He ran across a field but then, having entered a narrow lane, found himself facing a stone wall. Afraid now for his life, he threatened to shoot the men who had run after him. His legs were trembling.

At that moment, the opium-eater stepped into the middle. He turned to the crowd. Why are we doing this, he asked, why are we killing each other? For the past so many nights and days, had they not been trying to escape the horrible injustice of insane killings? He told the people that the boy needed to be given a trial, and if he was found guilty, the right punishment would be meted out to him. He entered the lane and took the gun away from Ehsaan and told him that he was to walk between two men like a prisoner.

That night, when a trial was held by firelight, the opium-eater was asked to be the judge. The father of the young woman cleared his throat and asked for permission to speak. He said that his daughter had said that the man who the boy had killed was about to rape her. The girl had described the boy as a hero.

The opium-eater became the acknowledged leader of the column, and he told Ehsaan that his name was Abdul Ghafoor. Ghafoor made all the important decisions and he also assigned duties to the guards. He carried out his tasks with a commanding dignity. His presence inspired confidence among the marchers but at night he confided his doubts to Ehsaan. Ghafoor would say that once they reached Pakistan they would find that their new leaders had already established themselves as the masters. Ehsaan understood him to say that in their new homes they were going to live as servants and not as brothers.

Finally, they came to Wagah where the border divided the two nations. Ehsaan looked at the woman in the tunic of white flowers before going his own way; he had killed a man for her sake, but he had not exchanged a single word with her. A taxi took Ehsaan to his family in Lahore. Seven months passed. One night, when he came out of a restaurant, Ehsaan stumbled over a figure crouching on the sidewalk. It was Abdul Ghafoor. Ehsaan called him by his name, but Ghafoor's addiction had returned and in his eyes there was no sign of recognition. Ehsaan began to shake him. Then, he himself stumbled and fell on Ghafoor and the two of them wrestled on the ground.

Ehsaan was angry but also sad. At last he got up and went home. He shut himself up in his room for three days. He didn't want to see others, and he didn't want to eat anything. He took a vow to become a revolutionary. And when he was tempted to take another road he always remembered Abdul Ghafoor.

In the Ehsaan Ali Archives at Hampshire College in Massachusetts, there is a letter from John Berger asking him if he approved of the brief narrative that he, Berger, had written about Ehsaan's past. I must assume that Ehsaan had liked the form that Berger had given to his story. I can only speculate that the choice of a fictional name for Ehsaan's character was necessary because one or both of these men—Berger and Ehsaan—understood that memory is unreliable. *Memories translate experience, and when we write about these memories a double translation takes place. This book, too, is an example of this uncertain process, Your Honour. I cannot claim any particular fidelity to facts. This arrangement of memories is my attempt to get to what is real.*

You can reach Irki, the village where Ehsaan was born, by road from Patna. I went there last summer. It took me about four hours. It was a hot July day, late monsoon season, and the highway went past paddy fields filled with water. Small towns appeared at regular intervals, and the car I was travelling in would need to slow down to a crawl. At one point we stopped to look at a crumbling mausoleum built beside a vast lake whose waters appeared a dark green, the mausoleum's archways framing the shadows of lovers. We continued on our way, passing tight clusters of crowds on the narrow highway, medicine stores, sheds for grinding wheat, cramped tailor shops, and stalls where chickens were sold from cages where the birds inside had plucked each other's feathers out. A thin road branched off from National Highway 83, past huts and houses built close together, and then a sharp turn to the left near a mosque, a sign that we were in a Muslim part of the village. If we had remained on the highway, in another hour we would have reached Bodh Gaya where Gautama Buddha had found enlightenment.

The house where Ehsaan was born has now been split up, divided between relatives by brick walls. A small metal gate stood locked near the wall where Ehsaan's father had been sleeping on the night he was murdered. I was asked to come inside through a door on the side. The middle-aged woman who answered the door introduced me to her mother, Sadrunissa, who was eighty-two years old and almost completely deaf. Sadrunissa was Ehsaan's first cousin. Her son-in-law shouted Ehsaan's name into Sadrunissa's ear and then, to make it clear who he was talking about, he patted in the air as if he was touching a child's head before miming with his fingers the gesture of a throat being slit.

Sadrunissa began to speak in a high-pitched voice. She had very few teeth left. She spoke of her father and then of her uncle. Ehsaan's father, she said, believed in justice and equality for all. He used to say, Do not oppress anyone. They killed him for it. She spoke of Ehsaan as if he was still alive and living in America. I didn't correct her. Her son-in-law told her that I was a journalist. Sadrunissa nodded her head and asked if I was from *The Searchlight* or from the *Indian Nation*. These had been the two Patna newspapers from my childhood; they ceased publication decades ago.

The azan sounded from the mosque. I had delayed things; it was time for my hosts to break their Ramzan fast. I was left alone while Sadrunissa and her family went inside to pray. While I waited in the verandah, small frogs hopped on the floor and a thin cat crawled down the clay tiles of the roof. After ten minutes, Sadrunnisa came out and sat down with me. She took a cracker from the plate on the table and drank water. Her daughter brought out slices of mango and a couple of glasses of Rooh Afza. The son-in-law was a journalist for a small Hindi paper with its headquarters in Punjab. He had stopped asking Sadrunissa the questions I wanted to ask and would try to give replies himself. He said that the family that had killed Ehsaan's father had met with ruin. Their two sons had both gone mad. The family had been cursed. Sadrunissa's son-in-law was curious to know about Ehsaan. He urged me to write about him because, he said, no one knew about him in his own birthplace. While he spoke, lizards darted swiftly on the green walls, trapping in their jaws the insects that were attracted by the naked lights. It was getting dark and I wanted to get to Bodh Gaya so that I could find a hotel to spend the night. Sadrunissa would interrupt our conversation to repeat, very loudly, what she had already told me earlier. When I got up to leave, she held my sleeve and said that the family had done well. By the time he retired from service, her father was a deputy superintendent of police and her son had become a doctor.

## Part VI

# Lotan Mamaji

*I want to share these lines from a xeroxed page left many years ago in my mailbox, with Ehsaan's scribbled 'EA' in the corner, after we had discussed my possible thesis topic. It is a quote from* Speeches on Religion to its Cultured Despisers *(1799) by Friedrich Schleiermacher:*

'What seizes you when you find the holy most intimately mixed with the profane, the sublime with the lowly and transitory? And what do you call the mood that sometimes forces you to presuppose the universality of this mixture and to search for it everywhere?'

*And this note I had scribbled along with a quote from Gandhi's autobiography,* The Story of My Experiments with Truth: *'I was devoted to my parents. But no less was I devoted to the passions that flesh is heir to.'**

---

*Morality is of interest to him, but morality that is always in conflict with itself. This is what makes the Mahatma more interesting than a box of tissue paper.

I remember being awoken once a little before dawn by a sound that I didn't recognize at first. An Indonesian student lived in the unit next to me in that apartment building on Morningside Drive; his girlfriend was visiting from Cleveland or Cincinnati or some such place where she too was a grad student. Was someone screaming? No, was she laughing? The sound, a moaning punctuated by rhythmic silence in a way that no ordinary screaming or even laughing can accommodate, went on for a while. Such unabashed glory. Alone in my bed, wide awake now, I marvelled at the matutinal sexual athleticism of the Indonesian fellow, Katon. He was thin, serious-looking, in wire-rimmed glasses. I think he was studying Forestry. What had he done to the white girl from Ohio, what forest spirit had he been keeping secretly stored in a bottle, what animal instinct for pleasure had he released in her now? She was shrieking with happiness and all the birds in the forest were surely going to wake up any moment now and release their song.

I waited till nine to call Cai Yan. I hadn't slept with her yet, although we had spent a lot of time together in classes and even at Ehsaan's home. I thought this could be the day. Katon had gifted me an omen. Cai Yan was grading papers for the International Relations class where she was a teaching assistant. I asked her to come over to my apartment; she could grade at my place while I cooked an early lunch for her. I told her I would keep up an endless supply of fragrant tea.

In half an hour, the bell rang.

I had an old pot, an antique piece that had been Nina's gift, and I set this on the small desk. While Cai Yan did her work, I prepared lunch. Kadhai chicken, fried gobhi-mattar, a tomato and cucumber salad on the side. For a thin girl, she had an enormous appetite. The rice was ready first and Cai Yan didn't want to wait, she scooped spoons of rice into a bowl and ate using a pair of old chopsticks that had come with a meal I had once ordered from Chinee Takee Outee.* Later, I gave her the rice with the cauliflower and the chicken. She devoured it all. It reminded me of a small animal, and it excited me to watch her eat with such hunger.

Cai Yan laughed easily but not when I flirted with her. That kind of play didn't appeal to her. She received each statement with some earnestness and then evaluated it seriously.

—Is it true that in China the word for 'hello' translates as 'have you eaten rice?'

She laughed and said yes. Then she said that actually it was usual for a hello to be accompanied by the second enquiry about food.

—Ehsaan is Chinese in that way, Cai Yan said. Oh, I like him so much.

We were sipping tea after lunch.

—I wonder whether there are other expressions that are also very different in Chinese. How might someone ask another person, 'So, are we on a date?'

*Your Honour, believing flirtatiousness to be foreign to Cai Yan, I spoke in an earnest manner. The gates didn't open. No one can keep the foreign away, or not for long, but Cai Yan was untouchable. Although she smiled she didn't seem to admit the thought that I was trying to seduce her. I stood, a stranger, a supplicant, a homeless alien, at the gates of an implacable continent. I saw her as if at a huge distance, standing alone at the end of a long road.*

—I don't think anyone says things like that. People just know.

Which, of course, left me not knowing much. Nothing troubled Cai Yan's serenity. She still spoke with a half-smile. If you were a poet, I guess you would say that her expression was as calm as the surface of an unruffled lake. While I waited, she remarked that she was making such swift progress, she must

---

*Your Honour, that name! You decide. Open and plainly literal pandering to the stereotype of a pidgin-speaking Oriental—or, instead, a playful linguistic mockery practiced by a consciousness primed by Asian-American critiques of representation?

keep grading papers. I left her at my desk and went away to read in bed.

Cai Yan finished all her grading work in the evening and announced that she was going to step out for an hour. She didn't give any reason why she was going to come back to my apartment. When she returned, she was carrying two heavy grocery bags. She had brought beer and also pork and shrimp for home-made dumplings.* We drank beer and after I had chopped cabbage, chives and ginger, Cai mixed them with the pork and shrimp she had put on rows of dumpling wrappers. The smell of sesame oil filled the apartment. Soon, it was time to eat. The dumplings were delicious. They were first dipped in ponzu sauce and we sprinkled scallion on them before popping them in our mouths.

I didn't think anyone else in the entire apartment building could be having better food that evening. It was a date, I felt I knew it. To make conversation, I said that I was ashamed that I had done so little work all week. This is the kind of thing all graduate students say. But Cai Yan paused. She wanted to know if I had ever felt shame.

*Real* shame?

I thought of the time I was caught stealing two books from the

---

*Cai Yan's report from her shopping expedition was that the cashier was a white girl dressed in all black and had black lipstick on. Her black t-shirt said in white letters: 'Jesus Saves I Spend.' When she was growing up, Cai Yan said, people in China wore clothes that were nondescript and didn't make any statement. It surprised her but also interested her that in America people wore t-shirts that made all kinds of bold assertions about the wearer. Had she observed this because she was Chinese? I didn't think so. I feel it is a shared immigrant trait. You come to America and just like you try to understand road-signs you also take note of t-shirts. The affluent-looking, middle-aged white man in Coney Island with the t-shirt shamelessly announcing: 'My Indian Name is Runs with Beer'. Or, more recently, the somewhat cheerful and overweight woman, possibly a Latina, who passed me on the street wearing a t-shirt that said: 'FCK,' and below that, 'All That's Missing Is You'. I should be taking notes! An essay about an immigrant navigating identity in America solely by reading what the natives had to say via their t-shirts.

book fair in Delhi. That had been embarrassing. I had professed shame and been allowed to let go after being made to sit in the heat for an hour. Frankly, I wouldn't even have got caught. It was just that my father was coming from Patna on a visit, and I was rushing to get back to the hostel before he arrived from the station. I was in a hurry and as a result had got caught. So, I was ashamed, yes, but I was also extremely irritated with myself. I thought about that incident and wondered whether it would count.

I didn't allude to this incident. Cai Yan was looking at me without any impatience or, for that matter, heightened expectation.

Then I remembered lying to my parents about my exam results when I was in high school. I wasn't ashamed of what I had done till my mother found out. There was also the shame of not having gone to see my friend when his father died. I was in my first year in college. My friend was someone I hung out with often, but I had never been to his house before, and I used this as an excuse to stay away. But it hurt when I saw him at the tea stall in Patna. He was standing there, his head shaven, and I had said nothing. Yes, it wasn't that I hadn't gone to his house. Instead, it was the fact that I hadn't had the courage or grace to offer condolences to a friend who had lost his father. I was ashamed also when a teacher I liked in school saw that I was cheating and turned his head away to give me a chance to hide my notes. All these incidents came back to me but, again, I didn't offer them to Cai Yan.

My silence didn't appear to disturb her.

—I was ashamed, Cai Yan said, when my cousin's husband called me on my phone and asked me to meet him. He was a doctor in Shanghai. I had just finished high school. He said he didn't love my cousin any more. When I didn't say anything, he said, I mean it, I don't even like her smell. I would like to take you out for a drive. I have bought a new car and when I bought it I told myself that I want to take my dear cousin-in-law Cai Yan for a drive. I know a place about an hour away where we can have a special lunch and then take a walk in a garden.

There are luxury cabins beside a lake if we want to rest. When he was saying these things, I said nothing. At a birthday party some weeks later, he pressed my breast and I felt I was going to vomit over his hand. I told my cousin what had happened. She slapped me on my left cheek but after that her husband never came near me.

I sipped my beer while Cai Yan spoke. She spoke matter-of-factly, with her mysterious half-smile, as if she was amused by what she was saying. When she stopped, I began talking, perhaps because I didn't know how best to respond to her.

Not long ago, I had gone to sleep thinking of my mother's recent illness and had a dream in which I was at a wedding. My mother and I were standing under a shamiana and a white cotton sheet had been spread on a mat beneath our feet. A man was rude to her and I threw him down on the floor. His head hit the ground hard and we knew instantly that he had died. I woke up from this dream and, though this memory was unrelated to the dream, I immediately recalled a half-forgotten incident from the time when I was a teen and my family had gone on a trip to Gujarat. I have repressed the name of the small town we were visiting. We had arrived at an old stone monument and looked around first for a bathroom. There wasn't one. Then we climbed up the monument, several floors of narrow stairs, and arrived at the top. My mother said she was helpless. She continued to apologize before I understood that she needed to urinate. I told her to use a corner of the room while I stood on the staircase blocking access. Where was my father? I think he had climbed down already. My sisters were with me. Ma chose to relieve herself near a small drain-hole in the corner. But this was a mistake. When we came down, it became clear that the men below, those who sold entry-tickets to the monument and also manned the tea shop, knew what had happened. Did I turn back and look up at the large wet patch visible on the wall high above? Perhaps that was the first sign. I remember clearly what the men were saying and without looking at her I tried to imagine the confusion and shame on my mother's face.

We talked like this that night and several other nights. I slept on the couch in Cai Yan's apartment; on one of those nights I said to her that we needn't sleep apart, we could share the bed, but it was as if I hadn't spoken at all. Her expression didn't change. She retained her serene half-smile and brought me a pillow and a blanket where I was sitting on the couch. I had begun enjoying these nights, finding comfort in the acceptance of a near-intimacy. One night, a cat was in her apartment. The cat was named Frida Kahlo and belonged to our friend Maya who had gone out of town for the week. Late that night, I lay on Cai Yan's couch watching television. The PBS station was showing a documentary on Christa McAuliffe, the schoolteacher who died in the *Challenger* disaster. Cai Yan had already gone to sleep in the bedroom. The cat was with her. When the shuttle had burst into flames, I was in high school in Patna but I had watched on television McAuliffe's students counting down five-four-three-two-one. From that moment on, their teacher lived for seventy-three more seconds. When the documentary ended, I realized that I had probably never watched the footage of the kids: we didn't have a television in Patna. It is possible I had read about it in the newspaper. McAuliffe had taken with her on the flight an apple that her students had given her. That is how I learned about this custom in America. The scene stayed with me. That scene as well as what Ronald Reagan had said to the schoolchildren using words that I later found out were borrowed from a World War II poet. 'We will never forget them, nor the last time we saw them this morning, as they prepared for this journey and waved good-bye, and slipped the surly bonds of earth to touch the face of God.' I went to sleep thinking that when I had read about the disaster I hadn't foreseen the trip to America and my life as a student in New York City. There was no way I could have imagined or expected the experiences I was going to have. This moment in Cai Yan's apartment, and all the moments that had preceded it during the past three years, were alien to me. There was nothing that connected them to what

I had known in Patna or the years I spent in college in Delhi. On those days when I sat in the university library, reading the *Times of India* or *The Statesman* that arrived from India a week or sometimes a fortnight later, I allowed self-pity to take root in me like an affliction. Sachin Tendulkar had scored a big century against England in Chennai, but by the time I read about it the next Test match in Mumbai was already over and India had won the series 3-0. Weddings and deaths happened at a distance, and the distance was also inscribed in time. Which is to say, if you'll indulge me for a drowsy minute, I had often felt as if I had been sent into space.

Sometime during the night, Cai Yan touched my shoulder and woke me up.

—Frida is impossible, she said. She is keeping me up. I'm going to put her here and close the door. You come and sleep in the bedroom.

Who was Frida? As I stumbled into the bed I remembered the cat and then promptly fell asleep. When I woke up again, it was still dark and I became conscious that I had my arm around Cai Yan. This thrilled me. I brought my face closer to her hair. The familiar smell of ginger was mixed with something else. I moved closer to her and felt her push her ass against me in her sleep. My heart was beating wildly, and I was certain that this hammering would wake her up. I put my hand on her breast. Was Cai Yan awake? She was. She turned towards me in the dark and allowed me to press my lips on hers.

The next morning she acted as if nothing had happened. She didn't talk about it and I didn't either, but it was impossible to go back. In March, I returned from a three-day visit to the National Archives in Washington, D.C. Cai Yan was very interested in my photocopied letters of Indian radicals and also the newspaper reports of Chatto's interrogation in Berlin. I read to her from a memorandum sent by the US Acting Secretary of State on 27 May 1916 to the US Attorney General ('with reference to the so-called Indian Revolutionary Movement in the United States') while reclining on her couch. I felt her toe on my feet and, since she didn't move it away, I slid my foot along the length of her shin. Then I put my hand there.

—Shin, I said. Is that the only part of the body that sounds Chinese?

—There's also chin, she said.

I kissed her chin.

—Tung, I said.

And sucked her mouth.

That was the first time we fucked.

8 October. Maya made pakoras using green chillies and invited Cai to her apartment. She told Cai that I was welcome too. Her apartment was on the next street and we took a bottle of wine with us. (Peter wasn't there. Maya said that he had bought a new translation of *The Brothers Karamazov* and had told her before leaving for a café in the morning that he wouldn't come back till he had finished reading the remaining four hundred and fifty pages. Cai told me later that Maya had confided in her that Peter was depressed and had been advised to take 'a ton of medication'. Maya had spoken to Peter's mom in Germany. The mom simply said that she was dealing with the same problem. Peter's father, she said, 'only likes his black dog'.) When I came back to my apartment with Cai Yan that night, I saw that there was a letter for me from Patna. The handwriting on the blue aerogramme looked vaguely familiar. It was a cousin on my mother's side called Pappu writing to inform me about Lotan Mamaji's death. Written in Hindi, the letter began: *It is with great sorrow that I'm writing to inform you…* The third line said that *it had been a matter of great hurt in the family that Lotan Mamaji had died under most unfortunate circumstances.* What the hell did Pappu mean? By the time I reached the end of the letter I had concluded that Mamaji hadn't died alone. Along with him, because of whatever circumstances that Pappu had hinted at, Lotan Mamaji's adopted son, Mahesh, had also passed away. Several months would pass before I learned the truth: Lotan Mamaji had been murdered by Mahesh.

Mahesh was in his teens when Mamaji adopted him. He was

the son of the woman who was Mamaji's mistress in Dhanbad. This is what Pappu had meant in his letter when he described the 'two-fold loss': Mamaji was dead and Mahesh was in prison. My sister told me when I was on a visit to Patna that Mahesh had tied Mamaji to a chair and then tortured him, asking him to sign over some property. Mamaji signed the legal forms readily enough but Mahesh wasn't satisfied. He wanted to avenge the humiliations of his past. How much more certainty seems to lie at the tip of a steel knife than it does in rumours about your parentage!

But when I had first received news of Lotan Mamaji's death, the letter, which I also translated for Cai Yan, was a puzzle. There was no way of unlocking the puzzle of the death that night. So long ago, it seemed, I had told Jennifer about the monkeys on Lotan Mamaji's balcony. The story of the monkey's suicide. It was a story from my infancy in Ara. In later years, of course, I had spun that personal story into a broader narrative. Monkeys as a metaphor for migration. The poor monkeys found electrocuted near the Hanuman Mandir in Connaught Place had lost their natural habitat. The modern-day menace of marauding monkeys, reported by Indian newspapers fond of alliteration, had to do with urban expansion and destruction of forests. That's what I had originally thought. Then came the discovery that another important reason was the massive annual export of young male monkeys right up to the 1980s. The monkeys from Indian forests were living and dying in American labs. This story rescued the monkeys of my childhood from where they were stranded in nostalgia; they were now swinging from branch to branch on the tree of history.

One newspaper reported the request made in March 1955 by India's finance minister that senior American officials in the US please explain why monkeys were needed from India. The Indian government had earlier been told that the monkeys were needed for scientific research on infantile paralysis and for the production of polio vaccines. Was there any reason to doubt this claim? The report didn't elaborate. Another account mentions that the Indian

Prime Minister Morarji Desai banned the export of monkeys in 1978 because the Americans had violated their promise that the monkeys would be used only for medical research. Desai had cause to suspect that they were being put to military use to test defence systems and new weaponry. NASA's public records indicate that on 11 June 1948, a V-2 Blossom launched into space from White Sands, New Mexico, carried Albert I, a rhesus monkey. On 11 June 1949, Albert II was sent into space, gaining an altitude of 83 miles. Upon return, the monkey died on impact. On 12 December 1949, the last V-2 monkey flight was launched at White Sands. On this occasion, the passenger was Albert IV. 'It was a successful flight, with no ill effects on the monkey until impact, when it died.' In September 1951, a monkey named Yorick was sent into space and survived.

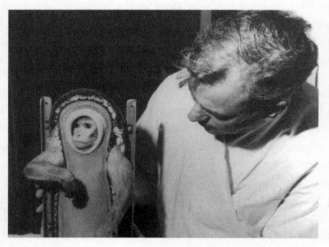

While reading about them I told myself that if at all I had been using the monkeys for autobiographical purposes I needed to stop and take note of the fact that they went further than I ever did. An adult monkey has the intelligence of a two-year-old human, and when zipped into its suit, locked into place in a metal case, its confusion and, if I can use this word, its courage, must have been extraordinary. The NASA site notes that without the use of these animals, in the early days of space testing in both USA and USSR, there could have been great loss of human life. 'These animals performed a service to their respective countries that no human could or would have performed.'

Was there a link between Indians and monkeys? The Republicans think so. In 2006, a Virginia senator named George Allen called an Indian-American youth a 'macaca'. Allen was on the campaign trail and the teen he called 'macaca' was working for his Democratic opponent. At his rally, Allen drew his supporters' attention to the young man, 'Let's give a welcome to Macaca here. Welcome to America and the real world....'

Then he began to talk about the war on terror.

I was only five months old at the time of the monkey's suicide and when I returned to Lotan Mamaji's house a few years later the monkeys were still there, removing and eating what my young cousin said were lice from each other's hair. Beneath the tamarind tree's branches the mohalla's pigs rested like sacks of rotting wheat. They were actually black in colour but were often coated with the dry brown mud of my birthplace. That summer I was quite taken with the pigs because they appeared in their loose packs, incessantly grunting, beneath the hole in the toilet, a wooden board placed a few feet above the ground, pushing their snouts inside the buckets under us.

I was already fifteen when, lying drunk on a mattress where I would find him the next morning sleeping in his own shit, Mamaji laughed at the old memory of my surprise at the sudden appearance of the pigs. The tears from his small eyes mixed with the red juice of the paan that bled from his mouth. We had come as members of the baraat party of the bridegroom for a marriage in a village called Garhi. It was about four hours' drive from Ara. Our hosts had made available the one large hall that was all there was to the village high school; sixty men were to eat and sleep and while away our time for the next two days in that room which was surrounded on three sides by the monsoon rains which had filled the village with water and the unrelenting croaking of bull-frogs.

Earlier that evening, I had watched Lotan Mamaji take out a moist bundle of hundred-rupee notes from under his sweat-drenched kurta and offer them, one at a time, to the dancer who had been brought from Calcutta for twenty thousand rupees. The elderly men from the district's landowning families had at last been able to watch live the dances first performed by Meena Kumari in *Pakeezah* a few months before she died of an alcohol overdose. The village had no electricity but a loud fuel-powered generator had been hired and brought from Ara. It lit three large bulbs which attracted millions of moths and more than two hundred villagers. The dancer didn't seem mindful of the rivulets of sweat flowing down her front and back. Mamaji was lying on a thin mattress, leaning on his left elbow, his back propped up by a pillow. In his right hand, he held a glass of Ambassador whisky that he would repeatedly refill. Whenever the dancer came close, he would set the glass down and grasp at her bangle-laden arm. If she lingered within reach or sat down in front of him, he would put a hand on her waist or push money down her blouse. Every time she bowed and salaamed, he smiled at her and touched his moustache like a villain in a Hindi film.

During one song performance, Mamaji allowed the woman to put in his mouth a paan that she had herself folded in front of him, placing a clove and a cardamom on the betel leaf with a show of delicacy. When she sat that close, she looked different. I saw the paint on her face and how sweat streaked the makeup on her cheeks. She had a hairy mole above her upper lip.

When the dance was over, a heavyset young man who had sat close to us through the whole evening helped carry Lotan Mamaji to the high school hall. The room was still bare even an hour after midnight except for an old man coughing in his sleep in the corner. Mamaji opened his eyes when I had settled his head on a pillow. He looked at the young man who was still standing next to me and then asked me if everything was okay. Then he drew out his .38 and pushed its barrel into my palm.

—To be or not to be, he said, quite meaninglessly. He said the words in English, a language that wasn't very familiar to him. His voice was lucid and unnaturally soft. A memory roused him momentarily and he laughed, the paan-juice bubbling out of his mouth. He had just remembered something from my childhood. He said that when I was four or five, I had told Lotan Mamaji that I was going to drink more milk. Why? My young self had explained to him that my pee was yellow and I wanted it to be a normal colour again.

My father's contempt for Lotan Mamaji, his brother-in-law, if described by means of a pie chart, would show thirty per cent coloured black for the lack of education beyond middle school. On that chart, another thirty per cent would be shaded differently for addiction to alcohol, while the last thirty per cent would be marked for adultery and lust. The ten per cent of the circle that remained would be a dappled slice attributable to other, unexplained sins. When I was growing up, the conversation between my parents made it clear that there were many flaws in Lotan Mamaji's character, but I was not very conscious of them. As a boy, I had watched him at sunset feeding the fish in his pond. He stood at the water's edge. His right fist moving in the air as if he were drawing in a kite that was the only one left flying gloriously in the sky, he threw puffed rice on the water whose surface was broken by the dark mouths of many fish. When Lotan Mamaji cast his line and drew out a rohu whose scales glinted silver and black, I was moved by his love for me.

I was telling Cai Yan all this, everything I could remember, all my devotion and my disappointment. If I wanted I could perhaps have used terms we bandied about in our seminars: about the unfulfilled lives or futile deaths of people—because of their class or upbringing—caught between an older feudal order and an emergent capitalist society. There was some pathos there but it was better to be clear-eyed about the harsh judgement of history. As grad students we showed ourselves eager to understand contemporary life, but, in reality, we were proclaiming our place in the future. I felt this most strongly when our friend Pushkin spoke of how the lives of the many anonymous others had been exceeded by the demands of hectic modernity. They were history's victims, the poor fucks, while we were not. I hated that brand of all-knowing academic talk. So, it is possible I mourned Lotan Mamaji's death, and my own childhood, in my conversation with Cai Yan that night, like a scene from a movie about a small town. There is a crumbling mansion in the background at the edge of a field. A large man with a moustache is sitting under a tamarind tree smoking a hookah. That morning the man sold to an antique dealer a portrait with an elaborate frame that had hung on his wall; the portrait was of his father who had been a minor landowning functionary under the British, and he got a price which he knew was low but he wasn't prepared to bargain. Money is scarce, it is needed for food or maybe even medicines, and yet there are also other uses. After he has had a drink, or maybe several, the man is going to lift his body that feels more and more tired these days and take a rickshaw to the bar near the movie hall.

By the time the spring semester arrived, our course work was almost done; each of us would now have to write a thesis. While Ehsaan gave Cai Yan books on insurgency in India, he also had a gift for me. Midway through the semester he called me into his office and said that he was going to recommend me for a Ford Foundation fellowship for summer research. The fellowship earned me a ticket to Delhi. Ehsaan wanted me to push further with my reading of Agnes Smedley and the Indian radicals in America. Late one night in early June, I landed in Delhi and the next morning took a train to Patna. I stayed with my parents for three days before returning to Delhi for my research. A taxi from Paharganj station brought me to Sutlej hostel in JNU where I had made a paying guest arrangement with a sociology student from Bihar. In the National Archives one morning, I found what I could start with. I had come across the letters of the Indian nationalist leader Har Dayal—whom Smedley had met in Berkeley. Har Dayal was the founder of the Hindustan Ghadr Party. The organization's newspaper was published from San Francisco but the letters in the file I found in the archives had been written from a small town in Algiers in 1910. These letters were addressed mostly to an older mentor, Mr Rana, and his wife, whom Har Dayal called 'Madame Rana'. In one letter, he had written to Madame Rana: *I shall write more later on. It has been raining all day today. I shall begin to learn your German in two or three months. Next year, I shall write to you in German. Then perhaps you will reply sooner!* Who was this woman, perhaps older, but also foreign, to whom this young revolutionary was pouring out his heart?

That morning, from outside the Reading Room, I could hear voices shouting in Hindi. Perhaps a wall was being painted. The librarian, a short woman with full, surprisingly pink lips, had been on the phone all morning. She would listen to the person at the other end, she would talk desultorily about work, and every few minutes begin to giggle, straighten her sari, and say lightheartedly, *Nahin, nahin.* I read the letters in the library and copied them in my notebook. The librarian went out for lunch to the canteen at the back that had yellow walls. I was alone in the Reading Room, sitting at my usual place. A painted sign to my right said *Please Maintain Silence* and, on the left, outside the door, on an iron frame, hung two red buckets with the word FIRE stenciled on them in white. I would pass those buckets each day of the fortnight I spent in Delhi: there was sand in them, presumably to be used to douse a fire, but there were also cigarette butts, crumpled paper, torn bus tickets, and clumps of dried paan juice.

I read more of the letters that Har Dayal had written. He was only twenty-six and already a prominent leader. But behind his discussion of politics, there stretched a vast solitude. (*I am doing well, though I feel awfully lonely. Several days pass without my speaking to anyone.*) There was a great deal of self-pity also. And moral sentiment, including advice on celibacy. It appeared that Madame Rana had a son called Ranji. Har Dayal wrote in a letter to her: *Never let him waste time on arranging his hair beautifully with care. Spartan simplicity should be enforced in youth, so that the character should be manly and not _____ [the last word was illegible]. Further, when he is a little older, don't take him into society where he should meet girls——parties etc. For between the ages of seventeen and twenty-two, much intercourse with girls should be avoided. It makes a man frivolous and produces the feeling of love precociously, and distracts his attention from studies and moral ideas.*

Har Dayal had been involved in what he called in one of his letters 'the bomb affair'. His studies at Oxford had been interrupted. But the rupture in his life was broader: *The suppression of the natural, filial, fraternal, conjugal and paternal feelings, the total estrangement from all early friends, whom I loved as the light of my life...* And the struggle was not only political. His disturbance was clearly more profound. Consider document number 2388 (11), Serial number 11. From the Hotel de la Californie, Algiers, on 13 June 1910. A Monday. Har Dayal had written a fourteen-page letter to Mr Rana. It passed from the seemingly personal—*I often find relief in crying*—to the plainly political—*I read in the*

*papers that thirty-three confessions have been made in Nasik Trial!*
*That is terrible.* Then, apparently only an hour later, he sat down
to write another letter to the same address. He declared in this
letter that he would take a vow not to ever again do two things:
*1. Money-making 2. Sexual intercourse, even with my wife.* And
then this despairing admission: *I have stooped to meat-eating, wine-*
*drinking, frivolity, sight-seeing, gossip, reading tales and novels, and*
*indolence in order to soothe my heart-pain and relieve my nerves and*
*get good sleep and appetite.*

I wanted to stop reading when, over and over again, I came
across such lines. The tone of self-pity was wearying, yes, but
what also depressed me was that the litany of regrets reminded
me of my journals.

And did 'frivolity' mean that he had gone whoring?

Sex and sightseeing and even reading novels all condemned
as sins!

What was this freedom that they were fighting for?

ᔑ

When I got back to New York at the end of the summer, Cai
Yan was getting ready to leave for India. Her stay was going
to be longer, perhaps up to a year. I was going to miss Cai; I
already missed her when I was in India. I remembered what
Nina had said about finding someone and loving her. I was in
love with Cai, I think. But love wasn't something I equated with
a person's life-goals. At that time a part of me considered such a
preoccupation selfish or immature or plainly reactionary.

On a rainy evening Cai Yan and I were walking through
the park to Ehsaan's apartment on Riverside Avenue when she
stopped to pick up a large magnolia blossom that had fallen from
the tree. The large white petals were heavy with water, but Cai
Yan just took the whole flower and pressed it against her cheek.
The expression on her face was one of surpassing sadness. Had
she shed a tear? Or was it just the rain? I didn't ask. Cai Yan
was very open and loving, but I always felt that there was an
inner knot of sadness that never loosened in her heart, and this

melancholy made her real to me. I wanted to surrender all my
sympathy to someone. To her. Embrace of sadness was okay, I
said to myself. It wasn't reactionary.

Ehsaan welcomed us, kissing Cai Yan on both cheeks. She
worshipped him, and so did I, but I could see how much she was
learning from him. I was failing as a scholar. My research was
always too scattered. Perhaps because I wanted to be a writer,
my academic questions kept getting entangled in some personal
enquiry I wanted to conduct into the complexities of the human
soul. Cai Yan had a clearer agenda and a much stronger focus.
When Mahasweta Devi came from India for a week's visit to
a seminar where her writings were being taught in translation,
Cai Yan met with her to discuss her thesis. With Ehsaan's help,
Cai was reading thick tomes on peasant insurgency in India;
she read books on history, literature, and even sociology and
religion. Also memoir and journalism, all the books arranged in
neat piles on her dining table. Of all the books I had seen in
her hands, I had read only one, a memoir by a young British
woman who had been jailed in Hazaribagh after her arrest in
the company of Maoists. That evening at Ehsaan's house, Cai
Yan was seated next to Ehsaan on the couch and was asking him
questions about the writings of an Oxford political scientist on
militancy in eastern India. Unwilling to join the conversation I
fussed with the bottles of wine and salted peanuts. But Ehsaan
wouldn't let me do that for long; he asked me to sit and listen
while he told Cai Yan a story.

—As a young man in Lahore, I must have been eighteen or
nineteen, I considered myself a communist.

—One evening I and my other communist friends were sitting
in a room in our hostel drinking tea. We lived in different rooms
but we shared what was called a ward servant. This would be a
male of any age, between maybe seventeen to seventy, who would
be responsible for anything from cooking to washing clothes to
buying newspapers. Yes, even though we were communists we
had a ward servant. He was a man around forty years in age.
His name was Qamroo.

—Now, this particular evening, Qamroo had made us tea and egg omelettes with green chilies in them. We were all feeling very grateful and kind towards Qamroo. Then, I said to my friends, This is all fine and good. But we are after all communists. We have to show Qamroo more respect.

—One of my comrades said that we ought to call our servant 'Uncle'. We should call him Qamroo Chacha. But this didn't seem radical at all. So, I suggested that we would now share Qamroo's chores. Whenever we could, we would step into the tiny kitchen with its black walls and ask if we could be of assistance to Qamroo.

—Now, I could immediately see that the response to this proposal was less than enthusiastic. My friends said that they were required to attend classes, they needed to go to political meetings, organize rallies. One of them, the son of a feudal landowner in Punjab who had pledged to fight for an egalitarian society, said that he didn't even have time to post a letter sometimes and had to ask Qamroo to do it for him. Another one pointed out that labour was not degrading; we only needed to make sure that Qamroo felt he got fair wages.

—But how to find this out? That was the question. Well, we must ask Qamroo himself. We called for Qamroo. The loudest of us shouted for Qamroo Chacha, and the man appeared with a grin on his face. He hadn't heard this name before. But there was an air of solemnity in the room. He was told that he was no longer our servant. He was our comrade. We would all treat each other equally.

—Qamroo was not grinning anymore. In fact, he looked a bit puzzled. He was not saying anything. So the boys explained that we were going to help him with his work whenever we could. Next, I asked him if he thought his wages were fair. Qamroo now looked a bit afraid, maybe because he thought that with this offer of help we were going to cut his wages.

—I understood this. I said to him that the reason why we were asking such questions was because we wanted to show him respect. In fact, I said, I don't know why you are standing. Please sit down on that chair.

—More than one chair was suddenly offered to Qamroo who had never before sat down in our company. We were all well-to-do people. He was our ward servant. During Eid, we would embrace him and say *Eid Mubarak* and give him money, but how many times in a year do you have Eid?

—He cooked for us every day; he washed our shirts, our trousers, and our dirty underwear. He swept the three rooms where we slept. We didn't even know the names of his two children who lived with their mother in the village. But we were now calling him Chacha and asking him about his needs. He had gastric ailments and his teeth chattered at night.

—We were stronger than him. We held his arms and asked him to sit in the wooden chair we had put in the centre of the room. Please sit, we said, please sit with us. Against his resistance, we pulled him down and released his arms only after he had seated himself. But once we loosened our grip on him, he found himself propelled out of the chair. He just couldn't sit there and since we wouldn't let him stand in the room he left at once despite our cries.

Ehsaan paused. He said to Cai, Do you understand what I'm trying to do here? I want you to remember this story and when you go and talk to the Maoist leaders who have spent their lives in villages, relate to them my story and ask them *why didn't Qamroo sit on his chair?* Let them hear my story and answer you. You will then have your book.

I remember that evening very clearly. I remember Ehsaan's story and what I also remember, as if it were a scene in a film, is the way in which Cai Yan and Ehsaan sat together discussing historical change. They were able to see the future, while I was either blind or simply too perverse to draw a straight line between my love for Cai Yan and the society they were describing. Cai Yan took Ehsaan's advice and wrote the book that he wanted her to write. About ten years ago I found her on YouTube discussing her new book. She was sitting on the stage under a white and red tent at a literary festival in Delhi. The man interviewing her was a BBC journalist and Cai was telling him about living in a village in Chhattisgarh and she then invoked her teacher who would have been pleased to see this book.

In that same video, you can see Cai Yan reading, interrupted only by laughter from the BBC man, a letter to Edward Said that Ehsaan wrote shortly before he died. Cai wanted the audience to appreciate Ehsaan's exaggerated and mordant style, the pleasure and flattery with which he offered his criticism on an op-ed by his comrade Said:

> Son of Palestine, Friend and Ally to the Wretched of the Earth, Keeper of the Flame in the World, the Text, and the Critic,
>
> I made a brave attempt to attend your talk yesterday but the press of bodies at the door was deeper and denser than even experienced in the tinbox buses on the crowded, sticky streets of Lahore or Accra. I saw the brief dazzle of your features and admired, from a distance, the elegant shine of your Savile Row suit. Then you began to speak! Such flowing oratory! Has anyone else ever been more eloquent on the narrow and constricted semantic field through which Islam is interpreted in the West? But I wanted to hear you and discuss these things with you in person, and not from behind a wall of perspiring bodies! When will you provide this timid and undeserving soul the benefit of your attention? I published the attached in *Dawn* last week—it was already in production, alas, by the time your own words on the subject fell like rain on my parched soul at your public address last afternoon—and I hope you will read it. I have tried in my own weak way to say something meaningful about Islam not only by saying that the Western construction of Islam is a fiction, a purely ideological construct, but by insisting on presenting the concrete, not to mention divided, struggles underway in polities that happen to be Islamic.

As always, with a sense of devotion that is your due and tender regards, I remain,

Ehsaan of no consequence.

*Part VII*

# Cai Yan

*I am interested in wisdom. I am interested in walls. China famous for both.*
                    —Susan Sontag, 'Project for a Trip to China'

'I used to think marriage was a plate-glass window just begging for a brick.'
                    —Jeanette Winterson, Written on the Body

Cai Yan and I stopped by Maya's apartment because she was coming with us to the Guggenheim Museum. We were going to see the exhibition of the works of the Chinese artist Liu Huong. In *The Times*, we had read that Huong's installations were 'quietly devastating'.

Maya had great affection for Cai and they got together often but I felt that Maya didn't like me very much. Even though she was always polite with me, I feared she saw me as unsophisticated and a bit of a lout. How did she form this judgement? Once there were five or six of us at her place wondering if we would have class the next day—the professor had gone to Paris earlier that week. I volunteered to go down to the pay phone at the corner and call the professor at home—if she answered, I'd hang up. When I suggested this, Maya looked at me and said, *Kailash, you're such a creep*. This was said with some conviction and it affected my behaviour with Maya. I became nervous. The next time we saw each other, it was again at her apartment. She hugged and kissed Cai Yan. Then I stepped into her doorway, but I didn't know whether I should kiss her or not. We hugged and I thought she was about to kiss me on my right cheek. Or was it the left? In my confusion, I ended up brushing her lips with mine. I didn't know then whether I would make it worse if I apologized and so I kept silent.

We took the 1 train down to 86th Street and then the M86 bus to the other side of the park. On the bus, I let Cai Yan and Maya sit together. I sat down next to a big sweaty man in a suit. He held a huge bouquet of flowers wrapped in tissue paper; water from the bouquet trickled towards the bus driver. After a short wait in the line at the Guggenheim, we produced our IDs for the student discount and then we were inside.

Liu Huong had been born in Beijing in 1950 and, unlike Cai Yan, he had lived through the Cultural Revolution. His parents were doctors who had been sent to the villages to work. Huong's portraits of his parents in Mao uniforms were austere and utterly devoid of emotion. There was no overt judgement but the blankness of their expression was haunting. The artist had also painted huge portraits of party officials and here the intent was less disguised: you saw the men, and one woman (probably Mao's wife), as scheming and complacent. They were painted, perhaps a bit ostentatiously, with a complexion that made them resemble pigs.

After the room with the portraits, we entered the next room that was dominated by two giant paintings that looked like posters. The caption for the first poster read 'Have Fewer Children, Raise More Pigs' and showed a man and a woman with a small child. On the opposite wall was the other poster with the caption, 'Long Live Our Brigade Leader'. This latter picture, as gigantic as the first one, showed a group of villagers sitting together in a room watching a woman on TV who was addressing them. Once again, the figures were so emptied of any genuine feeling they appeared as automatons, creatures driven by a controlling ideology.

This was absorbing but not deeply affecting. I was just forming this thought when we entered the third room and what I now saw made me change my mind. We were looking at an installation entitled 'Hunan School'. The whole of the long room had taken on the look of an abandoned, decrepit classroom. Benches were broken or overturned, pictures had slid out of frames, maps appeared bleached, and Mao's posters were stained with rainwater. Dust and a visible air of decline touched everything in sight. In dirty glass closets on the side there were on display old trophies but they too appeared lost to history: the triumphs they celebrated had faded forever. Huong had painted the walls red up to waist level, but the red paint, just like the white paint above it, was peeling. In a few discarded boxes on the floor there were test tubes, funnels, and some disintegrating books. Every object was evocative and, at the same time, represented decrepitude and death. At the far end were three showcases: desk-like structures with glass tops under which were displayed objects and brief accounts in Mandarin script. These were children's stories about

ordinary items they had picked up or otherwise come across
in their daily lives. There was a story about the painting of the
benches. Another one about a fly a kid had caught. Cai Yan
translated a third account written in a child's hand. 'With this
rope Li Chen tied the dog Hei Bao to the fence near the school
and he didn't untie him until the next morning. Hei Bao could
have died and Li Chen was expelled from school for a week.'

We left the museum half an hour later; we were headed to
Chinatown for a very late lunch. I was full of praise for 'Hunan
School'. The installation showed how the students were doomed.
I loved it. But Cai Yan wasn't so thrilled.

—How many visitors today were made to think of the
students killed in Tiananmen?

Maya and Cai Yan talked heatedly, each supporting the other,
just as they used to do in Ehsaan's classes. I knew better than to
challenge them but I could see absolutely nothing wrong with
what Huong had done. In fact, he had evoked an entire world
for me. I stayed silent. We got to Mott Street and when we
were waiting for the food, I heard Cai and Maya talking about
Peter. I hadn't seen him for a long time. As far as Huong's art
was concerned, it would take me a long time, at least months,
to reach a simple understanding of what Cai Yan and I had
experienced differently when looking at 'Hunan School'. For
me, the richness of the experience had been about conjuring
the mundane details of a point in time. Art as an attempt to
capture a mood, a feeling, which reflected what it meant to be
alive in that place at that time. It wasn't the same for Cai Yan.
The politics of equality and radical change that she cherished
had been sullied in China. That was the meaning of the massacre
in Tiananmen Square. She had been in school then, and there
was no mention in the news, but her uncle, her father's younger
brother, had come back from college in Beijing with a gunshot
wound in his arm. I didn't realize this at once but what I came
to see later was that Cai Yan went to India to find among the
peasants and the tribals in places like Chhattisgarh a purer idea
of politics. It was her quest, different from, and yet similar to,

the hippies going to India in the sixties. It was a tableau full of innocence and that is why the disappointment I later caused her was even more devastating.

ⵡ

Late one night in Lehman Library, I watched an old Hindi film about China. *Dr Kotnis Ki Amar Kahani.* The film had probably been made even before Independence. A young Indian doctor from Kolhapur decides that because of the assaults of the Japanese army the poor people in China need medical help. The film was set in the late 1930s. Five doctors from India went on this humanitarian mission, and the film was the story of the one who didn't come back. Young Dr Kotnis falls in love with a Chinese peasant girl, played by an Indian woman who speaks in a high, singsong falsetto. Their marriage is seen as a bond between the two nations; the next day the Japanese bombing begins. Amidst widespread death and destruction, the doctor cures diseases and then succumbs to them. The drama of return, etc.

The thought came to me: I could perhaps go to China if

I could find a connection with the work I had already done. I went to talk to Ehsaan about it. Characteristically, he asked me if I had eaten. He was looking at me with his wide-apart eyes.

—How are you? I get the feeling you are a bit adrift.

I shrugged.

Ehsaan said that it was useless to ask me about the future, I first needed to sort out the issues that were facing me in the present.

—There's a famous ghazal of Javed Qureshi's that begins *Dil jalaane ki baat karte ho...* The relevant lines for you are *Hum ko apni khabar nahin yaaron / Tum zamaane ki baat karte ho.*

He recited the Urdu couplet and smiled.

I knew the song. Farida Khanum's rich voice came back to me, a golden length of rough silk. *I have no news of myself, my friends / You are demanding a report on the world.*

Ehsaan was wearing a pale blue kurta over a black turtleneck. While he cooked, we talked. He was stirring the pot in front of him, not saying too much. He had leftover zucchini in the fridge and was making a chicken curry for us to eat with rice.

I said something about the men whose letters I had read, their strange relationship to sex and to loneliness.

After a pause he addressed the chicken in the pot.

—And Agnes Smedley?

I sensed an opportunity.

—What was she looking for when she fell in with the Indians? Was it the same impulse that took her to China?

More silence from Ehsaan. He was still looking away from me when he spoke again.

—Talking of the same impulse... Cai Yan is going to India. You are going to China. What am I to make of this?

—In the last couple of years, India and China are being talked about in the same breath. India is familiar to me. I want to go to China to look at India in a new way, to find—

I stopped, suddenly uncertain. But Ehsaan was nodding.

—It's not just the opium that went from India to China, he said. There was a flow of nationalist ideas. This flow, at different

times, was in both directions. As you know, Cai Yan is working
on Maoism in India...

I came back to my apartment well fed and slightly drunk. I
let the phone ring in Cai Yan's apartment for a long time and
debated whether I should leave a message. I began speaking into
the machine, but then she picked up.

—Hi.

—How was your dinner?

—I want to have a drink with you. You want to come over?

—I can't. I'm putting these highlights in my hair. Can't you
come here?

I was happy to walk over. Cai Yan had silver foil wrapped
in her short hair. There was a half-finished bottle of Chardonnay
in her fridge that she took out, and I poured the wine in two
glasses. She didn't touch hers. Instead, she took off her flip-flops
and stepped into the bathtub. I put down the cover of the toilet
seat and sat down on it. Dark colour flowed from Cai Yan's hair
when she bent her head and poured water over herself.

I took the mug from her hand. The water was warm. My
fingers touched the back of Cai Yan's neck. I lowered my face
and kissed her wet neck.

—More water, more water, please. Kailash!

After she was done, Cai Yan sat on her couch, a towel draped
around her head. I took a seat on the easy chair. I told her
that Ehsaan had encouraged me to look into Agnes Smedley's
friendship with the writer Lu Xun. He had said that I could go
to China for a semester. Cai was on her way to India but the
thought of me going to her country excited her.

—Will you go to Shanghai? You can visit Lu Xun Park.

—I don't know yet.

—You can take a train and visit my parents. It will take just
half a day to get there from Shanghai.

Her parents!

I had never met Nina's parents. She hadn't asked me to visit
Maine that summer. But here was Cai Yan proposing that I visit
her parents. What would she tell them about me? I kissed her

and then hurried back to my apartment because both of us had
to take care of our TA work for the next morning. I felt very
tenderly toward Cai. A circle was closing. I was happy that I was
going to China. I felt confident that I would do good work there.*
On the walk back, I thought about the first day of spring the
previous year. Small green shoots were already pushing out of the
ground. Some of the students chose to wear shorts and t-shirts at
least while the sun was out. Cai Yan said that we should get ice
cream. We walked past a bookstore which had taken advantage
of the weather to roll out bookshelves with used books piled on
them. A pink-covered book caught my eye because of the name
on it. Ismat Chughtai. *The Quilt and Other Stories*. The book
had been published by a feminist press in Britain. Two dollars
for a used copy. During the afternoon I had planned to grade
papers, but I set that aside and turned first to the short story
which had inspired the making of the film *Garam Hawa*. One
after another, I read more stories in the book. Ten years earlier,
I had first read some of those stories in Delhi, and now for the
first time I was reading them in English. I tried to remember
but the original words would not come back. I had bought the
book because it seemed it had been waiting for me there among
other books that spoke another language. We shared something,
this book and I, we belonged with each other. But where had
this obstacle come from? I passed my hand through the pages.
'The reflection from the red twill lit up her bluish-yellow face
like sunrise.' What would those words have been in the original
Urdu? What had Chughtai got in mind when she described the

---

*If you were settled in love, you could get your work done. This piece of
writing advice had come from Ernest Hemingway.
*Interviewer: Is emotional stability necessary to write well? You told me once that
you could only write well when you were in love. Could you expound on that a
bit more?*
Hemingway: What a question. But full marks for trying. You can write any
time people will leave you alone and not interrupt you. Or rather you can if
you will be ruthless enough about it. But the best writing is certainly when
you are in love. If it is all the same to you I would rather not expound on it.

face as 'bluish-yellow?' Is that what she had even written? At least I remembered the original title of the story. I remembered also the summer afternoon in Delhi when I had gone to watch the film for the first time, and how the sorrow had struck home. But here I felt stranded in language. I had become a translated man, no longer able connect completely with my own past. What else had I forgotten? The sorrow of the world, but sorrow also for myself, gripped my throat. Without warning, I began to cry.

Till then, Cai Yan and I had been reading in bed. We were lying at an angle to each other, our heads together but our legs pointing in different directions, so that our bodies formed a V. The first sob that was wrenched out of me provided such release that, with a small yelp, I turned and touched Cai Yan.

—What happened? She asked.

But I was like a child, hiding my tears by pressing into her cotton shirt. It was an expensive shirt: she had worn it that day to greet the first flush of spring. She realized after a minute that I was actually crying.

—Oh, Kailash, she said, and cradled my head in her arm.

I let the tears come; the sorrow I had felt was abating, and in its place a feeling of exhilaration was taking wing. After a few minutes, I felt empty, and free.

Cai Yan was looking at me, with a slightly worried look, and I explained to her that I had been moved by what I was reading. It reminded me of what one poet had called 'the gentle poverty of my homeland'.

I wiped my nose.

I thought of the day when, on a walk to Ehsaan's house, Cai Yan had picked up a magnolia blossom and begun to cry.

Without looking at her, I unbuttoned her shirt that was already wet with my tears. She began to laugh, a short, amused laugh. Wordlessly, I took her breast in my mouth and began to suck as I would a mango when I was a boy. I had been reading about an unmarried girl in Chughtai's story; youth was passing her by, she would never know a man's touch. But here was Cai Yan, already panting from the effort of assisting me as I stripped off her clothes. I felt my soul had been cleansed by sorrow: I was able to savour what I possessed. She slipped her body under mine, and delicately drew my cock inside her. We were good when we were together. Everything fitted around a memory of what we had always done. She didn't have the passivity of the sad and helpless girl I had been reading about in the story. When I started pushing into her, she unwrapped her legs and held them up in the air. Cai Yan was one of the quietest people I knew, in public and in private, but she always made noise when we fucked. Her moans came suddenly and resembled the rhythmic fugue-like grunting of geese as they flew overhead when you were lying in the grass beside a river.

Cai Yan flew to Bombay. She published a brief piece in the *Village Voice* and Ehsaan pasted the cutting on his door. The story was about the mauling of a child in a town called Akola in central India. A dog had attacked a two-year-old boy and gouged out his eyes. The child's parents were daily-wage labourers. They had been working nearby, mixing clay at a brick kiln, rags tied around their heads. Cai Yan had expertly linked the savagery of the attack, which read like a parable, to the relentless depredations of a system that had ruined farmers. The child's parents had lost their meagre farm and become migrant workers. The much-vaunted liberalization of the Indian market hadn't brought wealth to the poor; on the contrary, it had made them more vulnerable and left them helpless and alone.

Her next piece was a long interview with a young widow whose husband, a cotton-farmer, had killed himself by drinking the pesticide that was to be used on his land. The farmer was in debt to a village moneylender who charged five per cent monthly interest. The dead man also owed money to a bank. The expensive seeds he had bought had all gone to waste because the rains had failed. The widow had told Cai Yan that the litre-bottle of pesticide her husband had ingested had also been bought by taking a loan of three hundred rupees from a neighbour. The huge subsidies given by the US to its farmers lowered the price of cotton worldwide while the new laws in India meant that the small farmers there had to contend with reduced earnings and higher rates of interest. I saw Cai Yan's article and the photograph of the widow that had been taken by someone called Sebastian D'Souza. The photograph showed the widow holding a portrait of her husband: he was sitting on a chair in the studio, dressed formally in trousers and a shirt. On his feet he wore a pair of oversized slippers. On the farmer's right, the photographer had placed a tiny vase of white plastic flowers.

Cai Yan sent me a postcard and then nothing for a while. The postcard showed Salman Khan flexing his biceps. Cai had written that she had been busy and was looking for a change; she was going to move to Bhopal and work with an NGO. But that probably didn't happen because three months later, when we were still dealing with snow on our streets, Cai Yan published a long report. This one was about her travel in the nearby forests of Chhattisgarh with the Naxals who were fighting for land rights. This report, nearly five thousand words long, was published in *Mother Jones*. It was less an analysis of a skewed economic system, though it was that too, than a record of terrible violence against the protesting tribals. Police executions at the edge of the forest or sometimes even in homes; torture and killings in police stations; army combing operations that included rape and the burning of huts. The report described appalling acts, but the emotion that I felt most strongly was perhaps envy. Cai Yan was living in India and reporting on the changes that had come since I left. I lay sleepless in bed thinking about the thesis I first needed to write. I would have to do this soon. One night I woke up from a dream in which I had walked into the ocean with a book that I had been reading. Cai was standing on the beach. She was saying that we should be leaving now. But before I could get out, a wave washed over me and it swept the book away into the deep waters.

ᔥ

I had sent a brief missive to a journalist I knew, one of the most beautiful women I had ever laid eyes upon. She lived in Park Slope. *You wrote last week that you would write a longer note 'in a minute'. You didn't. I haven't moved since then. I haven't eaten, or slept, or made love.* Such longing.* Until that note got sent to Cai Yan by mistake, accidentally mailed to India along with the detailed letter I had written to her about my work, a mistake that resulted in the abrupt end of our relationship, I received her reports from Delhi or towns in Bihar or Madhya Pradesh where she was doing research.† She was studying Hindi while living

---

*'If you ask me what I want, I'll tell you. I want everything.' —Kathy Acker, *Pussy, King of Pirates*
†After we became lovers, one of the things we did was that we shared a notebook where we wrote down the new words we had come across. Both of us were immigrants and wanted to know the names for all kinds of objects and emotions. Cai Yan's first entry was 'dormer: a window that projects vertically from a sloping roof'. Her second entry was 'bunion: a painful swelling on the first joint of the big toe'. I remember my first entry in that notebook. 'Pyriform breast: pear-shaped breast.' Years after I had made the stupid mistake of sending Cai Yan the wrong letter, I found a word from the Congo in an article in *Time* magazine that I think would have helped me with my appeal: 'ilunga: a person who will forgive anything the first time, tolerate it the second time, but never a third time.'

for six months in a town called Amarkantak. It delighted her
that she had learned all the names of the local trees. The town's
inhabitants were fond of her—a Chinese girl in Indian clothes. A
nun had been raped in a village an hour away but the person who
gave her this news said that Cai Yan was safe because she wasn't
a Catholic. In her letter to me, Cai Yan wrote that she was going
to interview the nun.

In Delhi she watched a play called 'Netua'. A netua is a
man who puts on women's clothes and dances during weddings
and festivals in the villages of Bihar. The play was about a netua
called Jhamna who gets married and brings his bride back to
his village. During Holi celebrations, the drunken upper-caste
youth in his village watch him dance and then they come for
his bride. Jhamna lets go of his inhibition and hits out at the
oppressors, but when they flee he falls upon his wife. The writer
had skillfully transferred all the violence of the ruling class on to
poor Jhamna and his rage. Cai Yan wrote me a long letter telling
me that inspired by what she had seen our friend Pushkin do
long ago in his translation work, she was going to collaborate
on the translation of the original Hindi short story on which
the Jhamna play had been based. The writer was Ratan Varma
from Muzaffarpur and she was going to meet him in a fortnight.

This information startled me. Muzaffarpur was where my
father had gone to college when he left his village and I still
had distant cousins living there. One of them owned two buses
and another ran a timber business. I used to visit them when I
was in Patna. If my cousins saw Cai Yan, a Chinese woman in a
salwar-kameez, in a crowded street near their home would they
ever guess that she was my lover? No one there could imagine
how hard she had worked to journey to a place where her present
met my past. I also had other worries about Cai Yan wandering
around alone in a town like that. When I was a boy, maybe
seven or eight years old, I was on a visit to Deoghar, walking
on a street near a hill with my sister. Our parents had gone
to the temple for which the town is famous. The guest house
where we had found a room was a little distance away from

the centre of the town. It was a pleasant evening, small green trees, red earth, a winding road leading to the rocky hill maybe half a mile away. A motorcycle passed us and then after it had gone a few hundred yards down the road it turned around and approached us. There were three young men sitting on it. They parked the bike and then came to us. One of them asked my sister if she needed a ride. She didn't answer them. The fellow who had asked the question took out a small plastic comb from his pocket and started passing it through his hair. The youth ignored their bike and fell in step with us. My sister jerked my hand to make me walk faster. One of the young men, a fellow in a tight blue shirt, stepped close to my sister and just pulled her dupatta off. Neither my sister nor I said anything. We kept walking but I was conscious that my sister was breathing hard. Then I realized that she was crying. We walked like this for about ten or fifteen minutes, I'm not sure.

The boys trailed us. They sang songs and passed lewd comments, never letting us hope that they'd fallen far behind. Had one gone back to fetch the bike? I didn't look back. My sister didn't let go of my hand. Beyond a tree on our left, a path appeared leading down to a small cottage. I could now see an old couple sitting on cane chairs. My sister turned on to the path. She went to the old man, who was easily seventy or eighty, and wearing a dhoti and a vest.

—Those boys are following me, she said.

That was the word, *follow*. A simple word whose meaning for a long time held a specific threat in my mind. The old man and his wife both looked towards the road. The woman remained silent but after a while the man told us that we were welcome to go inside. The young men disappeared in the direction they had been originally going. While we were in the old couple's home, my sister had her asthma attack, the first of her life, and this added to her helplessness. Later in college, asthma would cripple her life and she was prone to anxiety attacks for many years, but that evening in Deoghar the old couple were calm and helpful, as if they were quite used to young women rushing into their garden and collapsing breathless on the ground. They suggested that my sister lie down on their bed and then gave her honey and ginger tea. My sister became calm, her breathing returning to normal, in about half an hour. It was still light out when we left their house. The old man accompanied us to the road. He carried a large flashlight in his hand.

Now when I thought of Cai Yan at the bus station in Muzaffarpur, or standing in the marketplace in Barauni, she took my sister's place in my mind and for a moment I was a boy again filled with fear. The problem, of course, was that I was older now and therefore closer in age to the young man I still remembered from the road in Deoghar, the one in the blue shirt who had snatched away my sister's dupatta.

∽

The only time that Cai Yan called me from India was to tell me that Peter had died. I had just woken up and was confused by the news. Cai was telling me that I should go and look after Maya till Peter's parents got there from Hamburg. The phone connection was poor. I asked Cai Yan where in India she was at that moment, but she didn't hear me. I went to the building where Peter and Maya had been living for the past six months; their apartment was larger because they had been given married students' housing. As I hurried along to the apartment, rushing past people who were headed for classes or for work, I wondered how Cai had heard the news of Peter's death. The answer presented itself when I arrived there. Ehsaan was sitting on Maya's couch with her. At my entrance, Maya got up and said that perhaps I could make tea for Ehsaan and myself. She said she was going to lie down for a bit. Ehsaan said to her, Yes, you go but know that we are here if you need us.

I stayed silent as I made strong tea, with ginger, cardamom and cloves thrown in. After the milk came to a boil, I let the mixture simmer. Ehsaan stepped into the tiny kitchen.

—This smells good. You know, make a bit extra. Let's try to get Maya to drink some tea.

He spoke in a very low voice, as if Maya were really trying to sleep in the bedroom. Naturally, I too fell into a whisper.

—Where is he?

—The police have the body.

—How?

—Hanged himself.

—In here?

—No. In the basement.

Ehsaan went out of the kitchen, perhaps to check if Maya's door was still shut. When he came back he told me that another resident had found Peter in the basement early in the morning and called 911. There was no medical intervention because a Fire Department squad arrived almost as quickly as the police and declared him dead. The belt that Peter had used was looped from one of the metal pipes that criss-crossed the basement ceiling. He had wrapped duct tape around his wrists so that his hands were tied together. He must have done this last before kicking away the stool. Ehsaan arrived at four in the morning after Maya phoned him. The police were in the apartment. They found a suicide note in Peter's pocket but Maya had put it away. When the police left with the body for the autopsy, Ehsaan urged Maya to call Peter's parents. She also called her own parents in Delhi and asked them to tell Cai Yan.

The tea was ready. Ehsaan walked back to Maya's room and spoke her name. He said that she should perhaps have a cup too. Surprisingly, she stepped out.

We drank the tea without talking. Maya's eyes, or maybe more the area around them, had become dark. She seemed miles away from us, sunk into a silence that also had a madness in it.

—The boy was in a lot of pain, Ehsaan said softly.

Maya pressed her lips together.

In a burst she was soon telling Ehsaan that just the following week the doctors were going to start ECT, electroconvulsive therapy. Peter ought to have waited. He would have been put under anaesthesia and the doctors would pass small electric currents through his brain. The delay had been caused because

Peter had withheld consent; perhaps irrationally, he feared memory loss. But it was the only hope. Neither the Nardol nor the Restoril was working, Maya said, as if we knew what those names meant.

—You can't blame him, Ehsaan said gently. He was sick. He was in a terrible place.

Maya allowed herself a single sob that was like a spasm.

—The drugs confused him. I suspect he was flushing them down the toilet or something, and pretending to me that he was taking them.

I remembered Maya sharing this fear with Cai Yan. I didn't say anything.

—I don't know what—

—You can't blame yourself, Ehsaan said. We should keep our best thoughts of Peter in our hearts and pray for him.

Tears sprang into my eyes. I sat down next to Maya and touched her shoulder for a few moments before taking the empty cup from her. I think she thanked me for the tea.

When Maya went back to her room, I learned from Ehsaan that Peter's parents would arrive by evening. I asked him if he had seen Peter's body and he said that when he arrived they had him on a stretcher downstairs with a sheet covering him.

—I removed the sheet from his face and then spread my hands and recited the Fatiha.

I had never known Ehsaan to be religious. Did I look surprised?

—Let me tell you a story about prayer, Ehsaan said.

He began telling me about the time he was in Beirut. He had gone to the Hizbullah headquarters in South Beirut with a French journalist who later became the ambassador there. Ehsaan interviewed the Hizbullah leader, Sheikh Nasrallah. The piece he wrote was published under the title 'Encounter with an Islamist'. There was so much irony in that title because the man he had met was unexpectedly practical and not terribly weighed down by ideology. There were very few armed men in sight at the headquarters and, to Ehsaan, this suggested intelligence and efficient security arrangements. The women were moving around freely, dressed modestly, of course, but not wearing the hijab. And then there was the Sheikh, quite free of doctrinal armour, a man unwilling to defend the eternal or universal nature of the Shariat.

But the main reason Ehsaan had wanted to meet Sheikh Nasrallah was because he was interested in him as a person. He had wanted to interview him ever since he had watched news footage of him on television. This is what he had seen: seven coffins had been placed in a village school in South Lebanon, close to the border with Israel. A convoy of cars drove up before the burial. Sheikh Nasrallah got out of one of the cars and proceeded inside accompanied by his son, Jawad. The bodies in the coffins were of Hizbullah fighters returned by Israel in exchange for the remains of an Israeli soldier. Nasrallah stopped in front of each coffin and offered the Fatiha. When he reached the coffin marked 13, he stopped and whispered in the ear of an aide. The aide summoned two workers of the Islamic Health Association, which is a Hizbullah outfit. They opened the coffin, exposing a body wrapped in a white shroud. Sheikh Nasrallah's eyes closed, and his lips trembled as he recited the Fatiha. The body was that of Sheikh Nasrallah's first-born, his eldest son Hadi, killed in battle with the Israelis. Slowly, Sheikh Nasrallah bent down and stroked the head of his dead son. Jawad, the dead boy's younger sibling, stood quiet and pale behind his father. Sheikh Nasrallah stood with his hand resting on the chest of the body in the coffin. A deep silence had fallen in the room.

—I was unsure whether death had granted these people a grandeur that was denied them all their lives. But I felt that through his prayer Sheikh Nasrallah was giving their suffering and his own suffering some dignity. You understand?

Pushkin Krishnagrahi had written a play—*Satish Sadachar in His Heavenly Abode*—about a man on his deathbed telling the story of his family. In the darkened theatre I immediately thought of Peter but Pushkin's character was an old Indian man. The bed was empty, the lights shining bright on a white sheet, while the man's disembodied voice filled the auditorium. Then the action started with all the other characters, his family members, in different corners of the stage. Whatever was new wasn't really better, but there was no reason to remain nostalgic about the old. This was the play's uncompromising message, its alert scepticism. I was sitting with Prakash Mathan and a girl from NYU whom he had started dating. Ehsaan was there by himself but he readily agreed to come to a bar with us. After we had got our drinks, he asked me quietly whether I had heard recently from Cai Yan. I told him of our breakup.

—Your decision or hers?

—Hers, I said. I didn't have the courage to tell him what lay behind the split.

—Is this what you want?

—I don't know. My head says I should write to her. My heart knows she won't have me back.

He gave me a half-smile.

—Thomas Jefferson wrote a letter to a woman in the form of a dialogue between his head and heart. Do you know about it?

I shook my head.

The love letter was addressed to a married woman named Maria Cosway, an artist. He wrote the letter after meeting her in 1786. Jefferson was the US Ambassador to France at that time. He had been out on a stroll with Cosway and he leapt over a fountain. He fell and hurt his hand.

—The letter was written slowly with his left hand because he had broken his right wrist when he fell at the fountain.

Maybe I ought to write a letter to Cai Yan with my left hand, I thought. But it was Jefferson's leap that I identified with. And the fall.

—The letter was several thousand words long, Ehsaan said. This was the same man who had composed, ten years earlier, the Declaration of Independence. Which, incidentally, was much shorter than the letter.

Ehsaan wanted me to visit the library and read the letter.

Then, he told me that Maria Cosway had remained with her husband until his death, and later moved to Italy to start a convent school.

—Ehsaan looked at me. He said, Her husband was said to resemble a monkey. Jefferson became president around 1800.

Prakash and his girlfriend Maeve were drinking cocktails.

I turned my back to them and, summoning some feeling of urgency, told Ehsaan that I shouldn't wait any longer.

—I must go ahead and do the work I need to do in China.

Ehsaan could deliver a lucid lecture at any place and at any time.

—You must remember three points...

Deng Xiaoping was going to die soon but he was the model that the Indians were perhaps following. Deng had said that he wasn't interested in a socialism of shared poverty; he wanted capitalist growth. How was literature and art going to respond to these vast changes? Ehsaan said that I could go ahead and write a bit about Lu Xun, and Agnes Smedley, and maybe Saadat Hasan Manto in the subcontinent, considering the role of writers during a time of great upheaval, but I had to remain mindful of the present moment. This third point he felt was the most important.

—So, what is your position? he stopped and asked. Where do you stand vis-à-vis the unfolding present?

My present position was that I was standing in a bar drinking a bottle of Brooklyn Lager.

A good thing about Ehsaan was that he would often answer his own questions.

—You must travel from Beijing to Shanghai and then to places like Guangzhou and Shenzen. The new zones wouldn't exist except for Deng. What is life like there? Take a look for yourself and let your perception frame how you write about the past in which Lu Xun lived. You know enough about India and Pakistan to write a commentary on Manto. Let's see how quickly you can do this so that you can then look for a job.

↵

For four months, at 10.15 in the morning on each weekday, I was to be found on the twelfth floor, in the class right next to the men's room, of the Beijing Language Institute. The institute was in the Haidian District. For an hour and a half, my official task was 'to share and advance the bilingual/bicultural competence, extra-linguistic/encyclopedic knowledge, and translation strategies/techniques' of about thirty students. The work was uninteresting because I learned nothing about the lives of the people I met. From time to time, a sentence would be read out to me in English and I would nod my head or try to reframe it. Simple sentences: You can't be too careful. *Is that correct?* Or I would be asked questions that I didn't have any answers for: Why does English have such extensive use of passive voice? Don't you think English has more impersonal structures than other languages? *Impersonal structures! What were they?*

I always arrived on time and Professor Ning would welcome me with a smile. After that, I was ignored. I didn't know any Chinese and my real responsibilities were close to nil. Professor Ning would write sentences on the board in English and answer all questions in Mandarin. When the bell rang, I was expected to leave and I did. My presence was simply proof of a business relationship between two educational institutions and nothing more; but it was of help to me because it got me a dorm room where I slept peacefully, my white bedcover tinged red by the neon sign outside that said Research Institute of Petroleum Exploration and Development.

During weekends, I visited monuments and parks, but on weekdays, in the afternoons, after my lunch in the dorm, I would read about Lu Xun and also Manto. In the Lu Xun Museum, I saw pictures of Agnes Smedley. On the cover of the German edition of *Daughter of Earth* she had written: *Presented to Lu Hsün in admiration of his life and work for a new society.* She had signed the book on 2 February 1930. She would go on to spend much of the decade in China, often reporting from the war-front for newspapers like the *Manchester Guardian*. When she applied for membership in the Chinese Communist Party she was rejected for what was seen as her lack of discipline. One account said that her activities in China included racing horses, cross-dressing, and providing instruction to women—on birth control, Western dance, and romantic love.

In contrast to Smedley's activities in China, my life was dull; I was poor and often cold. I went to the library and read the stories in Edgar Snow's *Living China*; then I read Manto's *Kingdom's End and Other Stories*. Sitting in my room, an electric

heater in the corner, I sipped pots of Da Hong Pao tea and began
writing a comparative study of Manto's 'Toba Tek Singh' and Lu
Xun's 'A Madman's Diary'.* This solitude in an alien land, as well
as the work I was doing, helped me; it made me think more
deeply about what I wanted to say about literature. But it is not
what I had wanted to do. My starting point had been different.
A man like Har Dayal, who had embraced revolutionary ideals,
writing letters to women about desire and loneliness. That was an
image in my mind. Or Smedley's marriage to Chatto, their long
embrace and falling out, the strain of being outsiders engaged in
subversive activities. I wanted to write about love and, although
I was blind to this at first, I wanted to be in love.

꙼

After I arrived in Beijing, everything reminded me of Cai. I
tried to suppress my longing. I knew that she wasn't wasting
time thinking about me; instead, she was filing away reports that
would become a part of her thesis. She was on her way.

I husbanded my energy. I seldom went out on weekdays.

---

*Pushkin provided me a letter of introduction to a Chinese writer in
Beijing, Yu Hua, who had written extensively about Lu Xun. I took a
translator with me for our meeting at a cultural centre. Yu Hua turned
out to be in his late thirties. He had a fine sense of irony, and a casual,
relaxed manner that was not diminished but only enhanced by the fact
that he chain-smoked while we talked. Pointing to his watch, he sketched
a circle and told the translator that Lu Xun's career had come full circle
in China. At first, he was an author and his writings created controversy.
Then, he became a catchphrase during the Cultural Revolution, more of
an empty slogan. When the Cultural Revolution ended, he was again an
author and his name caught up in controversies. But now, with the rise of
rampant capitalism in China, Lu Xun was once again a slogan, a name to
be included in ads. On a piece of paper, Yu Hua drew Chinese characters,
a long list that my translator transcribed for me thus: 'the characters and
places in Lu Xun's stories have been put to work as names for snack foods
and alcoholic beverages and tourist destinations; they serve to designate
private rooms in night-clubs and karaoke joints, where officials and
businessmen, their arms wrapped around young hostesses, sing and dance
to their hearts' content.'

When I ventured out in the city, as I did sometimes in the evenings, to look for a drink called Pingo Sou, I carried a red English-Mandarin phrase book. Using that book in Beijing during those months reminded me of the time I was a fresh immigrant in the US and everything was new. I drank my tea and was content to eat noodles and tofu, and sometimes, as a treat, shredded pork. Two blocks away was the Garden Restaurant, a shabby place with three tables covered with plastic tablecloths. It served my needs admirably. I ate at the same fixed time every day. The owner expected me and brought my food soon after I sat down. His daughter, a cute toddler named Mei Ling, would come and sit near me. She would babble in Chinese and I understood not a word but I was filled with happiness. Back in my room, I read more stories by Lu Xun and Manto, and I shaped chapters on subjects like truth and self-deception, satires against the powerful, the bodies of women and the body of the nation. The conceit that I had smuggled into the book was that it wasn't me but Agnes Smedley who was reading these writers: her passions, her prejudices, even her biography, shaped my reading of Lu Xun and Manto. The work was speculative, even imaginative, but it was also systematic, and when my time in Beijing came to an end, I had much of my thesis already finished.

As Ehsaan had instructed, I made the trip to Shanghai and went to Lu Xun's home, now preserved as a museum. I had the phone number for Cai Yan's parents but I didn't call. Someday, perhaps, I could visit them when Cai was with me. Only once, late one night, when I was lost near a library I was visiting, and was unable to find anyone who spoke English, the thought entered that I should perhaps call Cai Yan's parents. But then a cab appeared in the drizzle and I showed the driver the card from the hotel where I was staying. I had a good two days there. At the museum, I took photographs of Lu Xun's statue and of the cover of his book of stories translated into Hindi. At another museum I found wooden crates with Patna Opium painted on them, and the mannequins of Sikh policemen in uniform on the streets. Dioramas of Parsi businessmen and male Chinese customers with their hair braided and hanging down their backs. I was a tourist in Shanghai and did things that tourists do. For instance, I ate spicy chanzui frog at a restaurant where they also had live crocodiles with thick rubber bands on their snouts. Before I left, amidst the lights of the evening, beside a river full of glittering cruise boats, I took a walk on the bund.

From Shanghai, I went by train to Guangzhou. I saw the factories and then the new construction sites covered in a green mesh and the familiar gridwork of bamboo scaffolding. That evening, at a bar on Xiao Bei Road, I met an Indian banker named Zutshi who told me that no building in China can be more than seventy years old. When it turns that age, it is pulled down. I don't know why I was taking down notes.

—India has great scope, Zutshi said. We are good in IT. And then he added, But we will never overtake China. The Chinese have the habit of work and they are obedient citizens.

On the train back to Beijing I put down my impressions of the journey. Ehsaan had suggested I use my travel in China to write the preface to my critical study of Lu Xun and Saadat Hasan Manto. Was industrial development going to solve our social problems? Would the powerful and the very rich become more charitable if they had made enough profits? What was a writer to do as a witness in a changing world? What was the writer who was a traveller, an outsider as well as a woman, to do as an activist? I took notes in a brown notebook that said Tian Ge Ben and, back in Beijing, while I waited two more days before my flight back to New York, I typed up my preface on the computer. My thesis was done. On the British Airways flight back, after having eaten, and drunk the complimentary red wine, I felt relaxed and took out a fresh Tian Ge Ben notebook. I wished very badly to go back to what I had ignored in my thesis. I wanted to write about love. Not just the story of one love, its beginning or its end, but the story of love and how it is haunted by loss. On the sound system on the plane, I listened to the Jimmy Cliff song 'You Can Get It If You Really Want'. With my earphones on, I played the song over and over again.

I began to write the short story with which I end this book—it is the story I sent to Yaddo—*so many years had passed*—and requested a residency to write a book about youth and its search for innocence. The story remained with me because, when I wrote it, I hadn't anticipated that my own story would follow, in some measure, the path the narrator takes. In the future that I couldn't foresee while sitting in that plane surrounded by clouds was the year of my betrayal and subsequent loss. I wrote the short story on that flight to New York. And then I decided to return in this book to the past to tell the story of the time I first went to pick apples.

*Part VIII*

# Reeti

The above picture is in my notebook for this novel. I must have torn it from a magazine, maybe Outlook, during a visit home. A reproduction of some of Satyajit Ray's sketches when he was making his first film, Pather Panchali. This is the storyboard for the scene in which Apu and his sister Durga catch sight of a train for the first time. It is a scene celebrated in the history of cinema. As in all of Ray's work, simple scenes, elegantly framed, producing a cumulative emotional effect that is shattering. Nothing in my notebook to indicate why I have cut this out from a magazine. It is possible I was thinking of collage. I suspect I was thinking more of ordinary life being transformed into art. Not just in the final film, but in these sketches too. These drawings are like calligraphy, awash with movement, as if a subtle suggestion was blowing through them like an invisible breeze.

*Bad writing model in my notebook:*

> suit. His writing is affectless, but not in the way
> that Chekhov made affectlessness a supreme
> kind of art. Often the language is pedestrian; at
> times, it clangs. In "The Bare Manuscript," a
> novelist tries to revive his talent by writing on
> a naked woman's skin: "The broad expanse of
> her tanned back and global white buttocks was
> in violent contrast, it seemed now, to his desk's
> former devastated dryness."

It is June. This is what I've decided to do with my life just now. I'm at Yaddo writers' colony in upstate New York, working on this book that I have long wanted to write. Two windows facing my desk open to a view of white pine trees that stand very tall and straight, and on the left I can see a small cluster of Douglas firs. The windows have screens to keep out insects and bats. My room is called The Breast Room on account of the ceiling above the desk, a perfectly rounded mound with a light fixture that forms its ornate nipple. The woman who showed me the room said that Philip Roth wrote his novella, *The Breast*, here. Roth's novella is about a man, a literature professor, who has turned into a giant breast. One night here at dinner, a violinist seated next to me said that Roth, who often stayed at Yaddo earlier in his career, had sent a letter stating that the rumour was untrue, that his imagination had never been so literal.

It is likely that both these stories are false. More interesting, then, to examine why we tell the stories we tell. Here I am in middle age, taking a break from the demands of teaching and family life, writing about youth and love and politics.* I

---

*Mixing the aesthetic and naked desire, this line stolen from the review of a photography book: 'Nearly every composition rides that fine line between hand-to-hand combat and cunnilingus, as all art must.'

have brought old letters and my journals here with me. How important these pages, written long ago, because, after a while, everything fades, and even the body, maybe especially the body, doesn't remember anything.

In the letters written by Nina, for example, I see her compressed style, the skinny loops on her 'l's, the consistent slant of her alphabets, as if they were all helping her say the same thing over and over again. *Listen to me! Listen to me!* And a few postcards from my twenties that I have taped to the windows. The silence that surrounds me and the near-sense of enforced discipline appear at first to be at odds with what I want to remember in these pages, the wild enthusiasm of youth, its idealism, chaotic desires and confusions. But this distinction is illusory. It's as if I have one folder named 'Politics' and another named 'Desire', and they will ultimately merge, their distinction blurred, between the covers of my book.

I appreciate the opportunity to write, even though it is intimidating and, occasionally, it turns into a chore. The hours between nine and four every day, and again after ten at night, are observed as quiet time at Yaddo. It is common for the writers and artists to work in their rooms or studios. The day stretches out as an invitation and a challenge. Even before breakfast, the staff in the kitchen packs sandwiches and carrot sticks into lunch bags emblazoned with our names in black ink. I write for a couple of hours and afterwards, with a cup of hot tea, sit down to read. Then, back to writing. At the moment, I'm reading from a collection of short stories, *My Mistress's Sparrow is Dead.**

A catalogue with a green cover showing the gate to Yaddo's

---

*The book takes its title from the writings of the Latin poet Catullus who was born around 84 BC. In his introduction to the collection, Jeffrey Eugenides explains that two of the verses that Catullus wrote concern his lover, Lesbia, and her pet sparrow. In one, the sparrow is the object of Lesbia's affection and play, denying Catullus her attention; in the other, because the sparrow is dead, Lesbia is sad, no longer in a mood for love and, moreover, her eyes are swollen from crying. And there, in the structure of those two fragments from Catullus, writes Eugenides, lies the key to the love story: *either there is a sparrow or the sparrow is dead.*

leafy estate sits on my desk. A white label at the bottom has printed on it the following request: *We kindly ask that you not take this copy with you upon your departure.* Inside are photographs of the artists and writers who have been guests at Yaddo. In this long and illustrious roster, including as it does several of my heroes, there is one name that leaps out at me—Agnes Smedley. Her story is told in the green book in a separate chapter called 'The Longest Stay'. This title has a story behind it: Smedley was a guest at Yaddo from July 1943 to March 1948. She was here for five years; today, no guest is allowed a stay longer than five weeks. The essay is by Smedley's biographer, Ruth Price. Smedley came to Yaddo after the publication of her book, *Battle Hymn to China*, which she had written after her return from there in 1949. Smedley's complex and surprising life contains in some measure the pasts of several of the characters in the book I'm writing—she was a writer from the working class, an activist committed to the Indian nationalist struggle, a reporter and possibly a spy in China, lover of a man from another country, etc. When I was in China many years ago, I had gone to see her tombstone in Beijing, in the Babaoshan cemetery for Chinese revolutionaries. A slab of marble with gold letters commemorating the memory of the 'American revolutionary writer and friend of the Chinese people'. In my thesis I had written about her relationship with Indians and also the Chinese but now I have an additional interest in her. In her novel, *Daughter of Earth*, Smedley transcribed from reality. Her book is part documentary, part make-believe. Another way to put it would be: it is neither a memoir, nor simply a novel. Smedley provides me a model for this work I'm writing. Even the fictional name that Smedley gave to her protagonist, Marie Rogers, had its basis in reality. Marie Rogers was a name that Smedley had invented years earlier: she had used it to sign all her letters during her involvement with the rebellious Indian nationalists in America.

I admire Smedley's loves. Such a wild, determined, wide-ranging search. What interested me from the start about Smedley was Vivian Gornick's discussion of the central contradiction of

*Daughter of Earth*: the fact that its fiery political protagonist is drawn to passion and abhors herself for it. And that this hatred gives her narrator's voice its strength but also limitation. Gornick writes, 'Never once does she acknowledge the stir of sensuality within her own being.' I agree with Gornick and yet think that Smedley was more self-aware than she allows. Smedley wrote of Marie Rogers and her struggle with a fair degree of self-recognition: 'No decent woman feels sex desire, no decent woman faces responsibility for it, I thought! Such had been my mode of thought for years. It was more comfortable, more respectable, to think of myself as completely innocent...' When I came across such lines I thought, of course, of the young Indian nationalists with their loneliness and their lust. The guilt that burdened Marie Rogers was also a weight on Har Dayal's conscience.

And Ehsaan! When I remember how Ehsaan was tormented by the FBI, I also think more tenderly of Smedley. The Yaddo book informs me that Smedley was suspected of being a spy and the FBI was watching her. A group of other artists at Yaddo, led by Robert Lowell, protested against Smedley's political activities. Lowell charged that Yaddo had been permeated 'by moods or influences that were politically or morally committed to Communism'. Smedley was forced to leave. Only a few weeks later, Lowell was committed to a private hospital in a state that was described as 'very nearly psychotic.' By then, the assistant to the director of Yaddo had already resigned from her position after confessing that she had been acting as an informant for the FBI. She was in the habit of submitting to the Bureau reports on the guests at Yaddo whom she suspected of Communist sympathies. A year later, Smedley was dead but the House of Un-American Activities Committee held a posthumous hearing on her activities. Ruth Price writes that it wasn't until the 1970s that, after years of obscurity and historical neglect, 'Smedley emerged as an unblemished heroine of the modern women's movement' and '*Daughter of Earth* was reissued to critical acclaim.'

Ehsaan never found fame. (When a critic called the writer Richard Stern 'almost famous for being not famous' I thought of my old professor.*) While reading about Smedley's resurrection, I asked myself whether Ehsaan's reputation would enjoy a similar rebirth. When Ehsaan died, he was struggling to establish in Pakistan a university that would teach the humanities. The university was never built; according to *The Economist*'s obituary of Ehsaan, he 'died before a rupee was raised for it'. If he came close to finding a sudden, unexpected visibility after his death, it happened after the September 11 attacks when Ehsaan's 1998 speech on terrorism found a new life on the Internet. In that speech, Ehsaan wanted terrorism by disaffected groups to be seen in relation to the much wider, more destructive use of state terrorism. In a characteristic move, he began by pointing out that President Reagan had welcomed the bearded mujahideen from Afghanistan to the White House and called them 'the moral equivalent of our Founding Fathers'. Then, once the Soviet Union had pulled out from Afghanistan, the same people became terrorists in the eyes of the US. A host of op-eds quoted Ehsaan in the months after the attacks, calling him 'prescient' and 'the face of progressive, secular Islam'. All this praise compelled me to look on YouTube for footage of Ehsaan in the years before I knew him. There were several clips of him, not just years but decades before the September 11 attacks, warning the US that the support of covert operations worldwide would one day come back to haunt America. If the US was going to be undemocratic elsewhere, peace was also unlikely at home. In one video of a teach-in from the late seventies, you can see Ehsaan explaining this contradiction by telling his audience: 'A man cannot be

---

*Later, I read in Stern's obituary in *The Times*, the following comment from Philip Roth but this reminded me not of what I admired about Ehsaan but about Roth himself: 'One of the reasons he never became famous—he was most famous among famous writers—was that his tone was hard to grasp, and some readers didn't feel morally settled,' Mr. Roth said, 'not because he was difficult or abstruse but because he was generous to all his characters. And that befuddled them.' (On second thought, these words apply to Ehsaan too. His generosity to all parties baffled the righteous guardians on both the left and the right.)

violent and sadistic to his mistress and gentle to his wife.'

⌐

Arranged in a pile in front of me are several books that I have
brought with me to Yaddo. On top of the pile sit books by
Elizabeth Hardwick and Renata Adler. Orgasms of twenty years
ago leave no memory, wrote Elizabeth Hardwick in *Sleepless
Nights*. Hardwick was delivering judgement on her character
Elizabeth's experience of sex with a handsome man named Alex.
Hardwick had just cited Casanova's grand declaration: 'The great
exhilaration to my spirits, greater than all my own pleasure, was
the joy of giving pleasure to a woman.' To which Hardwick, or
her character Elizabeth, had added: 'Some reason to doubt the
truth of that.'

Hardwick was right about doubting Casanova, but I have
doubts about Hardwick. At a recent conference in Minneapolis, I
was shaken by a memory while eating a buffet lunch by myself at
an Ethiopian restaurant on the West Bank. Well, that's not entirely
accurate. I had originally gone to that part of the university buildings
with a vague intention of knocking on the office-door of someone
I had once known. She was not from Minnesota but now taught
there. We had slept together in Connecticut and she had told me
her sexual drive was stronger than mine. Now, her phone number
was available in the university directory but I hesitated and then
decided to just eat lunch. Once, twenty years ago, she had reached
me at an airport. This was long before cellphones. I had heard
my name on the public address system and then picked up the
courtesy phone. She was laughing at the other end. I thought of
her laughter and it brought up another memory. Late one night, I
had read a short story to her on the phone. Pam Houston's 'How
to Talk to a Hunter'. She had let me sleep with her for the first
time a few nights after I read her that story.

Do past orgasms leave no memory? I'm thinking now of the
day only last year when I had walked past the store above which
Jennifer had lived. (A phrase I have used before: *so many years
had passed*.) It was a cold autumn day. The pale green paint on

the wall of her apartment was still the same and looked dirty. The window where I had often sat and read books now had a white fan placed there. I wondered who lived in the apartment now. I thought I might buy something in the store. A large handwritten sign with jagged edges, orange in colour, had been pasted to the front door: *No Public Restroom*.

⌢

I have also brought with me to Yaddo a daily planner from those early years. This afternoon, it is raining heavily when I sit near the window and open its pages. My father was a bureaucrat and at the beginning of each year he received a lot of calendars and these planners that we called diaries. This new, still untouched diary—a gift from a steel company—was lying around when I was about to leave India for the first time. I wrote the addresses of various people in it. In the first half, the names of those I needed to contact when I reached the US, and in the second half, the people I'd need to write to in India. I hadn't touched this diary for years until I decided to bring these old forgotten materials to Yaddo. It is stuffed with slips of paper, business cards, even newspaper cuttings, all held together with a rubber band stiff with age. Each name in it is a story of an appointment, a search for a story, even a missed opportunity. At the back of the diary, I find a list of the things I wanted to buy when I had gone back to India for the first time. I had forgotten this list but when I see it now it brings back vividly a year in my life. Spices for my thesis adviser, Ehsaan Ali; a kajal stick and earrings for Cai Yan; toys for the children of the Jamaican professor who had hired me as his research assistant for the following semester; beedis for two of my fellow teaching assistants; an ankle bracelet for another professor's wife; tea for the two women who were secretaries in my department at the university; a VHS tape of a Shashi Kapoor movie (*Shakespearewallah*) for Maya because she wanted to write a paper on it for her postcolonial theory class; press clippings for someone called Ravi. Where are all these people now?

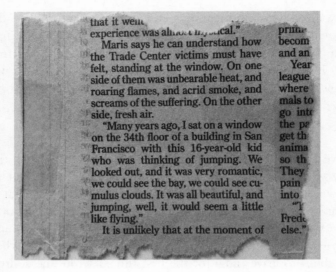

that it wen..
experience was aln..... u.,...cal."
Maris says he can understand how
the Trade Center victims must have
felt, standing at the window. On one
side of them was unbearable heat, and
roaring flames, and acrid smoke, and
screams of the suffering. On the other
side, fresh air.
"Many years ago, I sat on a window
on the 34th floor of a building in San
Francisco with this 16-year-old kid
who was thinking of jumping. We
looked out, and it was very romantic,
we could see the bay, we could see cu-
mulus clouds. It was all beautiful, and
jumping, well, it would seem a little
like flying."
It is unlikely that at the moment of

And do those people ever wonder where I am? Until recently,
just the last semester, in fact, I was teaching creative writing at a
small liberal arts college in Connecticut. For the past ten years,
I taught a variety of courses. The most popular course was one I
call 'Literature of 9/11'. It started as a report on what had been
written in the days following the September 11 bombings. I also
included what Ehsaan had written in the years leading up to the
attack. Then, my course widened into a study of novels by writers
across the world containing commentary on the attacks and their
aftermath. Over the years, I included in the course books on
Guantanamo and then the violence abroad. 'In the shadow of no
towers', to borrow a phrase from Art Spiegelman, except that the
shadow falls over Afghanistan and Iraq.

Another course that I taught more than once was called
'Professor of Desire'. We started with the Roth novel of that
name and then read Francine Prose's *Blue Angel*; *The Lover* by
Marguerite Duras and *A Sport and a Pastime* by James Salter; other
pieces and stories by Terry Castle, Nadine Gordimer, Jeanette
Winterson, David Wojnarowicz, Colm Tóibín. Also an excerpt
from Hanif Kureishi's *The Black Album*. The course ended with

a reading of J. M. Coetzee's *Disgrace*. The idea was to introduce into the space of the classroom, in a frank way, the issue of desire. At times, to celebrate the play of desire; at other times, to question it or condemn it. The course was successful because the students wrote essays that were themselves fresh and open, even if at times rigid and self-righteous. I wanted to risk putting on the table what had not been explicitly acknowledged in that space before. Not everyone liked the class, of course. The last time I taught it, one of the evaluations mentioned that the student felt uncomfortable throughout the course, especially during a reading of a story by Jonathan Ames. The story was about a creative writing instructor watching, with undisguised lust, the coeds at his Bryn Mawr-like college playing tennis. In the background, because these are the days following 9/11, the president has announced the bombing of Afghanistan. The narrator craves what he calls a 'womb shelter'. The evaluation said: 'As a student, and as a female, I felt totally objectified and it wasn't always clear how close or distant the instructor stood from what was being portrayed in the story.'

This past semester I was very excited about a course I was teaching for the first time. The course was titled 'In-Between Novels'. We read titles that were part-novel, part-essay. Most of the books that I have brought to Yaddo were on that syllabus:

> Elizabeth Hardwick, *Sleepless Nights*;
> Renata Adler, *Speedboat*;
> David Markson, *This is Not a Novel*;
> John Berger, *G.*;
> W. G. Sebald, *Rings of Saturn*;
> J. M. Coetzee, *Elizabeth Costello*;
> Lydia Davis, *Collected Stories*;
> Teju Cole, *Open City*;
> Jenny Offill, *Dept. of Speculation*;
> Ben Lerner, *10:04*.

My syllabus asked the students to keep a notebook. Students were advised to practice a type of reading that was slow, meditative, relaxed, so that the reading inspired students to write hybrid texts of their own. Perhaps trying too hard to sound poetic, although I felt I was only trying to be specific, I had written in the syllabus: 'Brief essays or fragments and sometimes photographs—like dried flowers found between the pages of a book.'* These essays could be only a line or two long, but I also urged them to write longer pieces. In the syllabus, I had provided the following instruction:

> Let the news that you encounter, as well as other knowledges, both old and new, enter into a chain of

---

*Annette, one of the students I liked the most last semester, wrote about her parents taking her to China. They arrived in Beijing and drove out four hours to a village where Annette had been found abandoned as a baby. The heat was intense. Annette was only twelve at the time of this visit. Her adoptive parents, who are white, wanted Annette to have a close connection to China. When they reached the village, they found rickety trucks loaded with green melons blocking the way. The entire breadth of the road was covered with smashed rinds rotting in the sun. Annette noticed that the black oxen pulling the carts loaded with melons used their tails to swish away the flies that were everywhere. Even now Annette remembers the smell, in the surrounding heat, of animal manure and rotting fruit. A translator had accompanied Annette and her parents. This was the first time Annette was among people whose hair was black like hers. She looked at the old women sitting on mats in the marketplace and at the others who were milling about or standing and staring at her. These were people who looked like her, high cheekbones, the same nose, slim build. About twenty villagers gathered around them and the translator asked the villagers if they remembered anyone who could have left a baby in the market twelve years ago. Annette wrote that there was a flutter in her heart, a struggle of hope. The villagers were kind, they said Annette did indeed look like them, but it was too long ago and they couldn't remember.

I liked the essay because it told me about the impossibility of return. The past has closed its doors and thrown away the key. You cannot go back home again. Annette's piece also reminded me of the time, about five years ago, when I was an adjunct instructor teaching in Rochester and a woman I was involved with suggested we adopt a baby from China. We went to a couple of informational meetings with adoption agencies in sad bureaucratic buildings downtown but nothing came of it.

reading and writing. I imagine us drawing our bright constellations of ideas, half-way between essay-writing and storytelling. This could be a daily practice, like a diary of your reading. Try to be real and inventive.

But the course could not be completed. Due to a minor controversy, two weeks prior to the end of the semester, I was asked to take a leave of absence. This isn't the occasion to discuss that matter. I'm not at liberty to share anything anyway. Suffice it to say that I've been turned into an object of curiosity. Allow me to narrate a different story.

Two years after being exhibited at the 1904 St. Louis World Fair, Ota Benga, a young man from the Congo, was brought to the Bronx Zoo and locked in a cage to be displayed under a sign saying 'African Pygmy'. Ota Benga was a member of the Congolese tribe of Mbuti pygmies; he stood less than five feet tall and weighed only 100 pounds. He spoke no English. He arrived at the Bronx Zoo wearing a white linen suit in the company of an anthropologist who was broke. Benga had with him a wooden box, a set of arrows, and his pet chimpanzee. The anthropologist had contacted the zoo's director in the hopes of securing an apartment for Benga on the zoo's premises. The director of the Bronx zoo decided it was better to display Benga in the orangutan's cage. 'Bones were scattered about the cage to add a whiff of cannibalism.' The zoo attracted as many as 40,000 visitors a day.

'Is that a man?' a visitor asked.

I too have been put in a cage. A cage that is invisible but no less real. He is not like us, these anthropologists of academic behaviour hiss around me. But the rest of the narrative runs in the opposite direction. I'm shunned. There are no visitors.

*Your Honour, before this disruption, I was planning a course on a particular kind of essay writing. Short, political essays. Nearly parables. In other words, I had a plan that has now been derailed.*

The photograph above, taken with my phone, is of one of the postcards I have brought with me to Yaddo. It stands propped against the wall to my left. On my first visit back to India, I purchased a whole set of postcards, cheap reproductions on paper that have begun to yellow now, at the National Gallery of Modern Art in Delhi. This one is a print of a painting, oil on canvas, by Vivan Sundaram. It is simply titled 'Guddo'.

Guddo is the girl on the right, beautiful and melancholic, but wraith-like, as if she were only spirit. Unlike the older woman in the background, who is substantially rendered, her skin brown and her eyes directed at the viewer, Guddo is like a ghost. Is it because she has removed herself, her spirit fleeing from what is being done to her, so that now she stands apart? Around the two women, the landscape, as if in an Indian miniature, is luminous and colourful. There are red flames on the roof of the structure to the left. It is a police chowki. Through the open window, we see a man in uniform, his trousers unbuttoned, pressing down on a body. Another man in uniform is drunkenly sprawled in the foreground. The painting had remained with me all these years because of Guddo's beauty and her silence, the thin dupatta draped across her chest, her hands quietly clasped before her: as a viewer you are held by the mystery and moved to a sense of anger because of the tableau of violence on which Guddo has been forced to turn her back.

Several years ago, I got a chance to meet Sundaram and ask him about 'Guddo'. I had just published my biography of the Bollywood actor Manoj Bajpai and had been invited to the Jaipur Literature Festival. I appeared on a panel with journalists who had written about Hindi films. After the panel had done its work, I went looking for a toilet. The venue used to be a palace, but there wasn't a decent bathroom to take a leak. I wandered into a courtyard where men sitting on their haunches around a fire were cooking food in huge vats. The scene reminded me of a Hindu wedding. Under a cement peacock, over a dark doorway, I found a welcoming pink curtain stirring in the breeze. This was the room I was looking for. Except that the person standing over the urinal, his hands and eyes focused on a hidden point below, was the right-wing historian Niall Ferguson. What was Niall Ferguson doing in India? This is what had happened while I had been gone from the country: India had changed behind my back. There were now huge literary festivals held here, and colonialism had become a respectable word again. I was washing my hands when Vivan Sundaram walked into the bathroom, a slight man in a Nehru vest, and easily recognizable from his photographs.

When we came outside, Sundaram and I stood under a tree and talked. Sundaram told me that it was when he returned to Delhi from London, where he was studying art at the Slade School, that he painted 'Guddo'. For his models, he used the woman who was a helper in his father's house and her daughter. 'Guddo' was a response, he said, to the Mathura rape case. The name stirred a memory. Mathura was the orphan tribal girl raped by two policemen in Maharashtra. The lower court judge had acquitted the rapists; the judge felt that Mathura's consent could be assumed because she was 'habituated to sexual intercourse'. The case went on to the highest court where, once again, the policemen were deemed not guilty. The judge declared that because Mathura 'was used to sex, she might have incited the policemen to have intercourse with her'. It was only after widespread protests led by a group of activist law professors that Mathura's story came to the attention of the public. A decade after she was raped in the police chowki—the building on fire in Sundaram's painting—Indian rape laws were changed. If a woman who had been raped stated that she did not provide consent to sexual intercourse then the court would have to presume the same.

⌐

Ehsaan's stories were never confessions or little accounts of the private self. Small details led you to the big picture. 'Why didn't Qamroo sit on his chair?' That question came at the end of a quick narrative that wasn't too much bothered about developing the interiority of a character. There was a certain flatness in the account, and a great deal of abstraction lay behind its telling.

His stories were almost parables. Similarly, when John Berger rewrote Ehsaan's story about his migration to Pakistan it became a parable about a revolutionary life.*

Some years ago, I travelled to Kashmir, a beautiful place devastated by war, to meet a nurse in a town called Sopore. I wanted to interview the nurse because her husband was on death row, accused of an act of terrorism, but she was sceptical of journalists and refused to talk to me. It was acknowledged by many that her husband had not received a fair trial. He had been badly tortured but he had nothing to tell. A police officer in Kashmir told a reporter that he had poured petrol into the accused man's rectum and had still been unable to get any information. In any case, the nurse brushed me away. A few months after my return from Kashmir, I heard on NPR that they were holding a short-story writing contest. A prompt would be provided and you could write a 600-word piece and submit it on their website. I thought of the woman in Kashmir when I

---

*On the night of 4 November 1975, Ehsaan delivered a lecture at a teach-in at the University of Chicago. Activist intellectuals had spoken all day. Ehsaan got up to speak when it was already past 11 p.m. The black-and-white video is available on YouTube. Ehsaan can be heard articulating his words softly and slurring a bit because, as he admitted during the talk, he was a bit drunk. He says, 'The Americans do not understand the war in Indo-China because they do not have a sense of the tragic. How is a sense of tragic to be acquired?' He describes a short film, fifteen minutes long, that would be shown before the main feature in theatres in the US. This was in the sixties. A man drives a long American car to a beautiful beach. Blue skies, blue sea. The man casts a line. The fish take the bait, and he catches one fish after another. You hear Ehsaan repeat the bit about how beautiful everything is, the sea, the sand, the sky. He dwells on the image of the hooked fish as they writhe in agony. Then the fisherman gets hungry and takes out his sandwich. He takes a bite and gets hooked. You see him dragged into the sea, making the same kind of movement the fish were making. You don't find the scene beautiful and this is the first time that you witness the scene from the point of view of the fish. The parable was about the need for a country that had never known defeat to be dragged out of its complacency. This happened when the war came home: with casualties in battle, with loss to the exchequer, Watergate. His voice rising, Ehsaan says that the universities ought to teach the children of America the meaning of tragedy.

got the prompt: *The nurse left work at five o'clock.* I was sitting in my office in Connecticut, looking at the red Japanese maples outside the window, a few students playing a game of tag in the distance. With Ehsaan in mind, and also Berger, whom I'd never met, I wrote this story and sent it to NPR:

The nurse left work at five o'clock.

She had seen the dead woman's husband sitting near the entrance under the yellow sign that Doctor Ahmed had hung some months ago. *While You Wait, Meditate.* He sat with his arms crossed, elbows cupped in the palms of his hands, and hadn't looked up when she passed him on her way out.

Just before lunch, a convoy had come from the Army camp. A dark-skinned soldier, holding a small rifle in his left hand, threw open the office door and announced the Colonel. Doctor Ahmed had automatically stood up.

The Colonel was plump. He looked calm and extremely clean, the way bullfrogs do, gleaming green and gold in the mud. He put his baton on the table and asked the nurse to leave the office.

When Doctor Ahmed rang his bell, the nurse went back in and was told to get his wife, Zakia, from their home on the top floor. Usually, he just called her on the phone. The nurse hurried up, guessing what she had to say.

Doctor Zakia was a paediatrician, good for offering women advice about breast-feeding, but she understood at once why she was to do the postmortem. The soldiers put the stretcher in the operating room and left. When the doctor removed the white sheet, she made a noise, and began reciting the Fatiha in a high voice. It was difficult for her to continue the examination—she had a grown-up daughter.

Then the nurse was alone with the young woman for over four hours, cleaning her of the blood and the filth, and then stitching her up. The abdomen and thighs had turned green, but this was to be expected. There was a pronounced swelling of the tongue and lips.

The nurse wondered whether the body would last till the funeral. If there was a protest, it would take the entire day in the sun for the procession to reach the cemetery.

A year ago, a doctor in the north had revealed that the corpse brought to him was of a woman who had been gang-raped. This was a mistake. The Army put out the story that the woman used to come to the camp for customers and that her husband found out and had probably got her killed.

The nurse, Sharifa, was thirty-three. Twelve years ago, her husband had disappeared. No one was likely to have performed a postmortem on his body, but she would have liked to know where he was buried. She stared at the back of her gloved hands. Then she turned them over, as if she were praying, and studied the film of dark coagulating matter on her fingers.

Doctor Zakia would probably tell the family that the body had been washed thrice. It wouldn't help—but how was she to save them? No one teaches you in nursing school to cover cigarette burns on the body or to stitch up torn nipples.

When she finally stepped out of the room she was startled to see a dozen soldiers in the hallway. She met the eye of the one closest to her and flinched, but he was quiet, even shy, like a dog that has brought in a squirrel and dropped it on the carpet.

At six, she was sitting in front of the television in her tiny living room. And there she was, the young woman in her wedding photograph. The newsreader said the body had been found in a ditch after the woman had gone missing for twenty-six hours. She had been struck sometime at night by a speeding vehicle.

✓

Authoritarianism is the mother (or father) of parabolic forms. With its control of the systems of signification, it forces a new, unnatural language: thus, with the ban on the use of 'June 4' in Internet postings in China, because of censors' sensitivity to any mention of the 4 June 1989 Tiananmen Square Massacre, the emergence of May 35th as a covert reference. Chinese writer Yu Hua has written: May 35th freedom is an art form. To evade censorship when expressing their opinions on the Internet, Chinese people give full rein to the rhetorical functions of language, elevating to a sublime level both innuendo and metaphor, parody and hyperbole, conveying sarcasm and scorn through veiled gibes and wily indirection.

ſ

My all-time favourite parable appears on the opening pages of Milan Kundera's *The Book of Laughter and Forgetting*. The communist dictator steps out on the balcony of the palace in Prague to speak to the crowd massed below. It is snowing. A solicitous comrade standing next to the dictator takes off his fur hat and puts it on the leader's head. A photograph from that day, of the dictator delivering his address, with his comrade standing next to him, is published in history books and national posters. A few years later, the comrade who had put his hat on the dictator's head is disgraced and hanged. He is banished from that photograph, and from history, by the propaganda department. Where he once stood, there is only the palace's bare wall. All that remains of the dead man in history is his fur hat.

ſ

When I find accounts of experiments and their results, they come to me as parables. Example: Psychologist Spike Lee found that telling harmful lies makes people desire mouthwash, whereas writing harmful lies makes people desire hand sanitizer. 'Findings', *Harper's* magazine, December 2010, p. 84.

Another example: if you were wearing imitation designer clothing or accessories, you were more likely to engage in cheating. Participants in a study were all given authentic sunglasses but some were told that they were wearing fake products. When subjected to a test, a much larger percentage of those who thought they had imitation products also cheated on their responses.

ſ

At Yaddo, I write every day and in the afternoon at 4.30 I do yoga. The class is led by a young American visual artist who learned yoga during her visits to India. Last night, this artist

screened her short film for those at the colony and, strangely
enough, because of the film I woke up this morning from a dream
in which I was smoking pot with Nina. The film was set in the
seventies in Pittsburgh during a Steelers-Raiders football game.
The two main characters are teenagers, a boy and a girl. The film
was about the city of Pittsburgh, and that is why I thought of
Nina, but it was also about the boy's inexpressible desire for the
girl. The two of them were smoking upstairs while the game was
on the TV downstairs. Standing near the window, after sucking
on the joint, the girl said that she didn't even like football. The
boy said that he loved it, and that watching football in his family
was like going to church. The girl raised her eyes and asked softly,
*Then why are you here instead of watching the game?* He hadn't been
talking much; he was shy but his look was filled with a kind of
dry-mouthed yearning. Now he appeared to be studying her face
before he kissed her for one fierce second. The next moment they
were on the bed where their movements built to a climax just as
the game ended with a dramatic touchdown.

The filmmaker is white and her skin is covered with tattoos.
On her right underarm are the dates that also appear at the
end of the film we watched last night—the date of birth and
death of her boyfriend. She has a tattoo of the Goddess Kali
on her right forearm. On her ankle, a red female pirate figure,
holding a camera. On her left shoulder, a peacock with its dark,
shimmering tail draped over her skin. When I remarked on
the fine dialogue between the youngsters in the film, she said
it hardly mattered what people said to each other—what was
important was everything that was left unsaid.

But that couldn't be true. I thought immediately of the women
I had loved. Then, I thought of the girl in the film, how she had
teased open a possibility by saying something. It *had* mattered,
what people said! Was the filmmaker saying something about *me*
when she made that remark about the importance of what has
been left unsaid? It is possible that she took note of my silent
scrutiny of all her tattoos, and reached a reasonable conclusion
about my curiosity.

I became a US citizen last year. The ceremony was held at noon on a Saturday in the high school in a town nearby. A table was set with twenty miniature American flags on it. And a stack of certificates. The ceremony got underway with three pudgy boy-scouts bringing on to the stage a large US flag. They held their fingers up in a salute, hands close to their temple as if they were in pain. We were informed that together we represented citizens of Somalia, Mexico, El Salvador, Jamaica and India. The Somalis were one large family, dressed in shiny clothes. The judge, a man of Filipino origin, asked us to repeat the oath. Like everyone else, I held my right hand up. Once that was done, the judge said, Congratulations, you are now citizens of the United States. You have forsaken the country of your birth in exchange for the rights and privileges of this country. He repeated the word privilege, saying, You are not entitled to be in the United States. Instead, it is a privilege. There is no better country in the world.

But I only felt like a man without a country and tears came to my eyes. I was crying perhaps only because the judge, in a poor, inaccurate choice of words, had used the word *forsaken*. The man next to me, a native of Guadalajara, thought these were tears of happiness and began to congratulate me.

The judge said that he was now going to ask a man 'who embodied the American experience and was a hero' to speak to us for a few minutes. A large black man with bad knees now climbed the stage: he had played for the Denver Broncos in the 1977 Super Bowl. I don't remember his name. The speaker said, 'It's been a long journey for you, you have endured pain and tribulation...' I wondered whether this was true of any one of us. The speaker wiped his brow with a handkerchief and the cloth, maybe because it was new, stuck to his forehead. He said that he appreciated diversity and was glad to welcome us to this country. Then a young girl named Rachel with drooping eyelids and a melancholic smile walked to the microphone and sang the national anthem rather beautifully. I was surprised that the Mexican gentleman to my right seemed to know the words to that song. When the ceremony was over, people took pictures.

In the car, certificate in hand, I wished I had eaten lunch before coming. I hadn't driven longer than two miles on I-84 when I saw the flashing lights of a police cruiser behind me. The cop was an elderly man with a thin moustache. When he asked for my licence and registration, I picked up the US flag and the certificate and showed them to him.

—Officer, I've just become a citizen. Only ten minutes ago. I was rushing home to tell my wife.

—Did you also get your licence today?

—No sir, I've been driving—no, I didn't get it today.

—Then I won't be needing these. Your license and registration, please.

The ticket he wrote was for a hundred and sixty-five dollars. I thought he had behaved fairly and hadn't questioned the lie about my having a wife—but I was also suspicious that I had been punished for having become a citizen.

As I proceeded to my house, driving under the speed limit now, I thought of Jennifer with gratitude. She had taken me to the DMV office in Harlem in her old blue Volvo. I had been living in the US for maybe four or five months by then. I drove her car for the test. The man who was the examiner turned out to be a Pakistani. I was afraid he was going to fail me. As I followed his instructions (please change lane, turn left, park on the right, etc.) the thought came that I should get on friendly terms with him. I tried to make small talk.

—Where are you from in Pakistan, Mr Alvi?

—Do not talk, he said, his eyes fixed on the road ahead. Please drive.

When the test was over, he said I had made one mistake but I had successfully passed the test. I said adaab to him. We shook hands. Jennifer said that she was quite sure, even when she had picked me up that morning, that I was going to get the licence. Then she laughed and said, I became certain when I saw that you were going to be judged by your brother.

That far-off winter day came back to me in the car when I was given the ticket after the citizenship ceremony. Must have been a day in early December. To celebrate we went for lunch to an Indian restaurant on Amsterdam Avenue. I was talking in Hindi to the Punjabi woman who was the owner, and Jennifer joked that after I had had my fill of white women I would return to India to live there and enter an arranged marriage. She imitated a head wobble and began to laugh loudly. She shut her eyes and her mouth formed a rictus. Her face had turned red. I had no idea where this sudden bitterness was coming from—her behaviour was unusual but it probably made me think that this was the real Jennifer. It is possible that *that* was the moment when I began to move away.

So, Jennifer, I don't have an Indian wife. And actually I'm a citizen now. This is not to say that you were wrong and I was right but simply that nothing turns out the way we imagine. (It certainly hasn't for me.) But thank you for taking me to the DMV.

*Your Honour, this is not a parable, of course. I have narrated this auto-story, ha ha, because I was in the car yesterday driving into Saratoga Springs to buy wine. On the car radio there was a report on children learning about death at a grief support centre. The children were being encouraged to process the death of a family member. So many kids whose fathers had committed suicide, in some* cases with a gun to the head. Today is Father's Day and I can't stop thinking of the voices of the children I heard yesterday. One little girl, the reporter said, had watched her mother have a heart attack. In the playroom at the grief support centre, this girl picked up the toy phone and spent the entire session dialling 911. 'Hi 911, my Mom's dying. Hurry. Come quick.' 'Hi 911, my Grandma's dying. Hurry. Come quick.' And listening to the show I thought of Jennifer. I said nothing, wrote nothing, to her after she asked me to leave her house. We never talked frankly about anything. The story I'm telling here of the trip to the DMV and to the restaurant is my first step in that direction.

> I can't write without a reader. It's precisely like a kiss—you can't do it alone.
>
> —John Cheever

At Yaddo, you aren't handed the WiFi password until you ask for it. The idea is to promote the kind of solitude that allows you to work. I haven't asked. I would like to keep the world at bay. I'll face what cannot be avoided any longer when I return. For such a long time, for years, I had wanted to write about the preoccupations that had taken root when I was young. But recent events in my life have stained this exercise.

The police was not involved in this case at any stage. I must first ask you to keep this in mind. Nor was there a manipulation of the sort that you come across every month in the news. Just last month I read of a famous philosopher at Yale accused of sexual harassment. An ethicist who used his power to lure young, idealistic women into his hotel bed. At a conference in a foreign city he told his female student sharing his room to come into bed. He wanted her to watch *The Constant Gardener* on his laptop with the lights in the room turned off. Later, when she resisted his advances, as the expression goes, he denied her a fellowship.

That is not me.

A female student of mine, prompted by another student and, I have reason to believe, a faculty member, approached the dean of the faculty with a complaint about an incident in my office one afternoon. And there is a procedure in place for such things—I was asked to go on leave while there was an investigation, but I decided to resign instead. Although I had only wanted to show my contempt for the proceedings it is more likely that others saw this as an admission of wrongdoing.

This faculty member in another department at my college, also of Indian origin like me, drew attention to the case of the law dean at UC Berkeley. This man had harassed his administrative assistant with demands for hugs and kisses. The administration had first gone easy on him, docking ten per cent of his salary and only requesting an apology; this year, the news came out that he had finally been asked to go on leave after the woman filed a lawsuit. The university will have to settle. This odious man at Berkeley, now back in his office on campus, is also Indian. I think this last detail might have helped my superiors make their decision against me.

These people know nothing. The Minister of Sport, or was he the Minister of Transport, I can't remember, a stocky, bearded man who rose through the rough ranks of Delhi hoodlums associated with various political parties, told reporters recently that the rape incidents in a Rajasthan school were just an example of young people having fun. Are my critics confusing me with that vulgar lout?

The girl at my college, the student who initiated the complaint, was a sophomore. An English and film double major. She would turn twenty, I learned later, two months after the incident. (Which means her birthday is right about now. I see her face close above the cake, blowing out the candles.) She was planning on going to London, to University College, for her junior year abroad. I do not know if she is still following her plans. I have been forbidden by my dean to contact her or say anything about the case.

Let me then talk about my dean instead. He is a mild-mannered scholar of Spanish Literature and a reputed pianist. My unmarried status had offered me the advantage of being welcome at several formal dinners at his home. Drinks in the living room, the large French windows flung open when the weather was warm.

A framed letter from Gabriel García Márquez hanging above the mantelpiece; next to it a photograph of the dean smiling beside a handsome Mario Vargas Llosa who sported a pale green shirt with the widest collar I've ever seen in my life. Dinner served in the adjoining room, almost always a catered affair with food from all around the world, Indonesian on one night, Mexican on another, or, once when there was a barbecue, the sausages and burgers helpfully identified as Canadian.

When I was summoned to the meeting, in an empty conference room next to the college president's office, the dean sat with a yellow legal pad and a pen on the other side of a large dark desk. He was extremely polite. I was handed a letter signed by the president. The dean said that I could take a few minutes to read the letter so that he could try and clarify anything that was unclear. The first two paragraphs mixed admonitory remarks with legalistic phrases that remained impenetrable to me. I was in no mood to ask questions. The compliance report I had submitted three years earlier in response to the Title IX seminar on campus was now being seen as contradictory and incomplete. The letter added that cognizance had been taken of the fact that I had taught a course in the past called 'The Professor of Desire'. The student evaluations from my past classes were going to be subjected to scrutiny for disturbing signs that had possibly been overlooked. I was free to respond or appeal within two weeks.

I didn't respond or appeal during the two weeks. But word was already out. When I took a box to collect the few books I had in my office, I saw a man in the parking lot duck back into his blue Prius to avoid me. I had often played squash with him when I first joined the college seven years ago. He was a professor in Psychology, working on a book on incarcerated youth and family ties. Inside the building, I had another bizarre encounter. The administrative assistant in my department's office had always been nice to me; we had exchanged bottles of wine at Christmas. She gave me a tight smile and found herself unable to greet me. I still had the empty box in my hand. When I turned

back from the mailbox in the office, she said, Have a nice day.
*Have a nice day!*

Am I whining? Do I appear to sound like a victim? Is this
beginning to tax your tolerance?

People can draw their own conclusions. What I resent most
deeply is that a whole lifetime of history of being around women,
the terrible negotiation of all relationships, and, above all, the
unknotting of pleasure because of what happens between people in
love and sometimes strangers, has been reduced to one encounter.
In the conference room that morning, I looked at the dean in his
crisp shirt and his stylish, expensive rimless glasses, his pianist
hands playing a slow adagio in the air, and wondered whether
he had revised every idea he had once had about me. The most
disappointing thing in the world is an apology. It would have
been pointless.

Nor did I want to proclaim my innocence. No, far from it.
Instead, if I wanted, which I didn't, I could tell him in great
detail about all my fuck-ups. The glory and the mess of it all.
Except, the terrible futility of writing official responses that no
one will ever read. I know that the dean likes Jorge Luis Borges.
He is no doubt familiar with a short prose-poem by Borges about
a man who looks like Borges in a stone tower in a deserted
place in Iran. He is sitting at a wooden table in a cell without
door or window. He is writing a poem about a man in another
circular cell writing a poem about a man who looks like Borges
in another circular cell.

Such writing is a dream of loneliness. I want to have no
truck with it.

I have seen the declassified FBI files on Ehsaan's activities
in this country. There is no element of doubt in those files, or
much of ambivalence; certainly there is no feeling; the masked
writer of those reports, name redacted, the anonymous hack
of the state, isn't required to risk vulnerability. All of which is
understandable, of course, but my purpose here is to engage in
magical thinking.

3. [X] Because of background is potentially dangerous; or has been identified as member or
participant in communist movement; or has been under active investigation as member
of other group or organization inimical to U. S.

4. [ ] U. S. citizens or residents who defect from the U. S. to countries in the Soviet or
Chinese Communist blocs and return.

5. [ ] Subversives, ultrarightists, racists and fascists who meet one or more of the following
criteria:

   (a) [ ] Evidence of emotional instability (including unstable residence and
   employment record) or irrational or suicidal behavior;
   (b) [ ] Expressions of strong or violent anti-U. S. sentiment;
   (c) [ ] Prior acts (including arrests or convictions) or conduct or statements
   indicating a propensity for violence and antipathy toward good order
   and government.

6. [ ] Individuals involved in illegal bombing or illegal bomb-making.

Photograph [X] has been furnished    [ ] enclosed    [ ] is not available
[ ] may be available through _____.

                                                        Very truly yours,

                                                        John Edgar Hoover
                                                             Director

1 - Special Agent in Charge (Enclosure(s) 1
U. S. Secret Service, Boston   (RM).

I'm back on a plane that has now reached New York City.
I'm returning from my research trip to China. The young woman
I'm in love with is neither from my country nor from the country
where I'm now living. We are working with a mentor we adore.
My Chinese lover returned just the previous week. She is back
in her university apartment and when I look out of the plane's
window I do so with the certain knowledge that of the millions
of glittering lights beneath me there is one light that is hers. This
naïve thought might be the result of my long travel, this sense of
exhaustion that I've endured during my research. It's also possible
that, just a generation removed from rural life, the trappings of
urban civilization dazzle me. In our mentor's class, a line from
Trotsky: 'Yet every time a peasant's horse shies in terror before
the blinding lights of an automobile on the Russian road at night,
a conflict of two cultures is reflected in the episode.' I am and
I am *not* the peasant; I am *never* not the horse. I marvel at the
fact that there is one phone number, the right numbers in the

right combination given to the phone operator, which will make
the phone ring in the room of the one person in the world who
is waiting for me. All of that is true. But there's more that I
want in that moment. I want to present my best self to my lover
and, tired as I am, I want to sleep with my limbs entangled in
hers. As I look out of the plane window into the night, I can
taste her in my mouth.

To end this book, then, here is the story I wrote for Yaddo.

But first a question: aren't we condemned to repeat our stories
and write the same book over and over again? Or, to put it
differently, don't we fall in love every time with the same person
and make the same mistakes? I sometimes feel that all my life
I've been faithful only to the fact of this experience—so that all
my nostalgia is for my familiar struggles and my all-too-familiar
failings. An account of what is familiar becomes the story of
one's life. *It is life.* I have always wanted to be in love; all I have
managed to do is tell a story. That is not entirely accurate. I'm
like the monkey who, crouching in front of a mirror, tries on a
hat. He is only imitating his master. But the monkey has plans
for this summer night. Although it is difficult to think clearly, or
to remember previous nights, not least because his idea of who
he is or *was* is mixed up with what he thinks he must become,
he would like to step out precisely at seven. He will pause to
sniff the open air. Then, he will sally forth. Hat on his head,
arm in arm with someone who knows about his journey, who
will turn her head and smile when he starts humming his song.

## You Can Get It If You Really Want

Reeti was the daughter of the Chief Engineer of the Public Works Department in Patna. I remembered having seen her father's name in the papers, but couldn't recall any specific details because one scandal soon gets swallowed up by another. I met Reeti at Stony Brook where we were both new international students and, when I found out she was from Patna, I asked her whose daughter she was. With the naïve and often assertive morality that had been a part of my upbringing, I looked at her face, so full of allure, and her beautiful, naked arms, and was surprised that she appeared so entirely untouched by her father's corruption.

This was more true at the beginning of our friendship. For her part, she was often unconcerned and not the least self-conscious about anything. Each week, I would find scattered about in the apartment or on the dining table pages from a letter written by her father. The words of the letter were arranged in neat blue lines on sheets that, on the back, had words and figures printed on them. Here is an example:

> TENDER Information
> TR 1977273 Drainage and Embankment Related works in Connection with Proposed Phulwarisharif-Pataliputra Line Bihar 3,50,71,376
> TR 1977063 14/12/1995 Hiring of Road Vehicle (TATA SUMO or similar) Bihar Value 6,97,837
> TR 1968823 Development of TT Parking Area at Patna LPG Bottling Plant, Gidhha, Bihar. Refer document 8/12/1995.

At Stony Brook, we had been friends for maybe three or four months before becoming lovers. Other Indian students, like Chawla or Rashmi, would talk to Reeti in English, but I didn't. *Kya madam, kya haal hai? Bahut sundar lag rahin hain aap.* She would smile and say, *Tum bhi na, ek dum...* Once, Perry Anderson came to our university and spoke about language and politics in

South Asia. I got up and asked him if he had thought of Hindi speakers, and speakers of other Indian languages, or whether his understanding was limited to English. Some of my classmates said things like *I liked your intervention* but I was more struck by what Reeti said. *Abhay, You sound just like my father when he speaks in public.* I felt slightly weird but I knew that this couldn't be all bad.

Then, it was Holi. To celebrate the festival, the Indian Students' Association screened *Silsila.* An hour into the movie, I began to weep. It was becoming embarrassing, and I turned to Reeti and said, as if I needed to explain something, *This is like being home again. We never watched movies without crying.* This was true. My father has been a stern, patrician figure, but when we got a TV, he watched the Bombay films and his cheeks were forever wet and glistening. I would look at him and find myself moved, at least when I was younger.

I think my tears and my cheerful confession affected Reeti that night. She cried too, and in the dark of the theatre she leaned her head on my shoulder. I did not want the film to end, and in a way it didn't, because without ever putting it into words, Reeti and I found that we had become lovers.

Reeti was a serious student. She never missed any classes and spent long hours at the library reading everything that her professors recommended. When I looked at her, I saw a very bright future ahead for her. I was studying history but I wanted to be a filmmaker. My plan was a simple one: I'd sell the land we had near Barauni, I had no need to be a farmer, and I'd use that money to make a film like *Teesri Kasam.* Of course, I had no training, and didn't know how I'd do it, but that was my dream. Unlike Reeti, I didn't have a straight path joining my present and my future. But I wasn't too worried. At the Dark Grape, a bar on Eisenhower Road, I had many times put quarters in the jukebox to hear Jimmy Cliff singing 'You Can Get It If You Really Want'.

I didn't go to classes as regularly as Reeti did; I certainly didn't spend as much time in the library reading. But, nevertheless, I tried to stay true to the idea I had developed about myself—I wrote a little, I watched films (becoming a fan of Truffaut's *Stolen Kisses*, which I saw seventeen times), and I began living with Reeti.

Reeti told her parents that she had found the person she would marry. It was a natural, uncomplicated feeling, which she accepted without ambivalence or doubt. I can honestly say that the discovery of this love, a love that stretched around me like the open sky, made me feel sometimes that I hadn't left home. And yet, I was not wholly satisfied.

Perhaps I wanted to be like Antoine in *Stolen Kisses*: when he is discharged and comes back to Paris, Antoine's girlfriend no longer loves him, at least not for a long time. Although this happened in a movie, I felt that is how it was supposed to be in real life. In real life, love was messy. And by that standard, I didn't feel I was living a real life. Reeti's love for me was so steadfast, so unlike what movies and books told me love, and thus life, was all about, that I almost resented it.

When I met Janet, who was a documentary filmmaker from Los Angeles, it struck me that instead of a feature film I might want to make a documentary in Bihar. Janet had beautiful clear eyes. She said she did yoga every day and had for the longest time wanted to go to India. I decided I wanted to tell the story of the elephants that were sold at the Sonepur fair. Who bought those elephants? Who sold them? They represented for me the signs of a way of life that was familiar to me from my childhood but was now getting lost.

The old zamindars were gone, their sprawling homes on their estates now decayed or turned into crumbling government offices. The landlords had maintained elephants as a symbol of sorts. They were used during weddings for the bridegroom's baraat, and during floods although there was danger in that. Or when a car got caught in mud or slipped into a canal, but now there were tractors that did the job. What place did those pachyderms have in our modern society?

When I mentioned this idea one summer day to Janet—describing in detail how, when I was a boy, I had seen my

grandfather bringing back bullocks from Sonepur, their hides
and horns painted in bright colours—she announced that she
would come with me. *You'll need some help with the equipment,
my friend*, she said with a smile. My eyes dropped to her feet,
and I pretended to be looking at the tattoo on her right ankle.

—She said, Do you think Reeti will be all right with it?

—Why not? I said, but was already afraid that I had hit a wall.

In the end, unwilling to make anything big out of it, I didn't
say anything to Reeti until the last week. I saw from the look
on her face that she was puzzled.

—She said, Is anyone else going with you two?

On our way to Sonepur, we spent a night in Patna. My
parents had no reason to doubt or question my statement that
Janet was a film-maker and was here to help me on a project.
She slept in her own room, of course. I would now and then put
my arm on her shoulder, as when we were crossing a road, but
there was no physical contact otherwise. Still, I felt guilty that
I had come without Reeti. I made it a point to go by myself to
Reeti's house. She had sent an electric toaster, a shirt, and two
bottles of perfume.

—Her mother said, Why didn't you bring her with you,
Abhayji?

—Her father put his hand on the shirt, shiny in its Brooks
Brothers box, and asked, She didn't send a letter?

Sonepur was only an hour away from Patna, but I didn't want
to come back. I found a two-storey hotel not too far from the
fair, and paid for two rooms next to each other. The hotel was a
modest affair but it was new and freshly painted. It didn't serve
any food on the premises and the carpets and walls didn't smell
stale. The fair was on the banks of the Ganga and a rickshaw took
us there. The man at the hotel had said we'd find the elephants
near the bank, often being washed, and this turned out to be
true. The beasts lay on their sides, lazily plopping their trunks
in and out of the grey water. The sun had peeled away all the
mist that had greeted us in the morning; all around us, there was
dust and smoke and sometimes the smell of marijuana. A man

was shouting or chanting on the loudspeaker, asking whether we wanted to kill all the seven generations of bedbugs in our home. He had the medicine if we hurried.

Janet asked me whether I'd mind if she started shooting some footage of the elephants. She rolled up her trousers to her knees and stepped into the water. More people gathered to look at her than those who had stood around watching the elephants. The exercise filled her with energy.

When she came out of the water, she said she wanted to explore. She let the camera stay on as she panned over the young women buying ribbons and bangles that glinted brightly in the sun. We saw sadhus with matted hair, quacks, sickly looking Pomeranians, lizards in small cages, women who were getting their ears cleaned. Late in the afternoon, Janet found a stall that billed itself as a drama company, but it was actually nothing more than a makeshift brothel. A Bollywood number was playing on a tape player and five Nepali girls, all teenagers, were rocking to the music. Men sat on chairs and drank toddy and country liquor. She said, *You might have found your subject.*

I looked at the girls, and then the men. None of them would speak to us, I was sure of that. Then, Janet moved away, captivated by the sight of two peacocks, with long, lustrous tails. The birds had thin metal chains around their feet and were tied to a peepul tree. An old man sitting beneath the tree was waiting for a customer. Janet took the camera to the birds. She had found in this camera her passport to enter India.

The elephants were there to be sold primarily to the officials from the Forest Department. The driver of our jeep pointed to a dwarf and said that the man was actually very rich, he owned a circus, and he would buy an elephant or two for his business. Janet thought if we followed the dwarf it would make an interesting documentary but it would be grotesque in a Diane Arbus kind of way. She was clear—she wouldn't let me do it.

This said, she didn't think there was anything grotesque in filming the Nepali girls from the drama company. On the second day, she proposed that we also film two young girls, maybe teenagers, who had come to the fair from a nearby village to buy something they wouldn't have got anywhere else. But I nixed the idea. Partly because I felt it would be much better to keep the focus on the Nepali dancers, and, if it became necessary, to splice contrasting footage from the dance sequences in *Teesri Kasam*. Also, I thought I couldn't let Janet determine everything that was going to happen in my film. This was not the reason why she had come to India.

In any event, as a result of my irritation, a quality of callousness had come into my dealings with Janet. The old feeling that someone owed me something returned to me, and I surrendered to it. I became determined that I would like to see Janet naked. She was slim with small, shapely breasts. She wore her hair high in a ponytail, and on that second day in Sonepur I knotted a red ribbon in her hair. I had picked it up from a seller's cart, a gaudy piece with golden brocade stitched to it. When she began to laugh, I also took a bindi and pressed it on her forehead.

—Tilting her chin up, I brushed my lips against her face and said, You look nice.

After that, I went back to the hotel and slept. For a while I lay facedown in bed and imagined Janet under me. She was still at the fair; I had felt unsure about leaving her alone there, but she had said she'd be okay. I gave the driver of our jeep a fifty-rupee note and said he should drink tea if he felt sleepy. He was to keep an eye on Janet and not let anyone molest her.

That night, I was very happy when they returned to the hotel. This was because while I had been taking my long nap, Janet had spoken to our driver and he had asked the dancing girls about their manager. Janet found him and arranged for us to have a conversation with the girls on camera. The manager claimed he was the uncle of one of the girls; he was dirty and unshaven, but he spoke English, and this impressed Janet. It became apparent to her that all the girls referred to that guy as Uncle. She didn't understand why they didn't call him their pimp. She wanted me to ask the girls all the necessary questions, and I asked her what she had told the man. She said, *Oh, I was careful. I told him we were interested in the dancing.* We would record their dancing, she had told him, and then suggested that there was money in it.

The girls had been waiting when we reached their tent. A few customers had already gathered to watch them, but the girls seemed unconcerned about this. I asked them questions and they ignored the camera that was being handled by Janet. Our talk didn't reveal much but we established a rapport. In the coming days, we would be able to do much more. The girls giggled a lot, and they stroked Janet's arms and feet. They told her they loved the ribbon in her hair. It made her look like a Bollywood star.

I had let our driver take the evening off because he was interested in watching a film. We took a rickshaw back to the hotel and on the ride back, I thanked Janet for having arranged the interview. This time, when she turned to smile at me, I kissed her on the mouth.

When we were back at the hotel, a surprise awaited me. Janet had put her afternoon in the market to use. She had bought tomatoes and given it to the wife of the guy who manned the register downstairs: after sautéing onions and garlic, the woman had added the tomatoes and allowed them to simmer in water. The soup was in an aluminum pot, to be heated on an electric coil heater. We ate it with warm rotis. Janet said she had had this fantasy about this simple meal the moment her eyes had fallen on the fresh tomatoes.

Then, once we had begun to kiss in earnest, she asked me to wait and took out from a little paper-bag fashioned out of a Hindi newspaper, a packet of condoms. The brand she had bought was Nirodh, whose red-and-yellow ads had been a part of my childhood. (Ah, the nostalgia for one's past! Even when cheating on one's lover!) While it was true that I had earlier harboured thoughts about being brutal with Janet, at that moment I felt only tenderness. It was not so much carnality I felt as much as an intimacy, and it made the experience of fucking Janet so much sweeter than I had imagined.

I had planned to stay in Sonepur for a week. Work was going well. Each day and even during the night, we shot footage: we had gone with one of the Nepali girls to a doctor; two of them had decided to buy a puppy and we went around with them, looking at all that was on offer at the fair until they selected a four-month-old black terrier; one night there was a fire in another section of the grounds when a electric spark set aflame sheets of plastic and then a section of bamboo fencing. Once, we were shooting one of the youngest girls making a telephone call at the STD booth to her elder sister, and I asked the owner if he also had an international line. Could I call Reeti in America? He said yes but then I decided not to.

On our fifth night, a Friday, when we had eaten and made love, I was awakened by the sound of knocking on a door. It was the door across from us on the other side of the corridor: I had earlier seen a short dark man wearing a white banian and lungi coming out with a bottle of water. Then I heard my name. Light seeped in from under the door. The man called out my name again. It was Girish, the man who sat downstairs at the counter, but there was someone else talking to him. I began to put on some clothes.

Standing outside with Girish was Reeti's father and another man I had not met before. I brought my hands together in greeting. Had they first been knocking on the door of the other room, the one in which Janet was supposed to be staying? They must have noticed the lock on the door. Had they got a message for her? That was the first thought that came to me. I thought, perhaps too hopefully, that someone had needed to get in touch with Janet urgently.

—I said, Is everything okay?... So late.

Reeti's father parted the curtain and nodded to the man with him who tried to step inside.

—But I stopped him. I said, One minute...

—Reeti's father only said, Why?

—I said, There are other people here. Let's go into the other room.

The key to the other room was on the small desk inside, but I didn't want to leave my post at the door. Janet had been lying naked in bed. All the conversation had so far been in Hindi, and she wouldn't have understood what was going on. Had she had the sense to slip on a t-shirt?

I saw that even Girish looked curious.

Then, a few seconds later, there was Janet beside me. She had come out to see what the matter was. She was wearing a simple grey sweater and pyjamas. Her hair was in a ponytail. Once she had appeared at the door, Reeti's father said, *One minute, excuse me* and pushed past her into the room. His sidekick quickly followed him inside. But there was nothing to see. A bed with woolen blankets where, till recently, two people had been sleeping. Two open suitcases. A video camera and a still camera. Some small yellow bananas. Janet's blue jeans and a red ribbon draped on a chair.

—Janet said to me, What do they want?

—Reeti's father said to her, in English, What's your name?

—She said, Who are you? and then, turning again to me, What do they want?

The previous night we had shot footage of sadhus beside a campfire smoking dope from fat chillums. At one point, one of them, an old sadhu with grey hair still thick on his head and his eyes twinkling, had given his fragrant bong to Janet. And she, smiling, full of assurance, had sucked on it. Instead of returning it to its owner, she had passed on the chillum to me. I had half-tried to give it back to the sadhu but he said it was God's gift and I shouldn't refuse it. When I pulled on it, I thought of Reeti. I told myself, I should call her. Rather, I felt that I should have called her during all these days I had been in Sonepur. It was as if she had ceased to exist for me. I froze. I found that my thinking had become blocked, and then wondered if it was the dope that had done something to me. I looked at Janet. She seemed unaffected. With a smile on her face, she had put the camera to her eye and kept it rolling, chasing the smoke as it spiralled into the mango leaves above.

—Reeti's father said, So this is the research you are doing?

—I tried to look offended. I said, I have been shooting every day.

—He said, I came because Reeti called this evening.

It must have been early morning there.

—She was very worried because she had received no word from you. I don't think she had slept.

—She asked has he fallen sick? Does he have diarrhoea?

I didn't look at Janet. She must have heard the English word 'diarrhoea'.

—She had this thought that you were lying sick somewhere in a room, stinking in your own shit, but—

He stopped and touched his collar. Then, turning away from me, he stepped towards the bed. Snatching the thin, ugly pillows from the hotel bed, he threw them on the floor. For a moment, I asked myself if he was going to ask his men to bundle me into his car. What would they do with Janet?

But Reeti's father wordlessly walked out of the room.

They were gone. I saw Girish turn the light off in the stairwell. Back in the room, I let out my anger and it took me a minute to notice that Janet was not responding at all. I realized she didn't yet know who the visitors were. I told her, and then apologized to her.

—I said, Let's go back to bed.

But she didn't move.

⌣

Five years have passed. I have made two more documentaries, one about a Hindu sacred thread ceremony on the banks of the Demerara in Guyana, and another about a Muslim wedding in a Tamil community near Durban, South Africa. What is the hybrid culture that groups of people scattered across the world, removed from their roots, have created in response to alienation and a kind of collective loneliness? I'm interested in the persistence of forms. The more things change, some things stay the same. I go back sometimes to my first documentary that I made in Sonepur. Elephants return us to our beginnings: they connect us to the woolly mammoth; they have lasted so long.

Recently I learned from a woman who was also in school with us that Reeti got married. She took her lover home to Patna and they were joined in a traditional Hindu ceremony under a mandap. The man she married was someone I knew slightly, a big, light-haired grad student named Doug Tauscher. They had twins, a boy and a girl. The person who was telling me this, Nandini, who had been in Sociology with Reeti, said that Doug was doted upon by everyone in Patna. He fell sick with diarrhoea during their trip, and Reeti's parents treated him like a son.

—Nandini said, looking at me intently, When Doug had diarrhoea Reeti's mother even washed his underwear.

Who had told her all this? Reeti? I asked these questions to myself, but I was also happy for Reeti.

When I came back from my India visit with Janet, I only had one question in mind: would Reeti's father have said anything to Reeti about what he had seen in the hotel room? Not only because there was something shameful about having to tell one's daughter about her boyfriend's infidelity, but also because he was a man who flouted laws, made illicit deals, and was perhaps quite comfortable with human failings. But when I got back, Reeti had already moved out of the apartment. She was polite with me when we met, but there was no going back. And I didn't feel the urge too strongly myself; I could see in her eyes that it was all over. I didn't seek out Janet either, though we met over several beers and talked about the work we had done in Sonepur. When I raised some grant money and hired an editor, I didn't call Janet to discuss the footage. We never talked about having slept with each other while we were together in India.

All of this came back tonight as I was rubbing a muscle relaxant on my back. I don't know how I strained it, but it's been hurting so much that I've been unable to move. When I rubbed the ointment on my skin, the smell transported me to those small, overheated rooms of my childhood. I was visiting an old relative in the winter. The door opened and I entered a room where the windows were shut and the walls were dark. A figure was on the bed, wearing a maroon sweater, with one or two blankets covering his body. On the floor there was a single-coil heater and the room had an overcrowded air. Even in the middle of an ordinary conversation, I could feel something huge tilting down and about to crash on me. But the defining feature was the sharp smell of the muscle relaxant in the room. Nothing from the outside world was going to come inside, nor was anything ever likely to leave. I'm not making excuses for what happened with Reeti. It has become clear to me in all these years that whatever I have done has been a way of escaping that room.

# AUTHOR'S NOTE

Immigrant, Montana, doesn't exist. Although I visited the town of Emigrant, Montana, in August 2008, immediately after Barack Obama accepted the Democratic nomination in Denver, I wish to state that the map presented here is faulty. Even the historical account accords only with what is remembered. Memory is real but it is not accurate. It is arguable that history is not accurate either; however, this novel isn't the place to stage that particular debate.

After Barack Obama was elected president I read about his courting Michelle. She had been his boss, assigned to advise him during a summer job, but Obama began to ask her if she would go on a date. Before the end of the summer, she agreed to go out for a movie—Spike Lee's *Do the Right Thing*—and an ice-cream cone at Baskin Robbins. The clipping in my notebook includes these lines: 'Vacationing on Martha's Vineyard in 2004, Barack met Spike Lee at a reception. As Michelle has recalled, he told Lee, "I owe you a lot," because, during the movie, Michelle had allowed him to touch her knee.'

Here is a partial list of those to whom I owe a lot:

for providing conditions to write, Lannan Foundation, Guggenheim Foundation, United States Artists, Norman Mailer Center, the Yaddo Corporation;

for help on sections of an early draft, Jeffrey Renard Allen, Scott Dahlie, Sheba Karim, Siddhartha Chowdhury;

for reading the final manuscript, Shruti Debi, Karan Mahajan, Kiran Desai;

for their various acts of encouragement and friendship over the years, my thanks to Rob Nixon, David Means, Ken Chen, Amit Chaudhuri, Teju Cole;

also, for their support, Ian Jack, Rick Simonson, Suketu Mehta, Erin Edmison;

for early conversations about Eqbal Ahmad, Zia Mian, Dohra Ahmed, Robin Varghese, Julie Diamond, Anthony Arnove;

for their expert care at Aleph, David Davidar (again), Aienla Ozukum, Simar Puneet and Bena Sareen;

for help with publication abroad, David Godwin, Susanna Lea, and Lisette Verhagen at DGA; Lee Brackstone at Faber; Sonny Mehta at Knopf; and all the other foreign language publishers.

This novel is about love, and since love comes at a price, I acknowledge my enormous and unpayable debt to my loving family, particularly Mona, Ila and Rahul.

Most quotations are accompanied by attributions in the body of the text. Where the source isn't provided, as with clippings from notebooks, a simple Google search will do the job. In addition to the titles mentioned in the novel, I have used the following books: Elizabeth Hardwick, *Sleepless Nights*; Grace Paley, *Just As I Thought*; Elmore Leonard, *Rum Punch*; David Omissi, ed., *Indian Voices of the Great War: Soldiers' Letters, 1914-18*; Harold A. Gould, *Sikhs, Swamis, Students, and Spies*; William O'Rourke, *The Harrisburg 7 and the New Catholic Left*. The reference to a prose-poem by Jorge Luis Borges is to 'A Dream', published in *The New Yorker*, 6 & 13 July 2009; in Part 5, 'The Lovers' by Picasso, reproduced with permission from © Succession Picasso 2017; the Pico Iyer quote is from *The Global Soul: Jet Lag, Shopping Malls, and the Search for Home*, and the response to it is taken from a review essay by Kai Friese, 'Global Trotter's Nama', *Outlook*, 28 August 2000; in Part 7, the art-installation 'Hunan School' is very much inspired by Ilya Kabakov's remarkable 'School No. 6' at the Chinati Foundation in Marfa, Texas; I had enjoyed my exchange with Yu Hua at the Asia Society and, again in Part 7, have quoted from his essay on Lu Xun; in Part 8, I quote from Charlotte Glynn's short film set in Pittsburgh, *The Immaculate Reception*; also, in the short story at the book's end,

I have drawn upon Saba Dewan's documentary, *Naach*; Ehsaan Ali is a fictional character but parts of him are based on my interviews with family, friends and former students of Eqbal Ahmad; I have relied upon Eqbal Ahmad, *Confronting Empire: Interviews with David Barsamian*; I also interviewed Stuart Schaar who is the author of *Eqbal Ahmad: Critical Outsider in a Turbulent Age*; my thanks to the staff at the Hampshire College archives for showing me the letter written by John Berger. I have drawn upon Ruth Price's excellent *The Lives of Agnes Smedley* while recasting details of Smedley's loves. Unless otherwise indicated, use has been made here of found images and I will make grateful acknowledgement if any further debts are owed.

'"Don't mess with Mr In-Between,"' my father would often advise me, but it seems to me that Mr In-Between is precisely where we all live now.' So writes David Shields in *Reality Hunger*. This is a work of fiction as well as non-fiction, an in-between novel by an in-between writer.

An excerpt entitled 'A Foreigner' was published in *Alchemy* and in *Tehelka*; the short story 'You Can Get It If You Really Want' was published in *Pratilipi*; and another brief excerpt appeared in *Seminar* under the title 'Revolutionary Road'.